The Age of Nightmare

Other Books of Interest from St. Augustine's Press

Jeremy Black, *The Importance of Being Poirot*

Jeremy Black, *In Fielding's Wake*

Jeremy Black, *Defoe's Britain*

Jeremy Black, *Smollett's Britain*

Thomas F. Powers, *American Multiculturalism and the Anti-Discrimination Regime: The Challenge to Liberal Pluralism*

Joseph Bottum, *Spending the Winter*

Marvin R. O'Connell, *Telling Stories that Matter: Memoirs and Essays*

Francisco Insa, *The Formation Affectivity: A Christian Approach*

Pete Fraser, *Twelve Films about Love and Heaven*

Peter Kreeft, *Ethics for Beginners: Big Ideas from 32 Great Minds*

Anne Drury Hall, *Where the Muses Still Haunt: The Second Reading*

Alexandre Kojève, *The Concept, Time, and Discourse*

David Lowenthal, *Slave State: Rereading Orwell's 1984*

Gene Fendt, *Camus' Plague: Myth for Our World*

Nathan Lefler, *Tale of a Criminal Mind Gone Good*

Nalin Ranasinghe, *The Confessions of Odysseus*

John Poch, *God's Poems: The Beauty of Poetry and the Christian Imagination*

Roger Scruton, *The Politics of Culture and Other Essays*

Roger Scruton, *The Meaning of Conservatism: Revised 3rd Edition*

Rainer Maria Rilke, *The Sonnets of Maria Rilke*

Allen Mendenhall, *Shouting Softly: Lines on Law, Literature, and Culture*

Marion Montgomery, *With Walker Percy at the Tupperware Party*

Stanley Rosen, *The Language of Love: An Interpretation of Plato's Phaedrus*

Will Morrisey, *Shakespeare's Politic Comedy*

Will Morrissey, *Herman Melville's Ship of State*

Winston Churchill, *The River War*

The Age of Nightmare
The Gothic and British Culture, 1750–1900
Jeremy Black

THE WEIGHT OF WORDS SERIES

St. Augustine's Press
South Bend, Indiana

Copyright © 2023 by Jeremy Black

All rights reserved. No part of this book may be reproduced, stored in a retrieval system, or transmitted, in any form or by any means, electronic, mechanical, photocopying, recording, or otherwise, without the prior permission of St. Augustine's Press.

Manufactured in the United States of America.

1 2 3 4 5 6   28 27 26 25 24 23

Library of Congress Control Number: 2023937113

Paperback ISBN: 978-1-58731-009-6
Hardback ISBN: 978-1-58731-008-9
Ebook ISBN: 978-1-58731-010-2

∞ The paper used in this publication meets the minimum requirements of the American National Standard for Information Sciences – Permanence of Paper for Printed Materials, ANSI Z39.48-1984.

St. Augustine's Press
www.staugustine.net

For
Michael Wheeler

Table of Contents

Preface ix
List of Dates xii

Introduction 1
1. Italian Horror with Walpole 9
2. Gothic Shadows Lengthen 23
3. After Otranto 39
4. Nightmare in London with Henry Fuseli 60
5. Staging the Gothic 74
6. The Terror of Revolution 81
7. Ann Radcliffe, the Queen of the Genre 97
8. In Ann's Shadows 121
9. Monk Lewis 135
10. Miss Austen Responds 147
11. Forgotten Decade 154
12. And So to Frankenstein 172
13. Enter Messrs Collins and Dickens 189
14. Echoes in Whitby 206
15. Conclusions 221

Selected Further Reading 230

Index 235

PREFACE

If reason, politeness and sensibility vie for our attention when considering the long eighteenth century, so also should shock, horror and nightmare. Centering on the Gothic novelists, this book takes us from the 1760s into, eventually, the Victorian age of horror, culminating with *Dracula* (1897) and *The Hound of the Baskervilles* (1902). By so doing, I will offer a different account of the period to the accustomed one, while also using an understanding of the period to throw light on the novels. Attention, moreover, will be devoted to the painting of horror, notably by Henry Fuseli, to the shock of revolution, the terror of social anarchy, and the presence of a lack of ease that could so readily develop into nightmare.

This lack of ease was presented not only in the dreams of the protagonists of Gothic fiction, but also in the physicality of sensation and shock. There could be a very disturbing physicality in the Gothic. In Charles Maturin's *Fatal Revenge* (1807), one of the most potent and sustained of the dramatic tales of supernatural challenge, the protagonist finds a dark cavity in which he sees 'a heap of bloody and decayed garments, pierced with more holes than those of decay,' and then:

> half smothered by the dust and rubbish, I scrambled through, crushing at every touch the eggs of the little domestic serpents, and displacing the nests of lizards and toads, whose cold slime made me shudder, as I crawled amongst them (16).

So also with the vistas, both claustrophobic and distant, that were offered. Thus, the capacity of woods to be horrific was captured in *Fatal Revenge* as the protagonist flees pursuit:

> how I listened in horror to the wind, and the hollow whistle that ran through the wood, mixed with it; how I thought the whisper

of murder was in the underworld, as it hissed in the breeze; and how often I recoiled as the tossing branches of the trees flung a sudden shadow across the way (16).

Trying to locate styles, topics and developments risks mistaking coincidence for cause. Furthermore, there is the risk of finding common characteristics among novels and novelists that, looked at differently, could be very different. Furthermore, it is overly easy to underplay the complexity of individual novels, and to quote accordingly. In *A Sicilian Romance* (1791), Ann Radcliffe is scathing about 'the enjoyment of the good things of this life' in a monastery in which the Superior toasts 'Profusion and confusion' (5), and she generally adopted a critical note, but, subsequently, she could praise the 'holy calm' of a nunnery (8). Similarly, the Gothic novels of the 1790s can be covered and explored in a number of ways. A glib one is to adopt a typology defined by Radcliffe and Lewis, sometimes referred to as 'female' and 'male' approaches, and to group the novels accordingly, not least in discussing them in related chapters. In this book, certain novels appear accordingly, but, in practice, essentially in order to undercut such a typology.

The organization of this book is used to group Gothic novels in order to make a range of points. For example, in the chapter 'Miss Austen Responds,' some of the novels cited by Jane Austen in *Northanger Abbey* are considered there. This underlines the extent to which contemporary, like later, classification has a strong element of the instrumental about it. Not least, there were many other works that Austen could have cited.

Lastly, the following chapter, 'Forgotten Decade,' provides the somewhat different classification by chronology, which would have captured the possibilities offered by new books, but not those provided by existing copies or new editions. Variety in repetition and repetition in variety, helped provide a theme of anxiety, if not nightmare. Fear and guilt are aspects of the longing that is part of the literature, alongside the reiterated admonitions about good behaviour. Incest is one overlap, as in *The Monk*, but so is murder; the two combining in the dysfunctional families of many of the novels. While literally in dungeons, man-made or natural, imprisonment is more terrifying and horrific because of the personal dynamics involved and the deceit entailed. Satan is not present in most of the novels, but the subterfuge

Preface

associated with him is very much there, not least as identities are adopted and manipulated.

I have benefited greatly from the comments of Grayson Ditchfield, Bill Gibson, Crawford Gribben, Will Hay, Murray Pittock, and Michael Wheeler on an earlier draft. As before, Katie Godfrey has proved an exemplary editor. It is a great pleasure to dedicate this book to Michael Wheeler, friend, scholar and fellow-clubman whose company I and very many others have enjoyed in the Athenaeum for many years.

List of Dates

Note on numbers

Those in brackets refer to chapter numbers unless otherwise indicated.

1764	Horace Walpole's *The Castle of Otranto* published.
1773	Anna Letitia Barbauld's *Miscellaneous Pieces in Prose* published. Joshua Reynolds' *Ugolino and His Children in the Dungeon* published.
1777	Clara Reeves publishes *The Champion of Virtue*.
1778	Clara Reeves' *The Champion of Virtue* republished as *The Old English Baron*.
1781	*The Count of Narbonne*, a dramatic adaptation of *The Castle of Otranto* produced successfully.
1781	Henry Fuseli paints *Nightmare*.
1782	Fuseli's *Nightmare* exhibited.
1782	Fourth edition of *The Castle of Otranto*.
1784	Joshua Reynolds' portrait of *Mrs Siddon as The Tragic Muse*.
1786	William Beckford's *Vathek: An Arabian Tale* published.
1786	Fifth edition of *The Castle of Otranto*.
1790	Fuseli becomes a member of the Royal Academy.
1791	Sixth edition of *The Castle of Otranto*. Ann Radcliffe's *The Romance of the Forest* published.
1794	Ann Radcliffe's *The Mysteries of Udolpho* published.
1796	Matthew Lewis's *The Monk* published.

List of Dates

1797   Ann Radcliffe's *The Italian* published.
           Jane Austen's *Northanger Abbey* published.
           Matthew Lewis's horror play *The Castle Spectre*.
1798   Regina Maria Roche's *The Children of the Abbey* published.
1802   Fuseli's *The Serpent Tempting Eve*.
1806   Charlotte Dacre's *Zofloya* published.
1807   Charles Maturin's *Fatal Revenge* published.
1818   Mary Shelley's *Frankenstein* published.
1820   Charles Maturin's *Melmoth the Wanderer* published.
1839   Edgar Allan Poe's *The Fall of the House of Usher* published.
1847   Emily Brontë's *Wuthering Heights* published.
1860   Wilkie Collins' *The Woman in White* published.
1870   Charles Dickens's *The Mystery of Edwin Drood* published.
1897   Bram Stoker's *Dracula* published.
1902   Arthur Conan Doyle's *The Hound of the Baskervilles* published.

INTRODUCTION

> I have a darker tale to tell than the owl that sits on the desolate ruin; than the raven that beats heavily at the window of the dying.
>
> Charles Maturin, Fatal Revenge (16)

The Age of Nightmare is not the usual term for the period from the 1760s to the 1810s, let alone the following century. Yet, in Britain, alongside transformative change toward greater international and economic power, it was an age of anxiety and fear. This was the case not least among both the élite and the growing middling orders, but also more widely. Successive crises defined the national mood, from fear in the 1760s about political breakdown to successful revolution in the British world from 1775 to 1783; from the concern that the French Revolution would spread to Britain to a traumatic war with Napoleon; from domestic traumas in the aftermath of the Napoleonic Wars to the more persistent anxiety about both circumstances and change; from a decline in religious observance to economic and social issues. The responses to these crises and this anxiety themselves also caused concern, whether millenarian movements or lawlessness.

That was the background and foreground to our book, and its topic is as much to be understood in terms of reader responses to Gothic fiction as of authorial interests and intentions. Reader responses is a phrase suggestive of a degree of passivity, but that is misleading, not least because there was room for choice in reader purchases. For example, a strong direction of reader interest toward millenarian works is of note, while, separately, the purpose of Gothic fiction was to thrill and entertain as well as to terrify.

More generally, this was a society in which evil for very many remained an active force. In 1765, Richard Browne had visited St Patrick's Purgatory, an island in Lough Derg in County Donegal, where each year over 10,000 Irish Catholics made a pilgrimage, finding:

a multitude indeed of both sexes mostly indeed of the poorer sort … in one place there are built seven small places of a circular form like pounds in which place the penitents are obliged to run so many times round barefoot on sharp pointed rocks repeating so many ave marias etc, in commemoration of the seven deadly sins … the next penance is to retire to a vault made purposely, where they must remain 24 hours without eating, drinking, speaking or sleeping, for they are sure if they do either the Devil has a power of carrying them away, and to prevent sleeping, everyone that goes in there supply themselves with pins which they thrust into anyone they find dozing … the last ceremony is washing in the lake, when they wash away all their sins.[1]

Yet, rather than seeing this as a Catholic primitivist survival, it is necessary to note the widespread character of providentialism. In 1758, writing to his sister from London with a long account of comets, John Rolls, who was not a Catholic, struck a common note:

Let not however any specious part of reason prevent our concern at such phenomena, but rather put us in mind of the end and final conclusion of all things … induce us to pay a more than common homage at the footstool of the throne of our good Almighty God, who with a nod or touch or breath can hurl us with fury and terrible destruction to all eternity.[2]

John Wesley was far from alone in claiming that divine intervention had occurred all through history and that miracles were therefore credible.[3] It was still widely believed that astrological anatomies and zodiacs were keys to character and guides to the future, that extraterrestrial forces intervened in the affairs of the world, especially human and animal health and the state of crops and the weather, and that each constellation in the zodiac presided over a particular part of man; with necessary guidance to this situation and

1   Richard Browne to his father, 24 August 1765, BL. RP. 3284.
2   Exeter, Devon County Record Office, 64/12/29/1/26.
3   Jane Shaw, *Miracles in Enlightenment England* (New Haven, Conn., 2006).

Introduction

its risks being provided by almanacs. This belief could overlap with a continuing interest in the occult, one that is overly neglected if the emphasis instead is on a British Enlightenment, however defined. Indeed, the *Reading Mercury* of 15 March 1773 argued: 'The ridiculous notion of witches and witchcraft still prevails amongst the lower sort of people, as the following account will sufficiently evince.' A context was that of a more direct providentialism. *Berrow's Worcester Journal* on 20 March 1766 provided:

> a very extraordinary instance of the Divine Vengeance…. One Richard Parsons, a young man of that place, was playing at cards, and he most prophanely wished his flesh might rot, and his eyes never shut, if he did not win the next game. When he was going to bed he observed a black spot upon his leg, from which a mortification began … he died in a day or two, his flesh being quite rotten; nor could his eyes be shut, notwithstanding all the efforts of his friends to close them. The truth of this fact is attested by many of the neighbours who were with him – *Read it ye Prophane, and tremble!*

Millenarianism was widespread.[4] In his *General History of the Christian Church* (1771), Charles Walmesley (1722–97), the Vicar Apostolic of the (Catholic) Western District of England, predicted the end of Protestantism for 1825. Among the Unitarians, both Joseph Priestley and Richard Price expected the millennium to follow the downfall of authority.

Far from ebbing, apocalyptic ideas were encouraged by the repeated crises of the French Revolutionary and Napoleonic periods. The search for providential support and struggle against evil were demonstrated by, and in, national prayer days, and also played a role in the discussion around particular items of legislation, such as the abolition of the slave trade.[5] These

---

4 William Gibson, 'Millenarianism and Prophecy in Eighteenth-Century Britain,' in Lionel Laborie and Ariel Hessayon (eds), *Early Modern Prophecies in Transnational, National and Regional Contexts. III. The British Isles* (Leiden, 2021), pp. 1–30.
5 John Coffey, '"Tremble, Britannia!" Fear, Providence and the Abolition of the Slave Trade, 1758–1807,' *English Historical Review*, 127 (2012), pp. 844–81.

themes remained strong. John Cumming (1807–81), a Scottish cleric prominent in London, used prophecy to claim, in a series of sermons and writings, that the 'last vial' of the Apocalypse was soon to be poured out. He also argued that sciences should only be studied in so far as they clustered round the Cross, a potent image and one that presented the Crucifixion as a continuing theme.[6]

Aside from apocalyptic thought, it was certainly the case that everyday life reflected religious commitment and custom. William Grasing, a Gloucestershire farmer who died in 1798, recorded, in his much-thumbed notebook, charms to be sure to bring health. That to stop bleeding was a statement of faith starting 'I believe Jesus Christ to be the son of God… This charm must be repeated five times.' As part of religious practice, there were also customs that went back to before Christianity. Those recorded in Edward Wakefield's *Account of Ireland* (1812) included swinging children over, and driving cattle through, fires lit on St John's Eve in order to ensure health and fortune. More generally, the religious positioning of Gothic writing has attracted very fruitful attention of late.[7]

Dreams played an instructive part in discussions of reason. They were a favourite subject of Wesley who regarded them as a means to communicate with the divine.[8] While some Gothic novels had the characteristic of a nightmare, notably Matthew Lewis' *The Monk* and Bram Stoker's *Dracula*, and others were given a dream-like character in part by being set in the past, individual nightmares were also frequent in the stories. In part, these are aspects of guilt and remorse. Thus, in *The Italian, or the Confessional of the Black Penitents. A Romance* (1797), subsequently referred to as *The Italian*, urged to new murder by Schedoni who knows his past, Spalatro replies:

> I wish I could forget; I remember it too well. – I have never been at peace since. The bloody hand is always before me! and

---

6   John Cumming, *The Millennial Rest* (London, 1862), *The Sounding of the Last Trumpet* (London, 1867), and *The Seventh Vial* (London, 1870).
7   Alison Milbank, *God and the Gothic. Religion, Romance, and Reality in the English Literary Tradition* (Oxford, 2018).
8   Phyllis Mack, *Heart Religion in the British Enlightenment: Gender and Emotion in Early Methodism* (Cambridge, 2008).

Introduction

often of a night, when the sea roars, and storms shake the house, *they* have come, all gashed as I left them, and stood before my bed! I have got up, and ran out upon the shore for safety! (II,9)

He sees again 'that dreadful hand ... with that blood-stained finger!' (II,9). Vivid nightmares included that by Ippolito in Charles Maturin's *Fatal Revenge* (1807) in which his father is poisoned in the Host at midnight mass by a pretend monk (17).

The cultural trends that led toward the Gothic and other aspects of the Age of Nightmare were varied. There was more than just the response to a sense of crisis, very important as that was. Instead, it is necessary to understand a number of elements. Three in particular deserve attention: the interest in what was termed the Gothic, for which see in particular chapter two; ideas of the sublime; and the more melodramatic aspects of Gothic novels, these aspects themselves in part answering to concerns about criminality and social disruption.

Novels as a whole had included a melodramatic dimension from the outset with threats to status, most commonly social or virginal, a key theme. At the same time, the attempt to provide an acceptable format in the shape of the sentimental novel was to be effected by the development of new qualities and forms of imagination, these leading towards the Gothic novel. This development drew on ideas of the sublime. The word sublime was used at the time for George Frederick Handel's music, which indeed sought a religious sublimity, but was defined by Edmund Burke as whatever led to ideas of danger, pain, or terror: he suggested obscurity, vastness, privation, and infinity, the sources of which could be imaginary. Burke's aesthetic *Philosophical Enquiry into the Origin of Our Ideas of the Sublime and the Beautiful* (1759) underscored the extent to which 'the sublime' could transform the reader and spectator, and emphasised that terror was important in creating the sense of the sublime. In a reaction against what was held to be the standard intellectual approach earlier in the century, one that matched the official approach to Christian exposition; emotions and potent sensory experiences, rather than reason and dignity, were here brought to the fore for Burke, whose work had great influence in the development of the idea of the sublime.[9] This was the aesthetic theory and experience that

9   Fred Lock, *Edmund Burke I, 1730–1784* (Oxford, 1998), pp.

the Gothic as a genre seemed almost manufactured to exploit or demonstrate. The word sublime was frequently used by Gothic novelists, notably Ann Radcliffe. The 'sublime grandeur' of the Alps was praised in *The Old Irish Baronet* (1808) by Henrietta Rouviere/Mosse (II,7). In Radcliffe's *The Italian*, a lengthy description of impressive mountain scenery in the Apennines was followed by an account of the impact on the protagonist, who is clearly intended to serve for the reader as well:

> To Ellena, whose mind was capable of being highly elevated, or sweetly soothed, by scenes of nature, the discovery of this turret was an important circumstance. Hither she could come, and her Soul, refreshed by the views it afforded, would acquire strength to bear her, with equanimity, through the persecutions that might await her. Here, gazing upon the stupendous imagery around her, looking, as it were, beyond the awful veil which obscures the features of the Deity, and conceals Him from the eyes of his creatures, dwelling as with a present God in the midst of his sublime works. (I,8)

Thus, the sublime was a matter of knowing God, with nature not an alternative to religion but part of it; all of which were conventional assumptions, and an aspect of the essential continuity, indeed conservatism, involved in the Gothic. Yet, drawing on the political reading of aesthetic debates in the 1730s and 1740s associated in particular with Mark Akenside and Edward Young, the sublime was also linked to ideas of individual fulfilment and, therefore, to a sense of Whiggish progress. Indeed, the idea of the Gothic as having an essentially conservative, even reactionary, character, can be countered by the discussion of the movement as Whig or Whiggish, with the Gothic looking back to the use of arguments from the Gothic or Middle Ages in order to justify calls for liberty, a process seen in English politics, and notably so from the 1620s, with, in particular the use of Magna Carta (1215) in anti-Stuart rhetoric. That discussion certainly provided an identity for the Gothic, but that was not necessarily the same for the Gothic novel. Moreover, the latter focused largely on an historicized version of the continent, specifically Italy, that scarcely matched English concepts of the Gothic.

Introduction

After the passage from *The Italian* quoted above, Radcliffe immediately pressed on with another conservative religious theme, one that served to minimise the activities and achievements of the armies of Revolutionary France:

> with a mind thus elevated, how insignificant would appear to her the transactions, and the sufferings of this world! How poor the boasted power of man, when the fall of a single cliff from these mountains would with ease destroy thousands of his race assembled on the plains below! How would it avail them, that they were accoutred for battle, armed with all the instruments of destruction that human invention ever fashioned? Thus man, the giant who now held her in captivity, would shrink to the diminutiveness of a fairy; and she would experience, that his utmost force was unable to enchain her soul, or compel her to fear him, while he was destitute of virtue. (I,8)

In historical and fictional terms, the melodrama was a key element in Gothic novels. In the shape of a woman seized and incarcerated in an asylum (a theme seen in the nineteenth century with Wilkie Collins' *Woman in White*), melodrama was already present in Tobias Smollett's novel *The Life and Adventures of Launcelot Greaves* (1760–1). However, melodrama was only a small part of that novel. Instead, the disturbing potential of medievalism was to be taken in a dramatically new direction with Horace Walpole's *The Castle of Otranto* (1764), the second edition of which was subtitled *A Gothic Story*.

A belief in the possible place of the occult was indirectly linked to a conviction of the dominant, albeit challenged, role of Providence, which drove aside malign forces, including those that were diabolical. Britain's fate was seen accordingly, as with *The Monitor*, an influential London newspaper, urging Caribbean conquests in its issue of 3 April 1762 and declaring:

> The late conquest of Martinique is such a peculiar mark of Providence, that we might, without presumption, look upon all the other islands in those seas, belonging to our arms ... permitted to pursue the course of Providence.

Providence acted through history, individual and collective, but delivered many of its lessons through nightmare, with the novelist providing an explanatory role akin to that of the clergyman. Charles Maturin, a clergyman-novelist, did both, and his most famous novel, *Melmoth, the Wanderer* (1820) provides in his protagonist's last desperate dream a warning of retribution that is at once religious and surreal. There is a quality of Dante in his imaginative writing. Having sold his soul for 150 years of life and failed to lead others into taking on his corrupt and corrupting bargain, Melmoth dreams he overlooks a fiery ocean of the damned, and then:

> He stood, in his dream, tottering on a crag midway down the precipice – he looked up ward, but the upper air (for there was no heaven) showed only blackness unshadowed and impenetrable – but, blacker than that blackness, he could distinguish a gigantic outstretched arm, that held him as in sport on the ridge of that infernal precipice, while another, that seemed in its motions to hold fearful and invisible conjunction with the arm that grasped him, as if both belonged to some being too vast and horrible even for the imagery of a dream to shape, pointed upwards to a dial-plate fixed on the top of that precipice, and which the flashes of that ocean of fire made fearfully conspicuous. He saw the mysterious single hand revolve – he saw it reach the appointed period of 150 years ... he shrieked in his dream, and, with that strong impulse often felt in sleep, burst from the arm that held him, to arrest the motion of the hand.
> In the effort he fell, and falling grasped at aught that might save him ... the rock was as smooth as ice – the ocean of fire broke at its foot! .... His last despairing reverted glance was fixed on the clock of eternity – the upraised black arm seemed to push forward the hand – it arrived at its period – he fell – he sunk – he blazed – he shrieked! The burning waves boomed over his sinking head, and the clock of eternity rung out its awful chime – "Room for the soul of the Wanderer!" – and the waves of the burning ocean answered, as they lashed the adamantine rock – "There is room for more!"

1. ITALIAN HORROR WITH WALPOLE

Widely presented as launching the Gothic novel, Horace Walpole (1717–97), from 1791 4th Earl of Orford, assaulted established practices by breaking with the existing conventions of the novel and its emphasis on realism, a theme he was to make explicit in his preface to the second edition of *The Castle of Otranto*. Instead, Walpole deliberately emphasised the need to employ 'fancy,' a form of imagination which included strangeness and uncertainty. In this novel, mystery was underlined by manifestations of the supernatural; and the reader, like the protagonist, was repeatedly unclear about what was happening. This lack of clarity was heightened to a nightmarish character by the accounts of menace, danger, pursuit, and assault.

At a time when his father, Sir Robert Walpole, later 1st Earl of Orford, was Prime Minister, Walpole[1] had visited Naples in 1740 as part of his Grand Tour, but did not travel on to the remote city of Otranto in Apulia. In 1786, when Elizabeth, Lady Craven, who had travelled there gave Walpole a drawing of the castle made in 1785 by Willey Reveley, the delighted author responded, 'I did not even know that there was a castle of Otranto,' which may have been a very good joke, although the book's descriptions of the castle and its environs are extremely sparse. Yet, replacing to a degree, or at least supplementing, the graveyards used by earlier 'Gothic' poets, castles and dungeons were key sites for Gothic fiction, focusing the menace and mystery that were more generally present in these novels and moving plots forward.

Walpole's novel very much influenced what followed, as in Clara Reeve's *The Old English Baron* (1778), which originally appeared in 1777 as *The Champion of Virtue*. That novel explicitly drew on *The Castle of Otranto*; as, very differently, in its name did Radcliffe's *The Mysteries of Udolpho* (1794), Udolpho strongly suggesting a link to Otranto, as did the

---

1   Timothy Mowl, *Horace Walpole: The Great Outsider* (London, 1996).

Italianate setting of many of the novels, such as both that and Radcliffe's *The Italian*.

A very different setting was offered by William Beckford in *Vathek: An Arabian Tale* (1786).[2] This novel engaged with the quest for deadly knowledge and legendary power in which the explicit defiance of established morality was in part expressed by a sexual adventurousness seen as part of its subject's desire to fulfil his sensuality. This looked to the exoticism of some Gothic fiction, and to troubled villains, such as Ambrosio, the protagonist of *The Monk* (1796) by Matthew Lewis; who, like Beckford and Walpole, was an MP when he wrote the novel. *Vathek* closed on a moral note:

> ... all testified their horror for each other by the most ghastly convulsions, and screams that could not be smothered. All severally plunged themselves into the accursed multitude, there to wander in an eternity of unabating anguish. Such was, and such should be, the punishment of unrestrained passions and atrocious deeds! Such shall be, the chastisement of that blind curiosity, which would transgress those bounds the wisdom of the Creator has prescribed to human knowledge; and such the dreadful disappointment of that restless ambition, which aiming at discoveries reserved for beings of a supernatural order, perceives not, through its infatuated pride, that the condition of man upon earth is to be humble and ignorant.
>
> Thus, the Caliph Vathek, who, for the sake of empty pomp and forbidden power, had sullied himself with a thousand crimes, became a prey to grief without end, and remorse without mitigation.

Thus, a book that aimed at the sublime ended with an appropriate moral.

The Gothic novel did not emerge from nowhere. Instead, it developed from the sentimental novel, and, more generally, brought to the fore many

---

2   Kenneth Graham (ed.), *Vathek and The Escape from Time: Bicentenary Revaluations* (New York, 1990).

of the emphases seen in previous English novels, a process that was to continue with the later 'Sensation Novel.' There was a continuance in elements of narrative and tone, but also differences between both individual novels and periods of writing, and, indeed, in the works of particular novelists. Thus, in Fanny Burney's second novel, *Cecilia: or Memoirs of an Heiress* (1782), there is the characteristic issue of a young woman growing up into society, seen for example in her first, *Evelina: or A Young Lady's Entrance into the World*, but, in this case, the upbringing is far less benign, notably with malevolent guardians and a melodramatic descent to insanity. The tendency of women in sentimental novels to lack self-restraint was presented as a sign of heightened nerves and emotions that could also be seen as an absence of maturity. Heightened nerves, moreover, were also a commonplace in sentimental plays, with the audience given clear clues; a process mocked in Sheridan's brilliant play *The Critic* (1779), with Puff's: 'when a heroine goes mad she always goes into white satin' (III,i). White, indeed, was the colour frequently worn by heroines in Gothic tales, for example Lucy in *Dracula*. It was part of the image of female purity, innocence and vulnerability that was so important to the novels, and to both their plot and their tone.

Walpole was not the originator of novels set with a medieval background. Indeed, although located in the present, Launcelot Greaves, the protagonist of Tobias Smollett's novel of that title (1760–1), was a medieval figure, but in the Don Quixote tradition of Gothic romance and a gentle humour rather than horror. Already in 1758, the anonymous *The History of Amanda. Written by a Young Lady* had offered a version of Gothic fiction. It was reprinted in Dublin in 1760 as *The Adventures of Miss Sophia Berkley*, an early instance of the role of piracy in the print culture of Gothic fiction.[3] This role was scarcely unique to Gothic novels, but was to be particularly the case with them. *Longsword, Earl of Salisbury: An Historical Romance* (1762) by Thomas Leland was an historical novel set in the reign of Henry III (1216–72), lacked any particular bite, and, despite such action as kidnapping and trial by combat, and troubling sites as the dungeons of a castle, reads without gripping, as in:

3   Christina Morin, '*The Adventures of Miss Sophia Berkley*. Piracy, Print Culture, and Irish Gothic Fiction,' *Irish University Review*, 49 (2019), pp. 229–44.

> In the religious house to which Oswald had retired, was a monk called Reginhald, whose mind but ill-suited his profession, or his residence in a seat of piety. He was brother to Grey, and by his interest had not been long since admitted into the monastery, and promoted to some degree of dignity and authority. His manners were equally brutal with those of Grey, but less disguised by art. (IV,i)

and so on.

Walpole wrote in a radically different fashion, one that captured his wide-ranging cultural interests, his mastery of a number of literary genres, the power of his eclectic intellect, and his delight in being distinctive and using his writing to establish his otherness of context, pose and content. Unlike Leland, there was the supernatural, which made the uncertainty of the developing plot more acute and open to authorial intervention. In *The Castle of Otranto*, Walpole gave an expression to his highly subjective portrayal of history, one that was different to the medievalism of his house Strawberry Hill, but an aspect of the same process of removing the experience from the exigencies of modern realism.[4] Deliberately written, as, in 1767, he informed his close friend Madame du Deffand, 'in defiance of rules, critics, and philosophies,'[5] *The Castle of Otranto* was very much an attempt to create a new genre, not least by bringing the supernatural into history, and as part of a use of mystery, imaginative terror, and a shock tactic of suspense. This model produced what was to be much later called the Gothic novel, but was then generally referred to as romance, a distinctive character and particular opportunity. The model also created a challenge for others writing later in what became a genre or, at least, a pattern and a template.

The first edition came out as a spoof, one that reflected Walpole's interest in authorship and sense of satire, an interest more generally seen in this period. Linked to that, there was in Walpole's spoof an irreverent tone

---

4   David McKinney, 'The Castle of My Ancestors: Horace Walpole and Strawberry Hill,' *British Journal for Eighteenth-Century Studies*, 13 (1990), pp. 199–214. See also, Crystal Lake, 'Bloody Records: Manuscripts and Politics in *The Castle of Otranto*,' *Modern Philology*, 110 (2013), pp. 489–512
5   Stephen Gwynn, *The Life of Horace Walpole* (London, 1932), p. 191.

1. Italian Horror with Walpole

that can be seen as subversive but that operated as a joke on a number of levels. The preface provided a totally fictional account of the origins of the work, saying that it was printed at Naples in 1529 and found in the library of an old Catholic family in northern England. The dating of the original text is given as probably thirteenth century and the episode described is dated between 1095 and then. Walpole then moved on to consider a change in culture and therefore literature:

> Miracles, visions, necromancy, dreams, and other preternatural events, are exploded now even from romances. That was not the case when our author wrote.... Belief in every kind of prodigy was so established in those dark ages, that an author would not be faithful to the *manners* of the times who should omit all mention of them.

This was a use of an historical setting in order to provide an opportunity to offer a radically difficult mental world. Moreover, Walpole offered a defence for doing so, instead of extrapolating modern views, notably what Walpole termed '*this* air of the *miraculous*,' upon the past. There was also a description of the intended impact and the method employed: 'Terror, the author's principal engine, prevents the story from ever languishing; and it is so often contrasted by pity, that the mind is kept up in a constant vicissitude of interesting passions.' Moreover, there was a defence of the work, one that employed the commonplace language of such defences in order to make fun of them: 'The piety that reigns throughout, the lessons of virtue that are inculcated, and the rigid purity of the sentiments, exempt this work from the censure to which romances are but too liable.'

In setting his story in Otranto, which was not part of Britain's Gothic, however defined, Walpole looked back to the obscure medieval significance of southern Italy as a contested zone, including in 1480–1 the site of a brief but bloody Ottoman invading presence. Otranto was also in an area that few Britons had visited.

Of those who had, St George Ashe (*c.* 1698–1721) visited Apulia in the late 1710s, with George Berkeley (1685–1753) as his tutor. Berkeley, who was very impressed by the Baroque architecture of Lecce, which he attributed in part to the influence of Classical Greek culture, went on to visit Sicily, including the 'Valley of the Temples' at Agrigento.[6] John Breval (*c.* 1680–1738), who claimed to have travelled abroad on ten occasions, and who certainly accompanied George Cholmondeley (1703–70), later 3rd Earl of Cholmondeley, as bearleader in 1721 and John Crawley (1703–67) in 1725, included in his *Remarks on Several Parts of Europe* plates of Agrigento, Selinunte and Taormina which encouraged interest in Greek remains in Sicily and southern Italy. John, Lord Brudenell (1735–70) went to Paestum in 1756 and such remote sites as Agrigento (1756) and Taranto (1757). William Young (1749–1815), later an MP, visited Apulia and Calabria in 1772, before sailing to Sicily, visiting Malta, spending a month in Palermo and returning to Naples. In Italy in 1784–8, Reveley travelled south from Rome in 1785, visiting Capua, Benevento, Salerno and Paestum, before travelling to the Adriatic coast where he visited Barletta, Trani, Bari, Brindisi, Lecce and Otranto. Sir Richard Colt Hoare (1758–1838), who had inherited the Hoare banking fortune, visited Classical sites in southern Italy and Sicily in 1789–90. In 1819, Hoare published *A Classical Tour through Italy and Sicily.*

Southern Italy's past had its interest, but British commentators saw its present as feudal, superstitious and poor, a perception that was reflected in the novels. In Ann Radcliffe's *The Italian*, Schedoni and Ellena travel through Zanti in south-eastern Italy, which is near Otranto:

> a small town ... where the poverty of the inhabitants seemed to forbid a longer stay than was absolutely necessary for repose and a slight refreshment. Spalatro led the way to a cabin, in which the few persons that journied this road were usually entertained. The appearance of the people, who owned it, was as wild as their country, and the interior of the dwelling was so dirty and comfortless, that Schedoni, preferring to take his repast in the open air.... (II,10)

The first chapter of *The Castle of Otranto* begins energetically and with a rapid setting, one in which a dire ancient prophecy appears in the very first paragraph. In the second, in which there is an interrupted marriage, a

---

6   Edward Chaney, 'Architectural Taste and the Grand Tour: George Berkeley's Evolving Canon,' *Journal of Anglo-Italian Studies* (1991), pp. 86–90.

1. Italian Horror with Walpole

key instance of both dynastic breakdown and of tragedy, there is a powerful sense of action off, with a servant 'running back breathless, in a frantic manner, his eyes staring, and foaming at the mouth.' When asked the matter, he points 'towards the court-yard,' crying out 'the helmet! the helmet!'

Manfred, Prince of Otranto, discovers his son, Conrad, destroyed 'under an enormous helmet,' an hundred times larger than one for any human. This helmet is identified as like that on a statue of Alfonso the Good, a former prince, which leads Manfred to fury. The helmet was indeed missing from the statue. Walpole then puts the readers in their places as many would have felt like the Otranto 'mob, who wanted some object within the scope of their capacities on whom they might discharge their bewildered reasonings.'

Manfred significantly seeks the darkness that was to be a feature of Gothic novels – 'Take away that light.' He then, in an echo of the murderous Richard III of England (r. 1483–5), a Shakespearian villain who also has a quasi-incestuous element, presses his case on Isabella, his once-putative daughter-in-law in a bid to keep his line going. The last was a frequent theme of Gothic novels, for many of which dynasticism was to the fore in context, narrative and assumptions.

Manfred is warned off first by the sight of the plumes on the helmet, and, secondly, by the portrait of his grandfather uttering a deep sigh and heaving its breast before descending onto the floor and beckoning him away, Manfred vowing to follow 'to the gulph of perdition.' This was really the language of an atheist who had rejected morality and overturned mortality. As such, Manfred was a far more profound villain than those in any sentimental novel. Isabella, whom Manfred pursued, in contrast, implores the assistance of 'every saint in heaven'; while the valiant peasant cites Providence against Manfred, only for Manfred to scorn Providence. This scorn is an aspect of the pride that the villains tend to have. In contrast, there was what Radcliffe in *The Italian* termed 'the justifiable pride of a principled mind' (I,1). Richard III was made a more vivid comparison by the strong Shakespeare revival associated in particular with the actor David Garrick who indeed was painted in that career-making role by William Hogarth in 1745.

In the following chapter of *The Castle of Otranto*, the exchange between Jerome, the friar, and Manfred draws out the clash between religious and worldly concerns and assumptions: 'If it is the will of the Most High that

Manfred's name must perish, resign yourself, my Lord, to its decrees; and thus deserve a crown that can never pass away.' The lack of a commitment to Christian burial is also pertinent to Manfred's values.

While these and other exchanges continued, the castle itself was a more powerful presence, notably when, in a vivid passage, Isabella sought to flee from Manfred through the subterranean passage from its vaults to the church of Saint Nicholas where she hoped for sanctuary at the altar. The description was one of menace:

> The lower part of the castle was hollowed into several intricate cloisters; and it was not easy for one under so much anxiety to find the door that opened into the cavern. An awful silence reigned throughout those subterraneous regions, except now and then some blasts of wind that shook the doors she had passed, and which grating on the rusty hinges were re-echoed through that long labyrinth of darkness ... a ray of moonshine streaming through a cranny of the ruin above shone directly on the lock they sought ... the trap-door ... beneath appeared some stone steps descending into a vault totally dark....

In specific terms, subterranean and other passages were a frequent setting for Gothic novels, one made more dangerous by pursuit, thus producing a very different tempo to the conventional novel. More generally, there was also a sense of nature and the natural world as becoming hostile and sinister, as in references to silence, wind, darkness and moonshine.

In turn, Theodore, the brave peasant, who, in a manner that was to become stereotypical, is revealed to be the son of the friar, who himself is really Count Falconara, flees imprisonment in the castle:

> to the forest ... he sought the gloomiest shades, as best suited to the pleasing melancholy that reigned in his mind. In this mood he roved insensibly to the caves which had formerly served as a retreat to hermits, and were now reported round the country to be haunted by evil spirits.... He thought the place more likely to be infested by robbers, than by those infernal agents who are reported to molest and bewilder travellers.

1. Italian Horror with Walpole

Forest, like castle and church, as both refuge and threat, helped provide a degree of inconstancy in this and other Gothic novels, and also contributed to the menace in suspense and suspense in menace. So also with passages, doors, gates, staircases, and keys. All could lead to safety or danger; and the drama of the stories repeatedly pivoted on this uncertainty, as well as with the particular problems of access. Even with buildings set close to the sea, there were still sinister passages, as with Schedoni's plan in *The Italian*:

> he resolved that Ellena should be assassinated that night, while she slept, and afterwards conveyed through a passage of the house communicating with the sea, into which the body might be thrown and buried, with her sad story, beneath the waves. (Ii,9)

The concluding chapter of *The Castle of Otranto* brings the return of horror in a revival of the drama at the outset: 'At that instant Bianca burst into the room, with a wildness in her look and gestures that spoke the utmost terror ... "It is come again! it is come again! ... Oh! the hand! the giant! the hand! ... I am terrified out of my senses."' Frederic is not impressed by Manfred's explanation that this is '"the delirium of a silly wench, who has heard stories of apparitions until she believes them,"' replying: '"This is more than fancy ... her terror is too natural and too strongly impressed to be the work of imagination."' After hearing the rattling of armor, Bianca has seen an enormous hand in armor on the great stairs of the castle, an image that had come to Walpole in the nightmare in which his novel originated.

The idea of an enormous threatening limb, in this case 'a gigantic outstretched arm,' was to be used by later Gothic novelists, notably Charles Maturin in the culminating nightmare in *Melmoth the Wanderer* (1820). The signs reported by Bianca convince Frederic 'that heaven declared itself against Manfred.' Subsequently, in a powerful image, in an oratory in the castle, Frederic:

> saw a person kneeling before the altar ... the figure turning slowly round, discovered in Frederic the fleshless jaws and empty sockets of a skeleton, wrapt in a hermit's cowl.

Frederic is then admonished to forget his 'carnal' drive, and left 'in a conflict of penitence and passion.' This is a frequent tension in the Gothic novel, one that brings to the fore issues implicitly presented in earlier novels. Sexuality is rarely in the background with the Gothic novel; and some of these novels, notably *The Monk* and *Dracula*, pushed the bounds with which sexuality was discussed.

In the great church at night, by the tomb of Alfonso, Manfred kills his daughter Matilda, mistaking her for Isabella, whom he thought unfaithful to his purposes. If this is a theatrical scene ready for the painter's brush, so also is the sequel, with the dying Matilda placed on a litter and carried by the monks from the church to the castle:

> Theodore supporting her head with his arm, and hanging over her in an agony of despairing love, still endeavoured to inspire her with hopes of life. Jerome on the other side comforted her with discourses of heaven, and holding a crucifix before her, which she bathed with innocent tears, prepared her for her passage to immortality. Manfred, plunged in the deepest affliction, followed the litter in despair.

Delirious, Theodore tries to marry Matilda before she dies, 'she shall be mine in death,' only for Matilda to die too swiftly. If that is not enough for the night, in a novel in which lurid events follow in unprecedented sequence and speed, and one that was rarely to be successfully surpassed in this, Matilda's death is followed by a potent and conspicuous supernatural intervention:

> A clap of thunder at that instant shook the castle to its foundations; the earth rocked, and the clank of more than mortal armour was heard behind. Frederic and Jerome thought the last day was at hand. The latter, forcing Theodore along with them, rushed into the court. The moment Theodore appeared, the walls of the castle behind Manfred were thrown down with a mighty force, and the form of Alfonso, dilated to an immense magnitude, appeared in the centre of the ruins. Behold in Theodore, the true heir of Alfonso! said the vision: and having

pronounced these words, accompanied by a clap of thunder, it ascended solemnly towards heaven, where the clouds parting asunder, the form of Saint Nicholas was seen; and receiving Alfonso's shade, they were soon wrapt from mortal eyes in a blaze of glory.

Resigning himself to the will of heaven, and therefore the injunctions of religion, Manfred proclaims the whole 'a warning to future tyrants.' His grandfather's murder of Alfonso and usurpation of Otranto are laid bare. Manfred is convinced by the supernatural: 'the horrors of these days, the vision we have but now seen, all corroborate thy evidence beyond a thousand parchments.' His is a repentance that is not to be seen with Ambrosio in *The Monk*.

Manfred's final response to evidence is a rejection of one type of legal proof, and as part of an affirmation of a broader ethics-based legality. The passage has been adduced by some as a reference to Jacobitism which, in the person of James II and VII, had been driven from Britain in 1688–9, launching a period of legitimist conspiracy and rebellion. Horace Walpole, the youngest son of a leading Whig, Sir Robert Walpole, leading minister from 1720 to 1742, might seem an unlikely supporter of the Jacobite cause. However, Horace had a highly conflicted personality, not least both politically and sexually. Moreover, once politically defunct, as it was after the crushing of the French invasion attempt in 1759, the Jacobite cause attracted a range of sympathy. This included even George III (r. 1760–1820), who saw his own claim to the throne as resting on past parliamentary action and his own duty, rather than on dynastic right.[7] This issue and approach offers a placement for the Gothic novel as part of the process by which conservatism was reconceptualized after Jacobitism,[8] which, from the 1760s, very much became a minority opinion, and was mocked accordingly.[9] Indeed, the Gothic became part of the new patriotism made possible by the defeat of Jacobitism. This also cleared the way for the use of the Gothic in

---

7   Jeremy Black, *George III* (New Haven, Conn., 2006), pp. 303–4, 379, 440.
8   Jim Sack, *From Jacobite to Conservative: Reaction and Orthodoxy in Britain, c. 1760–1832* (Cambridge, 1993).
9   *Felix Farley's Bristol Journal*, 23 November 1788.

a particular fashion in both Ireland and Scotland, expressing a sense of national identity and/or dilemma different to that of England.[10]

In the case of Otranto, there is a more specific reference to usurpation in the conflicts, after the death in 1250 of the (Holy Roman) Emperor Frederick II, 'the Wonder of the World,' over the rulership of the kingdom of Sicily [Sicily and southern Italy]. These conflicts involved Manfred, the illegitimate son of Frederick, who usurped rule over the kingdom of Sicily in 1258, only to be defeated and executed at Benevento in 1266. Conrad, his legitimate half-brother, had died of malaria in 1254, and the latter's infant son, Conradin, ruled from 1254 to 1258, being executed in 1268 when he tried to re-establish himself in Italy, only to be defeated at Tagliacozzo and betrayed to his rival, Charles I of Anjou, already victor over Manfred. There are no specific links between this struggle and that in Walpole's book other than the suggestive name Manfred; but the whole brought up the issues of usurpation, betrayal and sudden violence.

The Castle of Otranto was controversial, but commercially successful. Referring to 'the absurdities of Gothic fiction,' *The Monthly Review* saw the book 'as a work of genius, evincing great dramatic powers,' although its rival, the *Critical Review*, focused on 'the absurdity of its contents.' The first edition of 500 copies sold out in four months, leading, in April 1765, to a second printing of another 500 copies. In this, Walpole removed his disguise, adducing a 'diffidence of his own abilities and the novelty of the attempt' as his excuse for his earlier deceit. In a broad-ranging analysis of literature, Walpole explained his purpose:

> It was an attempt to blend the two kinds of romance, the ancient and the modern. In the former all was imagination and improbability; in the latter, nature is always intended to be, and sometime has been, copied with success. Invention has not been

---

10 Murray Pittock, 'What is a national Gothic?,' in M.A. Constantine and D. Johnston (eds), *Footsteps of Liberty and Revolt: Essays on Wales and the French Revolution* (Cardiff, 2013), pp. 231–45; Davison, 'The Politics and Poetics of "Scottish Gothic" from *Ossian* to *Otranto* and Beyond,' in Carol Margaret Davison and Monica Germanà (eds), *Scottish Gothic: An Edinburgh Companion* (Edinburgh, 2017); Christina Morin, *The Gothic Novel in Ireland, c. 1760–1829* (Manchester, 2018).

wanting; but the great resources of fancy have been damned up, by a strict adherence to common life. But if in the latter species Nature has cramped imagination, she did but take her revenge, having been totally excluded from old romances. The actions, sentiments, conversations, of the heroes and heroines of ancient days were as unnatural as the machines employed to put them in motion.

Instead, Walpole declared that he had sought to reconcile the two kinds of romance, and offered perceptive suggestions for how best to proceed:

> Desirous of leaving the powers of fancy at liberty to expatiate through the boundless realms of invention, and thence of creating more interesting situations, he wished to conduct the mortal agents of his drama according to the rules of probability; in short to make them think, speak and act, as it might be supposed mere men and women would do in extraordinary positions. He had observed, that in all inspired writings, the personages under the dispensation of miracles, and witnesses to the most stupendous phenomenons, never lose sight of their human character: whereas in the productions of romantic story [sic], an improbable event never fails to be attended by an absurd dialogue. The actors seem to lose their senses the moment the laws of nature have lost their tone. As the public have applauded the attempt, the author must not say he was entirely unequal to the task he had undertaken: yet if the new route he has struck out shall have paved a road for men of brighter talents, he shall own with pleasure and modesty, that he was sensible the plan was capable of receiving greater embellishments than his imagination or conduct of the passions could bestow on it.

Having created a new species of 'romance,' now in his own name, Walpole received a fresh coverage in the *Critical Review* which argued that it was important to keep branches of writing distinct. That criticism did not prevent pirated versions of both the first and second editions appearing in Dublin that year, followed by a third London edition in 1766 and a French translation in 1767. Yet, thereafter, *The Castle of Otranto* was not to the fore, with a fourth London edition not appearing until 1782, after which there were numerous printings.

Soon after *The Castle of Otranto* appeared, Pompeo Batoni painted his most dramatic portrait of a British tourist, that of William Gordon (1736–1816). This swagger painting of 1766 depicted Gordon in a toga-like tartan standing in front of the ruins of the Coliseum, near to where Edward Gibbon in 1764 had been inspired to write on the decline of the Roman Empire. In their very different ways, these works captured variations on the idea of the 'translation of empire' from ancient Rome to modern Britain. Thus, Gordon, a vigorous, manly warrior, was shown receiving an orb of authority and a wreath of victory from the figure of Rome, and against a background in which there were no Italians present. Son of William, 2nd Earl of Aberdeen, Gordon at this time was a Lieutenant-Colonel. He was to go on to be an MP, a Groom of the Bedchamber to George III, and a General. In turn, Gibbon was to describe how the Caledonians defied Rome, thus preserving their tribal virtue, while Walpole provided an account, in the case of Otranto, of the collapse of Italy through sin into ruin. Britain takes over the scene, the Gothic novelist, art patron, and historian, all three of whom were MPs, appropriating Italy past to the glory of Britain present, and also, in a number of genres, advancing differing accounts of how change had to occur. The use of Italy as a stage for Gothic novels captured this appropriation, and profited from it.

2. GOTHIC SHADOWS LENGTHEN

A fascination with ruins was seen in Britain from the mid-eighteenth century. Sometimes created anew as follies, ruins were increasingly presented as an innate part of the landscape, as in Thomas Warton's *The Pleasures of Melancholy* (1747) and William Mason's *The English Garden* (1772). The ruin was regarded as particularly suggestive to the human imagination, Thomas Whately writing in *Observations on Modern Gardening* (1770): 'At the sight of a ruin, reflections on the change, the decay, and the desolation before us, naturally occur; and they introduce a long succession of others, all tinctured with that melancholy which these have inspired.'[1]

This interest in ruins was related to the focus on mortality by those later termed the 'graveyard poets.' Locating their meditations in nocturnal churchyards, writers such as Robert Blair and Edward Young sought sublime effects that meshed religious thoughts and fine sensibility, moving beyond melancholia to find a more active reflection. An interest in ruins also reflected a concern with heritage and inheritance, as the longevity of a nation and society was an aspect of its legitimacy. The theme of meditation on death could be readily comprehended within Christian belief, as with Young's bestselling long poem *Night Thoughts* (1742–5), a precursor of the Gothic, although difficulties could be posed by the frequent resonances of Classicism, not least in the case of suicide. Furthermore, in Gothic fiction, monastic stonework and trees became ruined abbeys and sinister woods. Whether or not the foe was supernatural, these were ambiguous or controverted spaces, and, if the Gothic was understood as the ecclesiastical style, it drew, in part through location either (or both) in the past and/or abroad, on the controversial, if not disturbing or hostile, connotations of Catholicism. The Gothic was understood as the ecclesiastical style. Lewis in *The Monk* draws on a standard combination: 'The faint beams of the rising

---

1 Thomas Whately, *Observations on Modern Gardening* (London, 1770), p. 155.

moon scarcely could pierce through the gothic obscurity of the church' (I,1).

The Gothic had become more significant anew from the 1740s. In 1742, the first English book on Gothic architecture appeared, Batty Langley's *Ancient Architecture Restored and Improved by a Great Variety of Grand and Useful Designs, entirely new in the Gothic Mode for ornamenting of buildings and gardens*. Henrietta Howard, Countess of Oxford, rebuilt Welbeck Abbey in the Gothic style from 1752, and Alnwick Castle was remodelled in a Gothic fashion in the same period. However, the Gothic was used for rebuilding, not new seats, and Walpole's more modest Gothic suburban villa at Strawberry Hill, Twickenham, Gothicized an existing cottage. Gothic was not seen as a style equal to Classicism, or, rather, Neo-Classicism, until the work of architects such as James Wyatt at the close of the century and the arguments of John Carter, notably his *Essays on Gothic Architecture* (1802). Such work, however, led to an interest in buildings from the medieval past, as with George Cubitt the Younger's *Six Etchings of Saxon and Gothic Buildings now Remaining in the City of Chester* (1810–11) and his illustrations to the *History of the City of Chester* (1815), as well as extensive work on Windsor Castle.

In 1778, in occupied Philadelphia, the British army organised the Mischianza, an elaborate entertainment that included a pseudo-medieval tournament. This was intended to display noble martial identity and to call on the allegorical potential of chivalric romance, one that provided an instance of loyalist Gothic.[2] Loyalist Gothic was also seen in other arts, such as the paintings of Benjamin West, as well as in Gothic novels which became more fashionable in the 1790s, notably with the works of Ann Radcliffe. The role of the Gothic in late eighteenth century culture created a context more for artistic enterprise than for historical reflection. Yet, the two should not be too abruptly separated. There were important links, and both in content and tone. Indeed, the cultural dimensions of history need to be emphasised alongside the intellectual.

---

2   Daniel O'Quinn, 'Invalid Elegy and Gothic Pageantry: André, Seward and the Loss of the American War,' in Neil Ramsay and Gillian Russell (eds), *Tracing War in British Enlightenment and Romantic Culture* (Basingstoke, 2015), pp. 41–2; James Watt, *Contesting the Gothic: Fiction, Genre and Cultural Conflict, 1764–1832* (Cambridge, 1999).

2. Gothic Shadows Lengthen

An engagement with the Gothic helped ensure a stronger interest in the Middle Ages and in medievalism than had been the case earlier in the eighteenth century. George III's interest in the medieval period looked back to Henry, Viscount Bolingbroke's thesis of the Patriot King, an idea developed in his *The Idea of a Patriot King* (1749) and focused then on Frederick, Prince of Wales, before being adopted for Frederick's eldest son, George III,[3] although the latter contrasted 'our Gothic institutions' of state with taking the Sacrament which George did not wish to have the former prophane.[4] His coronation saw such 'institutions,' not least in the presence of the armour-clad King's Champion defying anyone to challenge the royal right to the throne, an instance that could lead to chaos due to the difficulty of controlling the horse.

The Patriot King was a theme readily located with Edward III (r. 1327–77) and Henry V (r. 1413–22), monarchs who were easily recovered through accessible Tudor, Stuart and Hanoverian histories, and, differently, with Henry VIII and Elizabeth I, for the sixteenth century was regarded as a continuation of the medieval ones. Other writers who looked to the Middle Ages, included Richard Hurd with his *Letters on Chivalry and Romance* (1757) and, somewhat differently, Thomas Chatterton (1752–70) who invented Thomas Rowley, a fifteenth-century British poet, and proved an iconic suicide. Medievalism had a number of forms and tones, as with Thomas Gray's poem *The Bard* (1757) which also presented an alternative to urban and rural restraint. Based on the subsequently discredited Welsh tradition, mentioned in Thomas Carte's *History of England,* that the conjuring Edward I ordered the execution of all Welsh bards, Gray had been inspired to complete the poem when he heard a Welsh harpist play at Cambridge. His image of the bard reflected the importance of picturesque landscape for bardic and primitivist literature:

---

3   Folke Nibelius, *Lord Bolingbroke (1678–1751) and History. A Comparative Study of Bolingbroke's Politico-historical Works and a Selection of Contemporary Texts as to Themes and Vocabulary* (Stockholm, 2003): 147–61.
4   Sir Nathaniel Wraxall, 'Anecdotes of My Own Times,' 31 Jan. 1805, Beinecke Rare Books and Manuscript Library, New Haven, Connecticut, Osborn Mss, c. 26.

> On a rock, whose haughty brow
> Frowns o'er old
> Conway's foaming flood
> Robed in the sable garb or woe,
> With haggard eyes, the Poet stood;
> Loose his beard and hoary hair
> Stream'd like a meteor
> through the troubled air.

Gray's poem was the basis of *The Bard*, a painting by Thomas Jones, the inspiration for later literary and artistic compositions, notably John Martin's painting *The Bard* (1817) which shows the last bard watching advancing English forces before he plunges to his death. The castle in Martin's painting is based on Harlech, but the landscape owes more to Alpine views and the dramatic crags near Allendale than to Wales.

Morality played a major role in the depiction of medieval figures. George, Lord Lyttelton, a onetime politician and, formerly, the friend and patron of Henry Fielding, devoted much effort to his *History of the Life of Henry the Second* (1767), in turn responding in 1772 to praise that

> it may be useful to the highest interest of mankind, by inculcating a right sense of morality and religion, which indeed I had at heart, above any other work, and without the hope of which I could not have gone through the drudgery of it with any satisfaction.[5]

Yet, as a reminder that the tone, content and genre of the Gothic could vary greatly, a somewhat different account of Henry II (r. 1154–89) to that of Lyttelton was offered by Thomas Hull (1728–1808), a leading London actor, in his most successful play, the tragedy *Henry the Second, or the Fall of Rosamond* which related to the king's love-life. First performed in 1773, the play appeared in four editions the following year, as did Hull's *Richard Plantagenet, a Legendary Tale*, a verse story based on the life of Richard, 3rd Duke of York (1411–60), the preface of which preached 'the duty of a

---

5   Lyttelton to —, April 5, 1772, BL. RR 2377ii.

patient submission to the destinations of Providence, in all vicissitudes and afflictions of life.' Hull's novel, *The History of Sir William Harrington*, also attributed to Anna Meades, had appeared three years earlier, and was to be reprinted in 1797 when medievalism was to the fore. It was also published in German (1771) and French (1775) editions.

Lyttelton also captured an international competitiveness which was an important background to the presentation of an English Gothic medievalism that underplayed the wider European span of the movement. Thus, in 1762, in this case with reference to Classicism, he commented on the grounds at Stourhead:

> The Pantheon [by Henry Flitcroft] is finished, and is an abode worthy of all the deities in Olympus.... I think I never saw the Graces of Sculpture and all the power of that divine art, before I saw them there. I would have every Frenchman that comes to England be brought to this place, not only that he may see the perfection of our taste, but to show him that we have citizens who have a truer politeness in their manners, and a nobler elegance in their minds, than any Count or Duke in France.[6]

The long-lived and victorious Edward III, the founder of the Order of the Garter, proved especially valuable as an example, as with both Reeve's *Memoirs of Sir Roger De Clarendon* (1793) and George III's sponsorship of the historical paintings of Benjamin West. West's *Edward III Crossing the Somme* (1788), an episode from 1346, showed how successful past monarchs could be portrayed in a dramatic and colourful fashion which reflected glory on their current successor. Moreover, James Northcote, a protégé of Joshua Reynolds and a popular royal academician, helped form an impression of the national past from 1784 with paintings including *Sir William Walworth ... Killing Wat Tyler* (1787), and *The Murder of the Princes in the Tower*, events in 1381 and 1483 respectively. Alongside this general impression of the drama of the Middle Ages, thus came potent individual images, the latter one painted by Northcote in several versions, most prominently in 1786, and followed by *The Burial of the Princes in The Tower*.

6   Lyttelton to Elizabeth Montagu, 21 July 1762, BL. RP. 2377i.

The latter topic captured a frequent Gothic concern, that of usurpation, and with the setting that of a grim castle. That was an image from a past kept alive by the publication of numerous national histories. A different issue in Gothic novels, that of mysterious heirs, was one that would have appeared more probable but also domestic to those reading newspapers of the period. Thus, the London news in *Jackson's Oxford Journal* of 3 July 1790 noted:

> Tuesday Evening, two women, supposed to be mother and daughter, knocked at the door of a single gentleman of large fortune at the West End of the town, and delivered a basket directed for him, which they said came from Clapham, and contained some fruit. The gentleman, on his return home, examining the contents, found, to his great surprise, a fine boy fast asleep, which appeared to be about three days old.

Earlier, on 31 July 1780, W.C., writing in the *Reading Mercury, and Oxford Gazette*, referred to 'spurious marriages' as a regular item in newspapers. They were an aspect of the challenge to realism posed by deceit, but also of the precariousness of credit more generally in society. The dubious nature of many marriages also related to questionable religious practices.

George Colman's play *The Surrender of Calais* (1791), a reference to Edward III's victory over France in 1347 not to English defeat at Calais in 1558, contributed to a different theme of triumphant medievalism, closing with:

> Rear, rear our English banner high.
> In token proud of victory!
> Where'er our god of battle strides,
> Loud sound the trumpet of fame!
> Where'er the English warrior rides
> May Laurelled conquest grace his name.

Medieval warfare with France was an important theme of the culture of the period, as with Robert Southey's epic poem *Joan of Arc* (1796), a work in which a patriotically disposed ruler played a role.[7] Although Southey gives Henry V a speech critical of clericalism, the plot downplays the role of religion and clerics. In part, Southey does so by ending before Joan's trial and execution, which would have provided a very Gothic theme.

Heroism was a characteristic of Gothic novels, and a heroism that was more prominent than in earlier novels, because threats were more immediate and terrible and the settings more sublime and horrific. This was true for both men and women, and each needed resolution, as each could be victims, as in Reeve's *The Old English Baron*:

> His father was assassinated by order of that wicked man ... his mother was, by his cruel treatment, compelled to leave her own house; she was delivered in the fields, and perished herself in seeking a shelter for her infant. (150)

If female protagonists, as in *The Mysteries of Udolpho*, could be somewhat weak, that was far from invariably the case, and, anyway, their circumstances were generally presented as pitiable and the context as malign. The context and content of male heroism varied, but it was an insistent theme, and related both to bravery in conflict, notably in duels, and also resolution in attitude. Thus, in *The Old English Baron*, Edmund:

> recovered both his voice and courage; he stepped forward, his person erect, his countenance assured, his voice resolute and intrepid. (96)

His romance with Emma takes a very different form to that of sentimental novels. Later in that novel, there is a judgment by group-conflict, which is shown to be an established process, one no longer pursued by the time of the novel.

In the nineteenth century, the Gothic was to become a theme linked

---

7   David Eastwood, 'Robert Southey and the Meanings of Patriotism,' *Journal of British Studies*, 31 (1992), pp. 271–2.

by many to contemporary Catholicism,[8] but that was not a necessary linkage in Britain then or earlier. Instead, far from the response to the medieval or the Gothic being constrained by anti-Catholicism, aspects of medievalism were of wide interest. Knowledge and understanding of the medieval period also benefited from the publication of sources such as Thomas Rymer's *Foedera* (1704–13), Thomas Hearne's publication of major chronicles, and the publication, from 1767, of the Rolls of Parliament. In historical terms, interest in the Middle Ages could lead to a degree of antiquarianism, but, more significantly, it ensured that national history was not solely a matter of the period from the Reformation or even the Glorious Revolution of 1688–9. This would have been the case had the relevance pursued been that of what was then held to be the origins of modern Britain. Equally, the focus on modernity encouraged a treatment of the Gothic, and the medieval more generally, in Romantic terms, one that was also to be evident in the Young England movement of the 1840s and its idealisation of the medieval past. Both tendencies were readily apparent in historical writing at the close of the eighteenth century.[9] They were aspects of the uneasy compound that constituted the developing historical sense of nationalism and, both linked and separate, the reaction to other historical cultures. This dimension was given added complexity in so far as Irish, Scottish and Welsh dimensions of the Gothic were considered.

Gothic novels dramatized the interest in medievalism. And, launched by Walpole, the drama gripped. Spending the night in hitherto closed castle compartments, two aristocratic youths in *The Old English Baronet*, in a scene depicted in the frontispiece, face first 'dismal' groans and then ghostly horror:

> a pale glimmering light appeared at the door from the staircase, and a man in complete armour entered the room: He stood, with one hand extended, pointing to the outward door (114).

8   Peter Nockles, 'The difficulties of Protestantism': Bishop Milner, John Fletcher, and Catholic apologetics against the Church of England,' *Recusant History*, 24 (1998–9), pp. 193–236.
9   For a different aspect, Mark Phillips, 'Relocating Inwardness: Historical Distance and the Transition from Enlightenment to Romantic Historiography,' in Adam Budd, ed., *The Modern Historiography Reader: Western Sources* (Abingdon, 2009), pp. 106–17.

2. Gothic Shadows Lengthen

There is an attempt at a cover-up: 'a piece of furniture fell down in the rooms underneath, which made the noise that alarmed them so much.' This device was to be used on other occasions, but cover-ups do not work in Gothic novels. Instead, they are about the revelation of truth. Harclay presents himself as 'only the instrument of justice in the hand of Heaven.' The villain, Lord Lovel, confesses that 'nothing can be concealed from the eye of Heaven,' a longstanding idea of its omnipotence that, as with the previous quote, captured the explicit physicality of the standard account. This approach would very much have accorded with the views of the pious George III, who had no interest in novels,[10] but was left meditative in 1788 by the tomb in Gloucester Cathedral of the murdered Edward II (r. 1307–27).

Heaven continues to be referred to throughout the novel and with a sense of its power, as in, '"Edmund," said the Baron, "you have a noble friend, but you have a stronger in my heart, which I think was implanted there by Heaven to aid its own purposes."' There is then an instance of a benign supernatural, while darkness is presented as Heaven's opponent:

> The sound of the horn announced the arrival of the commissioners; at the same instant a sudden gust of wind arose, and the outward gates flew open. They entered the court-yard, and the great folding doors into the hall, were opened without any assistance. The moment Edmund entered the hall, every door in the house flew open; the servants all rushed into the hall, and fear was written on their countenances.... Edmund [said] ... I accept the omen! .... let us finish the work of fate! ... Open the shutters ... the deeds of darkness shall now be brought to light.

The morality was reiterated in a novel without ambiguity: 'Behold the day of retribution! of triumph to the innocent.' Royal justice is also seen as exemplary because the king is 'good and pious.' The plot ends with the marriage of hero and heroine who have a son soon after, thus ending the family rift and sustaining the dynasty. Four sons and a daughter follow. The novel

---

10 Neither Arthur Burns nor myself have found any evidence of George's interest in Gothic novels.

closes with the affirmation that it provides 'a striking lesson to posterity, of the over-ruling hand of Providence, and the certainty of RETRIBUTION.'

This concern for morality and for deploying history accordingly was shared by novelists, Gothic and otherwise, and by historians, both talented, such as Edward Gibbon and David Hume, as well as less famous counterparts. This concern was at once timeless and located in particular moments, both religious and secular, past and present. Thus, Charles, 11th Duke of Norfolk (1746–1815), a firm Whig, a lapsed Catholic and a Unitarian, sought to commemorate the 600th anniversary of Magna Carta by building an octagonal Great Hall at his seat of Arundel Castle, a hall dedicated to 'Liberty asserted by the Barons in the reign of John.' Norfolk also acquired and prominently displayed Mather Brown's painting *Thomas Earl of Surrey defending himself before Henry VII after Bosworth*, a 1797 work referring to a 1485 episode involving the later 2nd Duke of Norfolk.

As an important aspect of British culture in this period, there was also a turn to a different landscape, one in which wildness was in the foreground. There was a major British dimension to this turn, but it was to be given fuller and freer rein in the discussion of foreign countries. The chronological dimension was indicated in the Gothic novels. *The Castle of Otranto* was not one about landscape, but those by Radcliffe were very different. Already prior to the 1790s, tourists had shown greater interest in wilder scenery and sensations. Thus, Switzerland became a goal, rather than an obstacle. It was no longer necessary for a mountain, waterfall or lake in Italy to have been mentioned by Virgil or Livy for it to attract tourists. By the 1780s, William Beckford was enthusing about wild, primitive scenery, while in Spain in 1786 Joseph Townsend rode on horseback from Leon to Oviedo:

> through the wildest and most romantic country which can be imagined, rendered tremendous by the rocks and beautiful by the wood and water.[11]

Radcliffe responded to this engagement with great skill. The wildness of Sicily was repeatedly asserted, and it is the setting in *A Sicilian Romance*

---

11 Jeremy Black, *The British Abroad. The Grand Tour in the Eighteenth Century* (Stroud, 1992), pp. 277–8.

(1790) for the 'banditti' as well as the counterpart to stormy weather. There is a much further development of this theme in her later writing. There is also the appeal of more attractive wildness in this novel:

> ... in a beautiful romantic country; and having reached the summit of some wild cliffs, he rested, to view the picturesque imagery of the scene below. A shadowy sequestered dell appeared buried deep among the rocks, and in the bottom was seen a lake, whose clear bosom reflected the impending cliffs, and the beautiful luxuriance of the over-hanging shades ... the rocks, stupendous heights and craggy steeps. (5)

Subsequently, the sublime is brought to the fore by Radcliffe in a lengthy passage about an evening walk among the mountains that provides:

> a view so various and sublime, that she paused in thrilling and delightful wonder. A group of wild and grotesque rocks rose in a semicircular form, and their fantastic shapes exhibited Nature in her most sublime and striking attitudes. Here her vast magnificence elevated the mind of the beholder to enthusiasm. Fancy caught the thrilling sensation, and at her touch the towering steeps became shaded with unreal glooms; the caves more darkly frowned – the projecting cliffs assumed a more terrific aspect, and the wild overhanging shrubs waved to the gale in deeper murmurs. The scene inspired madame with reverential awe. (7)

As a reminder of the extent and role of contrasts, this was also a time of growing urbanisation, notably the phenomenon of an apparently bloated London that variously (and strongly) dismayed George III, William Blake and William Wordsworth. In *The Monk*, Lewis presents Paris as a disgusting 'theatre of luxury' (I,3), while, in *The Old English Baronet* (1808) by Henrietta Rouviere (Mosse), a work the title of which looks to Reeve's *The Old English Baron*, virtue is found in country settings, not cities:

> In Ireland, England, France, Switzerland, and Italy, the industrious peaceful inhabitant of the fields is alike humane,

hospitable, and orderly: but these men are seldom employed as the engines of demagogic fury; it is the mob of cities that has wrought the woes of France; and ... the scenes in Ireland, the riots in London in 1780 [Gordon Riots], and earlier troubles ... prove that there, as elsewhere, the fury of the beast is in exact proportion to the energy of its exciting cause, and the weakness and tardiness of the force to be opposed to it. (II,4)

Yet, the Gothic largely abandoned the urban milieux of threat that had so challenged heroines earlier in the eighteenth century, for example Henry Fielding's *Amelia* (1751) and, instead, moved into the countryside. This was not the calm cultivation and stately homes of earlier novels, such as Richardson's *Pamela* (1740), but rather a marked accentuation of the menace of rural travels seen, for example, in Fielding's *Joseph Andrews* (1742) and *Tom Jones* (1749). In Gothic novels, travellers, often fugitives from danger, notably imprisonment in an intended but unwanted marriage, have the choice of the menaces of mountain or forest, desolation on land or storm at sea. Thus, Hippolitus in *A Sicilian Romance* faces 'high and savage mountains' or a gloomy forest, choosing the latter as it would provide shelter from the winds and the possibility of finding shelter by climbing a tree (13). This was a rural world very different to that discussed in English travelogues, notably by William Gilpin, and those who followed his pattern.

Aside from castles, monasteries were an important part of the standard landscape of the Gothic novel. In the second chapter of Radcliffe's *The Romance of the Forest* (1791), in the first setting described at length, La Motte finds 'the Gothic remains of an abbey,' overshadowed by trees which diffuse 'a romantic gloom.' The description is one that gathers pace, and the setting itself becomes part of the drama. It is worth quoting at length both in indicating the painterly character of descriptions and because Radcliffe greatly helped to push ruined Gothic abbeys to the fore, offering an alternative to castles:

> The greater part of the pile appeared to be sinking into ruins, and that which had withstood the ravages of time, showed the remaining features of the fabric more awful in decay. The lofty battlements thickly enwreathed with ivy, were half demolished and become the residence of birds of prey. Huge fragments of the eastern tower,

which was almost demolished, lay scattered amid the high grass....
A Gothic gate ... now obstructed with brushwood, remained entire
... the chapel of the abbey where the hymn of devotion had once
been, raised ... La Motte ... felt a sensation of sublimity rising into
terror – a suspension of mingled astonishment and awe! He surveyed
the vastness of the place, and as he contemplated its ruins, fancy
bore him back to past ages. (2)

La Motte refers to a place 'where once superstition lurked' (2), which suggests an ambiguous, at best, response to the awe of the Gothic. There is a more poetic reference to the 'mysterious accents of the dead' (2). As so often in Gothic novels, these 'accents' are brought to a head by night-time sounds, often from hidden chambers or passages. There is a clear juxtaposition in this novel between night and day, Gothic remains and natural purity, one seen when Adeline rhapsodically praises the dawn and, in doing so, brings Heaven into prospect and the text.

A background to such discussion was provided not only by earlier novels, by accounts of foreign travels, and the English landscape, and by the growing interest shown by travellers in Britain in medieval sites there,[12] many of which came with Gothic-style legends. Thus, in his *Tour of Scotland* (1771), a tour carried out in 1769 that included northern England and went into five editions by 1790, Thomas Pennant commented on Roman and medieval remains, offering anecdotes accordingly. Crossing the Lincolnshire Fens, he:

> passed near the ruins of Swineshead Abbey, of which there are not the least remains. In the walls of a farm-house, built out of the ruins, you are shown the figure of a Knight Templar, and told it was the monk who poisoned King John; a fact denied by our best historians,[13]

although asserted by John Foxe in his *Book of Martyrs* (1563).

12   Anne Janowitz, *England's Ruins: Poetic Purpose and the National Landscape* (Oxford, 1987).
13   Pennant, *A Tour in Scotland, 1769* (4th edn, London, 1775), p. 15.

Pennant was far from alone. In 1789, George Huntingford (1748–1832), from 1789 Warden of Winchester College, and, from 1802, a bishop, for first Gloucester and then Hereford,[14] wrote to his friend Henry Addington, then Speaker of the House of Commons and later Viscount Sidmouth and, in 1801–4, Prime Minister, who had been travelling in Hampshire: 'The old ruins of Beaulieu I know well, and remember with an impression bordering on superstition.'[15] Dissolved in 1538, Beaulieu Abbey became a ruin, part of which was turned into an aristocratic house. From the nineteenth century, there were to be many reported sightings of ghostly monks.[16]

Nearby Netley Abbey, a ruined Cistercian abbey in Hampshire that Jane Austen visited in 1807, was a site for the rise of Gothic tourism, with contrasting views about the supernatural character of such sites. Reports of ghostly activity at Netley were first described by Browne Willis in his *An History of the Mitred Parliamentary Abbies, and Conventual Cathedral Churches* (1718), in which a carpenter ignores apparitions, in particular of a monk, that warn him against improving the abbey, and is then killed by falling stones. The theme of these ruins as inhabited by ghosts was much advanced by George Keate in his *The Ruins of Netley Abbey: A Poem*, which was published in the same year as *The Castle of Otranto*.[17] In 1763, his poem *The Alps* appeared.

The abbey indeed became the setting for Richard Warner's *Netley Abbey: A Gothic Story* (1795), a Minerva Press publication that variously offered anti-Catholicism, the supernatural, sexuality, and mysteriously changing portraits. The villain, Sir Hildebrand, has designs on Agnes Warren who is imprisoned by his allies, the monks of Netley. Agnes's father, Sir Raymond Warren, the murdered uncle of Sir Hildebrand, appears as an armour-clad

14 A. Bell, 'Warden Huntingford and the Old Conservatism,' *Winchester College. Sixth Centenary Essays*, ed. Custance (Oxford, 1982).
15 Huntingford to Addington, 17 September 1789, Exeter, Devon County Record Office, 152M/C1789/F99.
16 David Scanlan, *Paranormal Hampshire* (Stroud, 2013).
17 Dale Townshend, 'Ruins, Romance and the Rise of Gothic Tourism: The Case of Netley Abbey, 1750–1830,' *Journal for Eighteenth-Century Studies*, 37 (2014), pp. 377–94, and *Gothic Antiquity. History, Romance, and the Architectural Imagination, 1760–1840* (Oxford, 2019).

2. Gothic Shadows Lengthen

ghost holding a lance. The ghostly figures are benign and ensure that justice overcomes Hildebrand. An American edition followed in 1796.

Ruined abbeys played a role in antiquarian travels, such as William Coxe's *An Historical Tour of Monmouthshire* (1801), dedicated to Sir Richard Colt Hoare, with whom he had travelled there in 1798 and 1799. Melrose Abbey was described in Walter Scott's *The Lay of the Last Minstrel* (1805), and was possibly the setting for his novel *The Monastery* (1820). When he visited Scotland in 1822, the first visit by a ruling monarch since the seventeenth century. George IV staged at Newbattle Abbey, the seat of the Marquess of Lothian.

Monastic sites had an additional significance as possible sites for a Catholic rejection of aspects of the modern, and this has been seen as a source of Gothic values and imagination. This, however, is a matter for suggestion at most, not least because there was variety in the attitudes of Gothic writers. In part, literature, most obviously the publication of the Bible in the vernacular, can be presented as a means to cope with the disruption of the Reformation, with some strands of that literature of the sixteenth and seventeenth century influencing what followed. Revenge tragedy in particular offered not only a theme that moved protagonists to obsessions and villains to evil, but also plot devices of horror, and the intervention of supernatural beings. Such works, however, were not solely the result of the Reformation. The revenge story in particular was long-lasting.[18]

George III gave up the title 'King of France' in 1801, but Gothic themes continued to be important in British culture. In large part, there was a degree of past values, as with the Prince in Sydney Owenson's *The Wild Irish Girl* (1806), a figure who prefigured Giuseppi Lampedusa's *The Leopard* (1958):

> … the splendid dwelling of princely grandeur, the awful asylum of monastic piety, are just mouldering into oblivion with the memory of those they once sheltered. The sons of little men triumph over those whose arm was strong in war, and whose voice breathed no impotent command; and the descendant of the mighty chieftain has nothing left to distinguish him from the

18 Nick Groom, *The Gothic. A Very Short Introduction* (Oxford, 2012), p. 43.

son of the peasant, but the decaying ruins of his ancestors' castle; while the blasts of a few storms, and the pressure of a few years, shall even of them leave scarce a wreck to tell the traveller the mournful tale of fallen greatness.[19]

To a degree, this was a British Gothic prefiguration of Percy Bysshe Shelley's *Ozymandias* (1818), and the theme of past glory and present challenge was present in both. While *Frankenstein* emerged from a discussion in 1816, *Ozymandias* followed another a year later. As with the Gothic, the past is strange and disconcerting, but the menace is not the active force of the Gothic, and 'The line and level sands stretch far away' of that poem is not the potently disturbing claustrophobia of the Gothic. Contexts led in different directions, and any discussion of causality has to be advanced with due caution.

19 Letter 6.

3. AFTER OTRANTO

In the second edition of *The Castle of Otranto*, Walpole claimed that Nature had 'cramped imagination.' Indeed, there was a somewhat limited character of science fiction in the eighteenth century, certainly in comparison to the last 140 years. With scant expansion in new directions, fantasy looked back to an established range of creatures, in large part due to the extent to which this was a society that was reverential of the past and referential of it.

There were intimations of a new world for the imagination. In his *History of the Present State of Electricity* (1767), Joseph Priestley claimed that recent discoveries of electrical phenomena, which even Wesley embraced as a therapeutic tool for melancholy, would extend 'the bounds of natural science.... New worlds may open to our view, and the glory of the great Sir Isaac Newton himself, and all his contemporaries, be eclipsed by a new set of philosophers'; but most, however, were less confident. Moreover, the contemporary ideas of species limited speculation. Few were led toward ideas of evolution. Most writers clung, instead, to the notions of the fixity of individual species and of a natural environment that would be static until the coming of the Apocalypse. Knowledge concerning the origin of animal characteristics, both as individuals and as a species, was still too limited to help to clarify theoretical speculation. At the same time, new movements and phenomena could attract attention, whether star-gazing, mesmerism (animal magnetism, which was in vogue in the 1780s), or electricity. That attention provided opportunities to consider new possibilities, a process that was encouraged by the popular notion of scientific discussion. Yet, the mathematisation of academic science possibly made the nature and constraints of theory harder to grasp. Indeed, the idea that personal moral faults, or the malevolent intentions of others, were responsible for mishaps, such as accidents, proved difficult to dispel, and that was the case whatever the current teaching on cosmology, physics and medicine.

At the same time, some theoretical discussion did lead in the direction of later science fiction. Thus, John Needham (1713–81), the first Catholic cleric elected a fellow of the Royal Society of London, published in 1749 his experimental proof of the theory of spontaneous generation, the idea that inanimate matter could come alive, and thus that mutations and new creations of species were possible. The fallacy of his experiment was not demonstrated until 1760. Somewhat differently, Giuseppe Balsamo, 'Count Cagliostro' (1743–95), began his career as an alchemist by seeking to transmute excrement, hair, herbs, minerals, urine, and wood into gold in London in 1776–7.

This was very different, in topic and approach, to the mathematisation of risk and options that was more significant, in part due to Newtonian physics but, more specifically, in part to developments in the analysis of probability and in life insurance. Richard Price (1723–91), an able mathematician (and radical Dissenter), provided reasonable guides which were of greater value because they were published, especially his *Observations on Reversionary Payments* (1771). The growth of the life insurance industry had little effect on the bulk of the population, but it reflected an attitude to risk and to the threat of calamity that was removed from fatalism or a reliance on Providence.[1] However, even with this new approach, there was little evidence of any widespread questioning of the notion of divine justice.

Furthermore, alongside support for new ideas, not least in medical care, there was also criticism. Thus, inoculation against smallpox was condemned by those who championed the doctrine of providential affliction; the notion that God was responsible and that His reasons should not be questioned or defied. Probably for most people, every disease and accident had a cause arising from the travails of the soul and the temptations of sin. Moral behaviour would be rewarded with health, and thus restraint in personal conduct was prudent as well as virtuous. At the same time, chance and uncertainty were always present, whether lightning and disease, or the dark and injury. All conveyed risk and menace.

Gothic fiction was produced against the background of a lasting search for stability and understanding in an essentially unstable and inexplicable

---

1   Geoffrey Clark, *Betting on Lives: The Culture of Life Insurance in England, 1695–1775* (Manchester, 1999).

world, a search that involved an attempt to reconcile divine justice with human suffering, and to order experience in a way that reflected the hard and apparently arbitrary nature of life. On a longterm pattern, religious world-views provided the most effective explanatory model, the best psychological defences, and the essential note of continuity. Gothic fiction provided an opportunity also to warn about the danger of turning to evil. It was not so much secular morality as religious admonition and entertainment.

The hostile environment was understood in terms of retribution, with the possibility, in turn, of winning remission by good actions; but the perception of the latter varied. For some, both bargaining and action could include satisfying the demands and temptations of the spirit world and the occult; and Gothic novels in part drew on this danger, although the degree to which this was made explicit varied. Separately, practices that derived their origins from pagan beliefs were not the same as paganism, as such beliefs and practices coexisted or were intertwined with Christian counterparts, with generally only limited awareness of any incompatibility. This was especially the case for ordinary lay people in the countryside. At the same time, this, essentially benign, account was challenged by writers such as Matthew Lewis, Charlotte Dacre and Charles Maturin who presented an antithesis in terms of a clear incompatibility, even if that was not always evident in the plot at first.

It is possible to point to an increasing questioning in the late eighteenth century of the notion of direct divine intervention in the fate of individuals and communities, as in growing scepticism that earthquakes reflected divine displeasure. Yet, this was very much not a secular society, and the contemporary notion of progress was not inherently sceptical. Instead, it rested in part on a diluted (or not so diluted) millenarianism, which was certainly much in evidence in the 1790s, as well as on the traditional conviction that God provided means to cure all ills if only they could be discovered, a means of incorporating science into religion. This approach, as well as British public culture and history, however, could make the position of the Catholic Church, which, for most Protestant writers, was inherently irrational, as well as overly powerful, a major issue, one that could be taken even further by Protestant writers in Ireland. Thus, Sheridan Le Fanu's novella *Carmilla* (1872), which, despite an Austrian setting, brings out the anxiety of the Irish

Ascendancy. The work influenced *Dracula*. Strong criticism of Catholicism was expressed by many Gothic writers, notably, but differently and not always consistently, by Radcliffe and Lewis. Criticism varied in its emphasis, whether on individual clerics or on institutions, but the common concern was that of excessive power and its use for malicious purposes. Popular belief in England, Scotland and Wales was not so much pagan as pre Reformation,[2] with a folk Christianity open to many of the elements of a struggle with diabolical forces, but against an anti-Catholic background.

The Protestant emphasis on a limited controlling role for any Church was presented by British commentators as necessary for the view and practice of knowledge and science as part of the divine plan; although Catholics believed the same about knowledge and science and divine intentions. At any rate, in the eighteenth century, knowledge and science were not solvents of religious faith.

Walpole, who had the time to do so, did not write another Gothic novel after *The Castle of Otranto*, but followed in 1768 with *The Mysterious Mother*, a Gothic tragedy set in the Middle Ages. Incest plays a key role in the plot, with the manipulative French countess committing suicide when her tormenting guilt is revealed. The Catholic clergy featured are dishonest and, for Walpole, she has reason to defy them and their attempts to make her achieve religious repentance. Guilt is a key theme in the play. The topic and outcome made the play inappropriate for the stage, but there were private readings and several editions.

The gap prior to the appearance of *The Count of Narbonne* did not mean that *The Castle of Otranto* fell from attention. Indeed, the book was cited as 'a very spirited modern attempt' upon the plan of the *Arabian Nights* 'adapted to the model of Gothic romance' by Anna Aikin (later Anna Bartauld) in her 'On the Pleasure Derived From Objects of Terror' which appeared in her *Miscellaneous Pieces in Prose* (1773). She provided in this piece an explanation of the sublime dimension of surprise including:

> the agency of invisible beings.... Passion and fancy co-operating elevate the soul to its highest pitch ... the more wild, fanciful,

[2] Michael Snape, *The Church of England in Industrialising Society: The Lancashire Parish of Whalley in the Eighteenth Century* (Woodbridge, 2003).

and extraordinary are the circumstances of a scene of horror, the more pleasure we receive from it.

Anna Aikin also focused on the consumerism of public interest: 'The Greediness with which the tales of ghosts and goblins, of murders, earthquakes, fires, shipwrecks, and all the most terrible disasters attending human life, are devoured by every ear,' and she added in Shakespeare as an instance of the process. The preface to *Miscellaneous Pieces* came with 'Sir Bertrand, a Fragment' (1773) by John Aikin (although often attributed wrongly to his sister Anna), an unfinished piece which provided a sinister, apparently deserted, Gothic castle with a mysterious moving flame, and a dead hand grasping the protagonist, both, notably the former, devices that were to be used frequently. The lid of a coffin flies open and:

> a lady in a shroud and black veil rose up in it, and stretched out her arms towards him.... Sir Bertrand flew to the lady and clasped her in his arms – she threw up her veil and kissed his lips; and instantly the whole building shook as with an earthquake, and fell asunder with a horrible crash.

This passage offered an early instance of the themes and images of illicit and dangerous sexuality, a veil, and earthquakes as both plot and an indicator of fundamental disruption. This sexuality was to lead to the nineteenth-century strand of Gothic vampirism. Anna Aikin (1743–1825) was to be a successful 'woman of letters,' particularly as a writer of children's literature. She was also a literary critic and a supporter of political reform. Her brother, John, was a doctor who became a writer, notably a biographer.

In turn, there was no preface to the next significant work, Clara Reeve's *The Champion of Virtue* (1777), but when it was published the following year as *The Old English Baron: A Gothic Story*, it had a preface that paid full attention to Walpole's novel, which was the defining point until Radcliffe's novels changed the paradigm in the 1790s. In this preface, Reeve presented her work as:

> ... of a species which, though not new, is out of the common track, the literary offspring of the Castle of Otranto, written

upon the same plan, with a design to unite the most attractive and interesting circumstances of the ancient Romans and modern Novel, at the same time it assumers a character and manner of its own, that differs from both; it is distinguished by the appellation of a Gothic Story, being a picture of Gothic times and manners.

Reeve argued that, to attain the uniting aim, it was necessary to have: 'a sufficient degree of the marvellous, to excite the attention; enough of the manners of real life, to give an air of probability to the work; and enough of the pathetic, to engage the heart in its behalf.' To Reeve, Walpole was excellent in the two latter, but, as she reasonably pointed out, although missing his intention, failed in the first:

the machinery is so violent, that it destroys the effect it is intended to excite. Had the story been kept within the utmost *verge* of probability, the effect has been preserved, without losing the least circumstance that excites or detains the attention.

Reeve then offered her account, one in which she tried to balance possibility, probability, credibility, and artistic licence. This balance drew on a problem that also faced the accounts of the future, as it were, that came from scientific research and technological innovation, the problem, seen for example with electricity, of the difficulty of establishing 'truth.' And so also with discussion of the past and, not least because, as Walpole had noted, the modern novel, with its emphasis on copying nature, matched in its stance that of histories. Indeed, many eighteenth-century novels were termed histories, although with the Gothic novels, and particularly in the early nineteenth century, there was to be a trend to calling them romances, which became the standard description. Discussion about the past and speculation about the improbable combined in the Gothic novel, but, in each case, there was an attempt at least to suggest verisimilitude, both for plot reasons and so as to engage with readers. Notions of plausibility in fiction, but also more generally, varied. Some of the discussion of plausibility in Gothic novels related to materialist issues of practicality, but there was also the more profound question of the relationships between realism and romance, and realism and the deceit offered by the forces of evil. The latter led to a fundamental challenge, one of the pursuit of the good life and the route to salvation, but in a universe bedevilled by contrary views and rival drives that had origins within individuals, in society and, most seriously, in the Manichean struggle between good and evil.[3]

The extent to which the Gothic novel could, should, or must, go in a distinctive direction was unclear. Reeve addressed this face-on in her preface, with reference to *The Castle of Otranto*, in order to distinguish her novel and to offer her own rules for the genre:

> For instance; we can conceive, and allow of, the appearance of a ghost; we can even dispense with an enchanted sword and helmet; but then they must keep within certain limits of credibility: A sword so large as to require an hundred men to lift it; a helmet that by its own weight forces a passage through a court-yard into an arched vault, big enough for a man to go through; a picture that walks out of its frame; a skeleton ghost in a hermit's cowl: When your expectation is wound up to the highest pitch, these circumstances take it down with a witness, destroy the work of imagination, and, instead of attention, excite laughter … the enchantment dissolved….

Reeve instead sought 'to compose a work upon the same plan, wherein these defects might be avoided.' This showed how from the outset, the Gothic novel did not have a template, despite critics who sought to mock it thus. Instead, these novels offered a range of vision and, in particular, moral approach.

Born in Ipswich in 1729, and, like Austen, both the unmarried daughter of a clergyman and the sister of an admiral, Reeve was, from 1772, a prolific author, including five novels, of which *The Champion of Virtue* was the first, as well as a history of prose fiction, *The Progress of Romance* (1785).[4]

---

3   Jonathan Greenaway, *Theology, Horror and Fiction: A Reading of the Gothic Nineteenth Century* (London, 2021).
4   Gary Kelly, "Clara Reeve, Provincial Bluestocking: From the Old Whigs to the Modern Liberal State," *Huntington Library Quarterly*, 65 (2002), pp. 105–25.

As with *The Castle of Otranto*, the first edition of *The Champion of Virtue* claimed to be an old manuscript, but this approach was dropped in the second. The story was set during the minority of Henry VI in the 1420s. Again, there is a murder, in this case of Arthur, Lord Lovel; a usurpation by his murderer, his cousin, Walter, Lord Lovel; and a true claimant who is ostensibly the son of a peasant, in this case Edmund Twyford, who is really Edmund Lovel, a posthumous son. Again, as with Walpole, there is a priest playing a positive role, Father Oswald; and a well-born woman, in this case Emma, in love with the peasant. There is also a 'Champion of Virtue,' Sir Philip Harclay, who had served under Henry V (r.1413–22), being victorious over the French, and also again over the Turks, who conquered much of Christian Europe in the fifteenth century, and remained a foe in the late eighteenth, with wars with Russia in 1768–74 and 1787–92. Repeatedly, Henry V was an heroic figure for this period.

For Reeve, emotional realism and the bounds of the probable were crucial, but Walpole was unimpressed, and found the novel uninteresting. The start was certainly heavy and lacked the arresting beginning of *The Castle of Otranto*. Reeve did not write with Walpole's economy nor convey energy with such lightness. The theme was one of the struggle between good and evil. Harclay reflects: 'This life, is, indeed, a pilgrimage!',[5] which was one way of presenting the journey to salvation. There was also a clear theme of equality between Harclay and the peasant, John Wyatt, who gives him shelter, but this equality is within a benign social structure of a paternalist hierarchy:

> they conversed together on common subjects, like fellow-creatures of the same natural form and endowments, though different kinds of education had given a conscious superiority to the one, a conscious inferiority to the other; and the due respect was paid by the latter, without being exacted by the former.[6]

The socially benign views of the good were captured by other novelists, as with Radcliffe in *The Italian*:

5   *English Baron*: 7.
6   *Ibid*.: 8.

3. After Otranto

> Ellena was not so wholly engaged by selfish sufferings, but that she could sympathise with those of others, and she rejoiced that the fishermen, whose boats she had observed, had escaped the threatening tempest, and were safely sheltered in their little homes, where, as they heard the loud waves break along the coast, they could look with keener pleasure upon the social circle, and the warm comforts around them. (II,8)

This was a very benign account of the sublime.

Reeve's account is given a Christian gloss, as befits Harclay, a former crusader:

> him I acknowledge for my Prince and Master, accepted the invitations of the poor, and washed the feet of his disciples.... They praised the creator for his gifts, and acknowledged they were unworthy of the least of his blessings.[7]

Harclay may lack plausibility, but was an instance of the potent role of archetypes in Gothic fiction, which was one of its characteristics, and can mean that assessments that fail to pay due attention to this feature can mislead in their critique of reason.

At the time, the nature of good lordship, and, indeed, good kingship, were very much matters of discussion, and as aspects of a situation in which there was concern about popular opinion. In 1763, Elizabeth Montagu, the wife of an independent MP, was shocked by the extent of critical sentiment in London:

> Alexander the Great was treated with contempt by a certain philosopher in a tub [Diogenes], but in this enlightened age the man who made the tub would use him with the same scorn.[8]

Yet, abusive power was also decried, and this was to be a standard theme in Gothic fiction. The Berkshire by-election of 1776 led to criticism of

7 *Ibid.*: 10, 11.
8 Montagu to George, Lord Lyttelton, 23 September 1762, San Marino, California, Huntington Library, Montagu papers 1420.

William, 6th Lord Craven, who dominated the county in alliance with Willoughby, 4th Earl of Abingdon, both supporters of the opposition to Lord North's ministry, for allegedly telling a county meeting: 'I will have it known there is respect due to a Lord.' Winchcombe Henry Hartley, who was elected unopposed, was a wealthy landowner and a particular ally of Craven. The argument that a wealthy peer was overriding the gentry was part of the social politics of the age,[9] and one repeatedly used against the aristocrats who opposed George III, such as the Cavendishes. This tension was seen in the plots of a number of Gothic novels.

A dream played a major part in the action of *The Champion of Virtue*. Harclay thinks he receives a message from an old friend, Arthur, Lord Lovel, to come to the castle, where the dead man leads him:

> into a dark and frightful cave, where he disappeared, and in his stead he beheld a complete suit of armour stained with blood, which belonged to his friend, and he thought he heard dismal groans from beneath.[10]

These were also to be heard in Radcliffe's *A Sicilian Romance*, as, in both, were such staples as haunted apartments, rusty keys, lamps blowing out, narrow passages, glimmering lights, and knockings at the door, all of which were to be subsequently repeatedly reprised by other writers. As with Radcliffe, Reeve located her story in a religious setting:

> I will not injure those who may be innocent; and I leave it to Providence, who will doubtless, in its own best time and manner, punish the guilty ... acquiesce in your conclusion, that Providence will in its own time vindicate its ways to man ... put your trust in God.[11]

These themes were frequently repeated: Edmund prays 'for a thousand

---

9   Anon., *A Heroic Epistle to the Right Honourable The Lord Craven* (1775); *The Heroic Epistle Answered* (1776).
10 p. 12.
11 p. 45.

3. After Otranto

blessings upon every one of the family of his benefactor,'[12] while Harclay declares, 'We want no light but what heaven gives us.'[13]

In turn, a nunnery was the setting for the first of the three Gothic novels by the obscure Irish writer Anne Fuller (d. 1790), *The Convent; or, The History of Sophia Nelson* (1786). She went on to write *Alan Fitz-Osborne, an Historical Tale* (1787), a tale with ghosts, caverns and murders set in the thirteenth century, and *The Son of Ethelwolf: An Historical Tale* (1789). With a dedication to George, Prince of Wales, which was an expression of opposition (Whig) sentiment, the last has a female character fight in disguise alongside Alfred the Great against invading Danes in the late ninth century. Alfred is praised as a model ruler who seeks justice for the peasantry. He had been an opposition hero earlier in the century, notably in *Alfred*, a masque of 1740 that later became an opera.

With xenophobia so often finding a home in the Gothic, *The Convent* has a cruel French father who disinherits his younger son, the Comte de St Pierre, and then imprisons him for marrying below his social rank, while the beloved Hortensia is abducted and imprisoned at the father's will. There is also a woman, Sophia Nelson, a heroine, who is abducted by her uncle and placed in a French nunnery in order to force her to marry his son. There she meets Hortensia. Men are both villains and heroes, whereas, in this story, women are resilient victims. Fuller is now forgotten, but her second novel was translated into French, and the third praised in the *Monthly Review*.

A focus on religion across much Gothic fiction was in accordance with contemporary culture. God had been deployed against the Jacobites in 1745–6, notably with biblical reference to Sennacherib's invasion of Judah.[14] The *Leeds Mercury* of 4 July 1795 observed: 'The resurrection, and a general judgment (essentials in the belief of a Christian) are the most awful ideas that can possibly occupy the human mind.' The Methodist and Evangelical movements were central to a broader engagement with a side of religion that focused on Providence, and possession by the spirit, rather

---

12   p. 99.
13   p. 128.
14   Françoise Deconninck-Brossard, 'The Churches and the '45,' in W.J. Sheils (ed.), 'The Church and War,' *Studies in Church History*, 20, pp. 253–62.

than a rationalism that removed emotional commitment. This was to be taken forward by Joanna Southcott (1750–1814), a religious prophetess from Devon who presented herself as the Woman of the Apocalypse, and claimed that she would give birth to the new Messiah. One of a number of prophetic and apocalyptic figures who emerged in the years after the French Revolution, Southcott left prophecies in a sealed wooden casket.

There was a major growth in this period in the religious periodical and newspaper press, with, for example, the foundation of the *Evangelical Magazine* (1793), and of a whole series of periodicals linked to different sects, notably Wesley's *Arminian Magazine* from 1778.[15] Many of the themes overlapped with Gothic novels, as in the confessions, often lurid tales of sin, redemption and retribution, pious deaths, and elements of the supernatural. These offered accessible individual morality tales, and, in this, both novels and newspapers paralleled crime literature. Both, however, found it difficult to match the attraction of chapbooks, the inexpensive, more crudely-produced works that expanded the audience for stories. However, in the early nineteenth century, lurid accounts of crime were provided by the developing Sunday press, the extensive readership of which demonstrated reader interest in such accounts.

The Count of Narbonne (1781), the play, left out the more exotic parts of *The Castle of Otranto*, including the animated picture which was suggested by a portrait in Walpole's Gothic-style residence, Strawberry Hill.[16] Portraits were to be a Gothic fictional device, one revisited in the identification of Stapleton's background by Holmes in *The Hound of the Baskervilles* (1902).

Aside from the clear religious and intellectual aspects of the issue, the debate about best practice that was developing was in part an aspect of the broader-ranging discussion about novels. Yet, other elements also played a role, notably the relationship between history and 'romance,' which Walpole found little different, and, more specifically, the issue of medievalism and how best to engage with the medieval past. Moreover, the bitter controversies over Ossian and Chatterton had lent particular interest to the

---

15 Josef Altholz, *The Religious Press in Britain, 1760–1900* (New York, 1989).
16 Jakub Lipski, 'Moving Pictures: The Animated Portrait in *The Castle of Otranto* and the Post-Walpolean Gothic,' *Image and Narrative*, 18, 3 (2017), pp. 64–79.

3. After Otranto

question of authenticity and very much related it to elements of the premodern. Such controversies take us toward the issues created by the lengthening Gothic shadows discussed in the following chapters.

The *Critical Review* was hostile:

> Why must all poetical justice be thus sacrificed to inculcate an idea that is shocking to truth and equity?.... What conclusion can be drawn from hence, but that oracles, divinations, and prophecies, should be believed, and must always be fulfilled? Such notions can only tend to enslave the mind, and bring us back to the long exploded errors of ignorance and barbarism.

Exploration, meanwhile, especially, in the case of Britain, the much-reported voyages of James Cook, George Vancouver and others to the Pacific, encouraged an interest in other, terrifying, non-Christian practices, notably cannibalism. Another aspect of a primitivism that suggested different values to those of modern Christian Europe came from the Ossian cult. James Macpherson (1736–96) published poems which he claimed to have translated from the Gaelic of a third-century Highland bard called Ossian. His *Fragments of Ancient Poetry collected in the Highlands* (1760) brought him fame, being followed by *Fingal* (1761), dedicated to George III's favourite, John, 3rd Earl of Bute, the preface of which proclaimed the superiority of Celtic to Greek heroic poetry, and also by *Temora* (1763). These works, in part Macpherson's own creation, in part based on genuine Gaelic poems and ballads, enjoyed a phenomenal success. Endowed with a primitivism that appealed to fashionable pre-Romanticism, they were translated into several European languages, including French (1777) and Russian (1792), and were to influence Byron, Coleridge, Goethe, Schiller and Napoleon, among others.

Impressed by Macpherson, Thomas Percy (1729–1811), a grocer's son who sought to show his descent from the medieval Dukes of Northumberland, published *Five Pieces of Runic Poetry, translated from the Icelandic* (1763) and *Reliques of Ancient English Poetry* (1765), an edition of old ballads which promoted a revival of interest in the subject. Indeed, there were four editions by 1794.[17]

17 Nick Groom, *The Making of Percy's Reliques* (Oxford, 1999).

Medievalism as practice was certainly in decline if not ruin. In *The Castle of Otranto*, the castle in question was very much set in Italy and in a timeless past, whereas the situation in Britain when Walpole was writing was very different. The suppression in 1746 of the major Jacobite rising of 'the '45' had been followed by a process of new fortifications in Scotland, notably Fort George near Inverness. A state-of-the-art bastioned fortress, this would not have made a plausible setting for a brooding tragedy, and was not to be used for one. There were no shadows in such fortresses. So also with the barracks erected from 1792 as war with France neared.

Nor were stately homes likely to fit the bill. Castle Howard, the name for the seat of the Earls of Carlisle designed by Sir John Vanbrugh earlier in the century, was no castle. Built for a famous general, John, 1st Duke of Marlborough, Blenheim Palace was also unfortified. So also with other aristocratic houses, other than in the shape of estate walls, gates, lodges, and, from the late 1770s, the spring guns and mantraps used against poachers. The approach from landscaped grounds to the house was easy for people, with the major obstacle being the ha-ha, a ditch to keep the castle away from the house itself.

In turn, the new Gothic style of the later eighteenth century was not designed to provide strength and was almost a parody. Indeed, castellated features very much became an architectural device; one that lacked any defensive capability. Modern stately homes were often near older ruined fortresses, for example at Sherborne and Wardour. This underlined the contrast of the past as both role and image. During the '45, the Jacobite rebellion of 1745–6, John, Lord Glenorchy, a government supporter and Scottish landowner, wrote to his daughter:

> I have often repented taking out the iron bars from the windows and sashing them, and taking away a great iron door, and weakening the house as to resistance by adding modern wings to it. If it had remained in the old castle way as it was before, I might have slept very sound in it, for their whole army could not have taken it without cannon.[18]

18 Bedford, Bedfordshire CRO., Lucas papers, 30/9/17/3.

3. After Otranto

The 'great iron door' and 'the old castle way' sought by the Gothic writers were not characteristic of contemporary Britain. Matthew Lewis, in contrast, described one in Germany in *The Monk*:

> ...the stillness of the scene inspired me with melancholy ideas not altogether unpleasing. The castle, which stood full in my sight, formed an object equally awful and picturesque. Its ponderous walls, tinged by the moon with solemn brightness; its old and partly ruined towers, lifting themselves into the clouds, and seeming to frown on the plains around them; its lofty battlements, overgrown with ivy.... (II,4)

In *The Italian*, Bonarmo finds the ruined fortress of Paluzzi near Naples, one that is described as a Roman fort but was clearly longer lasting not least due to the reference of a strong 'battery' or artillery position:

> ...he found himself on a terrace, that ran along the top of the arch-way and had once been fortified.... Some remains of massy walls, that still exhibited loops for archers ... led to a watchtower ... that crowned the opposite cliff ... served not only for a strong battery over the road ... citadel, a round tower, of majestic strength ... [plus] a mass of ruins near the edge of the cliff. (I,1)

As far as England was concerned, Elizabeth Montagu, however, reflected in 1762:

> A virtuoso or a dilletanti may stand as secure in these times behind his Chinese rail as the knight on his battlements in former days.[19]

There was a parallel in stories for British children which tended to provide a benign account not only of the present, but also of the past, as in the prolific Lucy Peacock's *The Knight of the Rose. An Allegorical Narrative* (1793).

19 San Marino, California, Huntington Library, Montagu Papers, no. 4557.

Some English castles were still aristocratic residences, such as Alnwick (Duke of Northumberland) and Powderham (Earl of Devon), but they were now stately homes, lacking military forces of their own. Instead, Britain had plenty of medieval castles in ruins. A traveller in 1735 noted that most castles 'are at present quite neglected.'[20] Ludlow Castle, once the headquarters of the Council of the Marches, was typical in being disused and decayed. Ruins became sites deemed picturesque. Richard Wilson, who visited Okehampton Castle in 1771, soon after painted a Romantic vision of that hilltop castle with its ruins silhouetted against the evening sky. There was no menace, and scant suggestion that these would make an appropriate setting for a present-day horror story.

In her posthumously-published essay 'On the Supernatural in Poetry,' Ann Radcliffe was to write of Windsor Castle, recently-enhanced as a royal residence as a Gothic work, as a setting that was effectively suggestive, although novelists made this 'work' by looking for plots located in the past, and drawing on its drama and sense of difference:

> I have sometimes thought as I walked in the deep shade of the North Terrace of Windsor Castle, when the moon shone on all beyond, that the scene must have been present in Shakespeare's mind, when he drew the night-scenes in Hamlet; and, as I have stood in the platform, which there projects over the precipices, and have heard only the measured step of a sentinel or the clink of his arms, and have seen his shadow passing by moonlight, at the foot of the high Eastern tower.... All has been so still and shadowy, so great and solemn.[21]

As with the work of Clara Reeve, it was seen as necessary to look back in time for settings and plots. This characteristic of the Gothic novel greatly increased its feel as exotic and remote. The emotions might be similar to those of modern society, but the difference of the setting could make it difficult, or alternatively safe, to identify with what readily appeared as

---

20   J. Dodd, tour, BL. Add. 5957 fol. 20.
21   Ann Radcliffe, 'On the Supernatural in Poetry,' *New Monthly Magazine*, 16 (1826), pp. 145–52.

3. After Otranto

escapist. There was also a requirement on the part of the novelist for more knowledge than if writing about present-day Britain.

Separately, locating Gothic perils abroad or in the past appeared in line with a public culture that devoted attention to lurid crimes both abroad and in British history. If the murder of the Princes (Edward V and his brother Richard, Duke of York) in the Tower of London, probably in 1483, was an instance of the latter, albeit with the standard account challenged, notably by Wesley in his *Concise History of England*, the coverage of crime in 1772–87 included such topics as a Portuguese mass-murderess, a mass-poisoning in Amsterdam, and a tale of sex and violence in Paris.[22]

Using foreign lands or the past as a setting provided an opportunity to reflect on all aspects of modern society. Thus, Sir Philip Harclay in *The Old English Baron*, like Smollett's *Sir Launcelot Greaves*, is a reproach to many in the modern British social élite, and, to that end, the protagonist, while a knight, lacks the aristocratic title that it might be thought they deserve:

> Sir Philip maintained twelve old soldiers who had been maimed and disabled in the wars, and had no provision made for them; also six old officers who had been unfortunate and were grown grey without preferment ... there are many others ... his ears are ever open to distress, his hand to relieve it. (122)

So also, at great length, with Sir Thomas O'Callaghan in Henrietta Rouviere/Mosse's *The Old Irish Baronet* (1808). Not a peer, he is generous, caring, and comprehensive:

> He fed the hungry, clothed the naked, relieved the indigent, and visited the sick.... He was literally adored in the neighbourhood; nor could his magnificent fortune be envied him, while he spent it in his own country, amongst his own people, and for the good of mankind.

---

22 *Darlington Pamphlet*, 4 September 1772; *Reading Mercury*, 2 May 1774; *Newcastle Chronicle*, 17 February 1787.

After Reeve, Walpole remained a point of reference for later Gothic writers. A quotation from him begins the second chapter of Radcliffe's *The Romance of the Forest* (1791). *The Castle of Otranto* as a readily-grasped image of a site for mystery went on echoing into the nineteenth century. Thus, set near Naples, Charles Maturin's *Fatal Revenge* (1807), has Castle di Muralto, which was described as unusual by the standards of modern Italy:

> The castle had been built in the time of the Norman kings of Sicily (1130–1197); it possessed all the rude and massive characters of that age, darkened by the injuries of time, and the gloom of antiquity ... the remains of the gigantic statues. (8)

Subsequently, from within:

> What a prize to the inquisition, or to a banditti, would this castle be, with its passages and vaults, and chambers in the solid wall, without window or loo-hole, or a single avenue of human comfort, and air that our lamp could scares burn in – air, like the breathings of a vault! (16)

Separately, while not matching the subsequent focus on, and from, mountains, that on landscape in the early Gothic novels matches the similar interest shown by William Gilpin and other picturesque writers. Although easy to overlook, the shore is a significant setting in Gothic novels, including in Charlotte Smith's *Emmeline* (1788) and Radcliffe's *A Sicilian Romance* (1790) and *The Italian* (1797). There, Vivaldi provides an account that shows how much the Gothic novel is not all castles, abbeys and mountains:

> ...he left the palace, and strolled down to the sea-beach. A few fishermen and lazzarone only were loitering along the strand, waiting for boats ... paced the edge of the waves, listening to their murmur, as they broke gently at his feet, and gazing upon their undulating beauty, while all consciousness was lost in melancholy reverie.... The sea fluctuating beneath the setting sun, the long mole and its light-house tipped with the last rays,

3. After Otranto

fishermen reposing in the shade, little boats skimming over the smooth waters, which their oars scarcely dimpled. (I,9)

Radcliffe was to return to praise of the seashore.

In *The Old Manor House* (1793), Charlotte Smith (1749–1806), a friend of Radcliffe, took Gothic elements into the modern day, with the vaults of an ancient British building the setting of part of the plot, but so also action in North America and a setting at the time of the American War of Independence (1775–83).[23] Moreover, with reason, the novel has been understood as taking a stance on current politics that certainly did not accord with the conservative views of Edmund Burke.[24] At the same time, there is, in this novel, the established fictional interest in inheritance.[25] Smith criticized the slave trade as well as war (II,8). The protagonist is captured by Native Americans, which provides a captive-narrative (II,11) that is different to the stereotypical Gothic one. Yet, the problems that malice threw at young love were capable of application in many contexts. Indeed, slavery recurs as a theme with reference to a cruel aunt being so keen to get rid of her niece 'that I believe she would have been glad to have sold me to Sir John Belgrave' (II,24) for marriage. In Smith's *Marchmont* (1796), there is a Mr Vampyre, but he is a lawyer, a group she had personal reason to despise, and he is not a satanic figure.

Whatever the setting, the language used in Gothic novels reflected both the pattern established in sentimental fiction, as well as much of the language and tone used more generally in correspondence of the period, correspondence which itself was affected by the fiction. Thus, in 1822, George IV wrote as 'a most affectionate friend' from his London palace at Carlton House, possibly to a 'Mrs M,' for the recipient is unclear:

23 Janina Nordius, '"A Kind of Living Death": Gothicizing the Colonial Encounter in Charlotte Smith's *The Old Manor House,*' *English Studies*, 86 (2005), pp. 40–50.
24 Simon Parkes, '"More Dead than Alive": The Return of Not-Orlando in Charlotte Smith's *The Old Manor House,*' *European Romantic Review*, 22 (2011), pp. 765–84; Carmel Murphy, 'Jacobin History: Charlotte Smith's *Old Manor House* and the French Revolution Debate,' *Romanticism*, 20 (2014), pp. 271–81.
25 Jacqueline Labbe, 'Metaphoricity and the Romance of Property in "The Old Manor House," *Novel*, 34 (2001), pp. 216–31.

You may easily imagine, warm and sincere as my affections are towards you, I have had but little rest, since we separated last night. The fear, that I may, possibly and unfortunately in a hurried moment when my mind and heart being torn in fifty different ways from fifty different causes have let an unjust or a hasty expression escape me to any one (but most especially to You, who I so *truly love* and who are so *invaluable* to *Me* as my *friend*) is to *me*, a sensation much *too painful* to be *endured*; therefore, let me *implore* of You, to come to me, *be it but for a moment*, the *very first thing* you do this morning, for I shall hate myself until I have the opportunity to express *personally* to You, those pure and Genuine feelings of affection for You, which will never cease to live in *my Heart*, so long as that Heart itself continues to beat. I am much too unhappy to say more.[26]

Such overwriting could make the dialogue in the Gothic novels, and in fiction more generally, seem almost commonplace. The same was true of fictional plots many of which did not appear overly remarkable in their personal relationships, although the Gothic added the reality or frisson of pure evil.

The great popularity of *The Castle of Otranto* was in part arresting due to the context. While the Middle Ages might seem distant, there was a social and cultural continuity offered by aristocratic landownership and Christianity, and certainly a continuity not present in the case of the Classical world, a point noted by Edward Bulwer-Lytton in the preface to his highly-successful 'Sensation Novel' *The Last Days of Pompeii* (1834):

With the men and customs of the feudal time we have a natural sympathy and bond of alliance; those men were our own ancestors – from those customs we received our own – The creed of our chivalric fathers is still ours – their tombs yet consecrate our churches – the ruins of their castles yet frown over our valleys. We trace in their struggles for liberty and for justice our

26 *Maggs Catalogue*, 1345, no. 88.

3. After Otranto

present institutions; and in the elements of their social state we behold the origin of our own.

But with the classical age we have no household and familiar associations.

These associations helped provide a thrill of horror for the readers and viewers of the Gothic.

4. NIGHTMARE IN LONDON WITH HENRY FUSELI

A Gothic fantasy that offered a powerful vision of the mysterious and the subconscious, *Nightmare* (1781) is a painting that grips as it disturbs and disturbs as it grips. Anglicising his name as Henry Fuseli, the Swiss painter Johann Heinrich Füssli (1741–1825) spent much of his life from 1764 in England, becoming a member of the Royal Academy in 1790. He was an aspect of the European character of the Gothic as well as its overlap with other movements. Influenced by reading Rousseau, Fuseli was a precursor of Romanticism, arguing, notably in his *Remarks on the Writings and Conduct of J.J. Rousseau* (1767), that the arts were a divine gift which elevated man by their force, impact and terror. Exhibited at the Royal Academy in 1782, *Nightmare* attracted much interest. The painting was sold in 1783, while an engraving by Thomas Burke did very well, earning over £500, and was accompanied by a poem 'Night-Mare' by Erasmus Darwin that emphasized female vulnerability:

> So on his Nightmare through the evening fog
> Flits the squat Fiend o'er fen, and lake, and bog;
> Seeks some love-wilder'd maid with sleep oppress'd,
> Alights, and grinning sits upon her breast.

Nightmare was terror as felt experience, rather than the horror as story presented by Joshua Reynolds, the President of the Royal Academy, in his *Count Ugolino and his Children in the Dungeon* (1773). The latter was a dramatic history painting, then a popular artistic genre. This genre could be closely configured with the Gothic imagination with, in particular, the Gothic as historical story. Based on a real-life episode described by Dante's in the *Divine Comedy*, the painting depicted the imprisoned Count Ugolino della Gherardesca having to decide to starve to death or eat his similarly imprisoned sons and grandsons when they die. This painting caused a stir when exhibited at the Royal Academy and was bought by John, 3rd Duke of Dorset for a great sum.

In contrast, Fuseli offered visions of more horrific fantasy. Producing works designed to arouse the imagination, not least for the Shakespeare Gallery and to illustrate Milton's *Paradise Lost*, Fuseli painted visions that exposed the limited sway of social order and psychological balance and harmony, as well as depths in human experience which reason could not explain. His paintings looked toward the unfixed, metaphysical quality that was to be so important to so much Romantic work. Whereas Ann Radcliffe, at the end of her novels, provided a rational explanation to what had appeared supernatural, there was no such structure or reveal to a Fuseli painting. Fuseli's unsettling *Titania's Awakening and Bottom* (1790), an episode from Shakespeare's *A Midsummer Night's Dream*, was followed by the alarming *Macbeth, Banquo and the Witches* (1793–4). *The Night-Hag visiting the Lapland Witches* (1796) showed Fuseli's interest in witchcraft, while *Richard III Visited by Ghosts* (1798) captured another nightmare as part of his commitment to presenting Shakespeare.

Fuseli had trained as a cleric and been ordained, although he lived as an artist. Initially, encouraged by the French Revolution, Fuseli, like many others, turned against it in reaction to its growing radicalism and expansionism, and became a relatively prosperous establishment figure who was buried in the crypt of St Paul's Cathedral. Fuseli influenced writers, notably Mary Shelley.[1]

Paintings inspired other Gothic tales and writers, notably Percy Bysshe Shelley, and Shakespeare dominated the English paintings on medieval, and later Gothic, themes. The painting of Shakespearean scenes by Fuseli and others was part of a reconceptualization of the playwright that focused on his sublime character. Indeed, the growing vogue for the playwright from the 1760s reflected the strength of Gothic themes in culture. 1769 saw the Shakespeare Jubilee as well as the publication of Elizabeth Montague's *An Essay on the Writings and Genius of Shakespeare*. There were editions and commentaries, including by Samuel Johnson (1765), Edward

---

[1] Maryanne Ward, 'A Painting of the Unspeakable: Henry Fuseli's *The Nightmare* and the Creation of Mary Shelley's *Frankenstein*,' *Journal of the Midwest Modern Language Association*, 33 (2000), pp. 20–31.

Capell (1768), Isaac Reed (1785), John Monk (1785) and Edmond Malone (1790), and, earlier, by Warburton and Pope. Shakespeare influenced the Gothic novels, and was quoted by Radcliffe at the start of many of her chapters. Thus, *The Romance of the Forest* included several quotes from *Macbeth*, including one predicting 'A deed of dreadful note.' The quotations were frequently evocative of more of a danger than in practice was the case, as with the chapter in *The Italian* (I,3) beginning with a quotation from *Julius Caesar*, a play in which the ghost of the murdered Caesar plays a significant role:

—Art thou any thing?
Art thou some God, some Angel, or some Devil
Thou mak'st my blood cold, and my hair to stand?
Speak to me, what thou art.

In 1798, Radcliffe was referred to by the critic Nathan Drake in his *Literary Hours* as 'the Shakespeare of Romance Writers.'[2] Walpole had earlier quoted Shakespeare in the preface to the second edition of *The Castle of Otranto*, and Matthew Lewis also quoted him. Henrietta Rouviere/Mosse's *The Old Irish Baronet* (1808) was launched with a Shakespeare quote that set the tone:

No natural exhalation in the sky,
No shape of nature, no distemper'd day,
No common wind, no customed event,
But they will pluck away its natural cause,
And call them meteors, prodigies and signs,
Abortives and presages, tongues of Heaven,
Plainly denouncing vengeance.

Subsequently in this play, 'our immortal Shakespeare' is cited in terms of his ability to highlight the danger of rebellion and how this prefigured

2 Rictor Norton, 'Ann Radcliffe, 'the Shakespeare of Romance Writers,' in Christy Desmet and Anne Williams (eds), *Shakespearean Gothic* (Cardiff, 2009), pp. 37–59.

the 1793–4 Terror of the French Revolution (II,4). In method, there is a comparison with painting:

> He identifies himself so closely with the characters he draws, that even such of them as were then imaginary, and have appeared since, bear witness to the skill of the painter, and prove that, in copying from himself, he copied from nature. His most exact portraits are those whose originals existed only in his own fancy; and he is happier in his likeness when left to himself, than where he is aided or rather fettered by historic outlines. (II,4)

Shakespearean description and occasion appealed to the imagination of many, which was unsurprising as Shakespeare was so frequently staged. The noted travel writer Thomas Pennant concluded his account of a journey from London to Dover in 1787 by taking aim at Samuel Johnson:

> I shall conclude this journey with mention of the cliff immortalised by Shakespeare in his tragedy of King Lear. It is a vast precipice of chalk, impending over the sea; a lapse has robbed it of part of its height; but still there is enough left to terrify those who have curiosity to peep over the brink. Doctor Johnson, amidst a waste of notes on this celebrated author, observes, that the overwhelming idea is dissipated and enfeebled by the minutiae of the description; the choughs, the crows, the samphire-men, and the fishers. With all respect to so exalted a name, had Shakespeare divested it of these images, it would not have been any description whatsoever; but the reader would have been as divested of ideas as poor Gloucester, had Edgar permitted the good old man to have taken his desperate leap. But I can still sympathise with the terror which must affect every reader at the extraordinary imagery, the fine creation of our matchless Poet:
>
> 'How fearful
> And dizzy 'tis, to cast one's eyes so low!

> The crows and choughs that wing the midway air
> Show scarce so gross as beetles: half way down
> Hangs one that gathers samphire, dreadful trade!
> Methinks he seems no bigger than his head:
> The fishermen, that walk upon the beach,
> Appear like mice; and yond tall anchoring bark,
> Diminish'd to her cock; her cock, a buoy
> Almost too small for sight: the murmuring surge,
> That on the unnumber'd idle pebbles chafes,
> Cannot be heard so high. I'll look no more;
> Lest my brain turn, and the deficient sight
> Topple down headlong.'

This is the powerful end to the volume, one preceded by an engraving of 'Shakespeare's Cliff.'[3]

Somewhat differently, in a product of the strong interest in Shakespeare but also an echo of the more general usage of forgeries, William Henry Ireland (1775–1835) produced what he stated were original manuscripts of hitherto unknown Shakespeare plays, all set in post-Roman or medieval England: *William the Conqueror, Henry II*, and *Vortigern and Rowena*, the last of which was unsuccessfully staged at Drury Lane in 1796. Ireland also wrote Gothic novels: *The Abbess* (1799), *Rimualdo: Or, The Castle of Badajos* (1800) and *Gondez the Monk* (1805).

Bringing the past under scrutiny was a feature of much cultural activity including not only Shakespeare, real and imagined, but also other Gothic fiction, plays, painting and architecture. The claims to authenticity seen from *The Castle of Otranto* on were an aspect of this scrutiny, as well as of the melding of history and fiction presented in earlier British novels.

This melding continued to be a feature of the historical novels of the years of the highpoint of Gothic novels; but with the addition of melodramatic features drawn from the Gothic imagination. Thus, Rosetta Ballin, in *The Statue Room; An Historical Tale* (1790), a melodramatic historical novel in which Elizabeth I was a villain, as she was for example, due to her (in

---

3   Thomas Pennant, *A Journey from London to the Isle of Wight* (2 vols in one, London, 1801), I, 205.

4. Nightmare in London with Henry Fuseli

practice fictionalised) treatment of Mary, Queen of Scots, in John Wesley's *Concise History of England*, has the heroine search for her imprisoned lover. Ballin offered an alternative history that was in accordance with the dynastic inheritance puzzles of so many Gothic novels. Catherine of Aragon is (falsely) described as pregnant when rejected by Henry VIII, and her suppositious child, who is given the Saxon name of Adelfrida, secretly marries the Duke of Alençon, only to be poisoned on the instructions of Elizabeth, while Adelfrida's daughter, Romelia, is also the target of the Queen. A vision leads her to seek to murder Elizabeth, only to fail and then commit suicide.

There were also developments in tone within this process of the scrutiny of the past, with the change in the depiction of Shakespearean scenes being instructive. The first known painting of a Shakespearean scene, William Hogarth's *Falstaff Examining his Recruits* (1730), which may also have been the depiction of an actual performance, was essentially comic and non-suggestive. The situation, however, subsequently changed, with a probing of more mysterious aspects. Related but separate, the Hogarthian comic dimension of the novels of Fielding and Smollett was relegated to the servants in Gothic fiction, a genre in which heroism and humour were generally kept apart; although they could interact in plot terms as in Radcliffe's *The Italian*.

In the painting of the period, there was a strong interest in mystery. Thus, focusing on the magical *Tempest*, Francis Hayman, George Romney and Thomas Jones all painted Prospero and Miranda spying the shipwrecked Ferdinand from *The Tempest*. Romney (1734–1802) was particularly interested in Shakespeare, offering a nightmare scene, *King Lear in the Tempest Tearing off his Robes* (1760–1), as one of his first major paintings. In parallel, nightmare Shakespearian lines were deployed by writers, as with:

I am settled, and bend up
Each corporal agent to this terrible feat. (II,8)

In his second Discourse as President of the Royal Academy, that of 1769, Joshua Reynolds suggested that, once thoroughly grounded in the discipline, the painter might 'try the power of his imagination.... The mind that has been thus disciplined, may be indulged in the warmest enthusiasm, and venture to play on the borders of the wildest extravagance.' The following year, he added that a true painter 'instead of endeavouring to amuse mankind with the minute neatness of imitation ... must endeavour to improve them by the grandeur of his ideas.' Theatre provided Reynolds with such a way. His 1784 portrait of *Mrs Siddons as the Tragic Muse* depicted the leading tragic actress of the age in a way that presented the theatricality of the Gothic, and, in this, the extent to which the potent psychology of the paranormal that the Gothic had come to express could be channelled to dramatic effect. This rich, dark painting, with its figures of Pity and Terror, was a great success, praised by James Barry as 'The finest picture of the kind, perhaps in the world, indeed it is something more than a portrait.' Sarah Siddons's most famous role was that of Lady Macbeth, which she first performed in 1785. Siddons also played many other Shakespearean roles, including Hamlet. Her powerful performances led audience members to the 'Siddons Fever' of hysterical reaction. She formally retired from the stage in 1812, but her last performance was in 1819. Her brother John, Philip Kemble, was also a major Shakespearean actor.[4] Other major actors, notably Edmund Kean, made their name in Shakespearean roles, he opened as Shylock at Drury Lane in 1814. Kean restored the tragic ending to *King Lear* in place of the happy ending by Nahum Tate used from 1681.

Reynolds's later portraits indeed moved away from conversation pieces and toward a style that was more otherworldly, with more clouds and smoke. Moreover, his massive *Macbeth and the Witches*, painted in the late 1780s, echoed aspects of Fuseli's work. Fuseli had produced a *Lady Macbeth Sleepwalking* (c.1781–84), a painting of staring eyes, shadows, and a wavering candle barely in control. More generally, Macbeth fixed attention, Romney's painting of the actor John Henderson in this role (c.1787) capturing the intensity that tragic actors sought and tried to communicate. *Macbeth* continued to echo in nineteenth-century Gothic novels, for example in Charles Dickens's *The Mystery of Edwin Drood* (1870).[5]

Differently, but also in an influential fashion, Shakespeare was staged by John Boydell who, in the 1790s, used his Shakespeare Gallery in London to display paintings of Shakespeare's plays.[6] Many of these paintings were

---

4   Tom Mole, *Romanticism and Celebrity Culture, 1750–1850* (Cambridge, 2012).
5   Chapter 12.
6   Jane Martineau (ed.), *Shakespeare in Art* (London, 2003); Stuart Sillars, *Painting Shakespeare: The Artist as Critic, 1720–1820* (Cambridge, 2006).

influential in helping to fix the public sense and understanding of particular episodes and plays.

Many of the descriptions in *The Castle of Otranto* would have done well as topics for Fuseli's paintings, not least in its Shakespearean dramatic style. So also with the other Gothic novelists. As aspects of a more general interaction, quotations from *Macbeth* are freely scattered in Gothic novels.[7] Radcliffe also made much reference to Shakespeare in her 'On the Supernatural in Poetry,' an essay published posthumously in 1826. Initially intended as a section of the prologue of her posthumously-published last novel *Gaston de Blondeville: Or, The Court of Henry III* (1826), the essay adopted the form of a dialogue on 'the illusions of the imagination.' 'Mr S' praises Shakespeare:

> Where is now the undying spirit that could so exquisitely perceive and feel? that could inspire itself with the various characters of this world, and create worlds of its own, to which the grand and the beautiful, the gloomy and the sublime of visible Nature, upcalled not only corresponding feelings, but passions: which seemed to perceive a soul in every thing: and thus, in the secret workings of its own characters and in the combinations of its incidents, kept the elements and local scenery always in with them, heightening their effect. So the conspirators at Rome pass under the fiery showers and sheeted lightning of the thunder-storm, to meet, at midnight, in the porch of Pompey's theatre … the sheeted dead were seen in the lightning to glide along the streets of Rome … the sublimity of these attendant circumstances … the whole soul is roused and fixed, in the full energy of attention.

Cymbeline, *Macbeth* and *Hamlet* are the other plays discussed, as is the work of Milton and Dryden.[8] *Gaston de Blondeville* has ghosts, a villainous abbot, and murder, but lacks drive to match its medieval detail.

Radcliffe's novels showed an interest in painterly qualities, notably in the use of light, which she often discussed and which, while it can take

---

7   For example, *The Mysteries of Udolpho*, I, 10.
8   Ann Radcliffe, 'On the Supernatural in Poetry,' *New Monthly Magazine*, 16 (1826), pp. 145–52.

precedence over that of sound, is generally matched by the latter. Thus, Cornelia's death in the abbey in *A Sicilian Romance* finds Julia:

> In her way to the church, the gleam of tapers on the walls, and the glimpse which her eye often caught of the friars in their long black habits, descending silently through the narrow winding passages, with the solemn toll of the bell, conspired to kindle imagination, and to impress her heart with sacred awe. But the church exhibited a scene of solemnity, such as she had never before witnessed. Its gloomy aisles were imperfectly seen by the rays of tapers from the high altar, which shed a solitary gleam over the remote parts of the fabric, and produced large masses of light and shade, striking and sublime in their effect.
>
> While she gazed, she heard a distant chanting rise through the aisles; the sounds swelled in low murmurs on the ear, and drew nearer and nearer, till a sudden blaze of light issued from one of the portals, and the procession entered. (11)

In the following chapter, the painterly challenge was that of the countryside:

> They travelled for some hours through gloomy forests of beech and chestnut; and their way was only faintly illuminated by the moon, which shed a trembling lustre through the dark foliage, and which was seen but at intervals, as the passing clouds yielded to the power of her rays.

So also for the sea, with first 'the bold concave of the heavens uniting with the vast expanse of the ocean.... a *coup d'oeil*,' which, in peaceful weather and seas, is described as sublime. This is followed by a tempest.

Artistic references and echoes were also much to the fore. In *The Mysteries of Udolpho*, the burial of Madame Montoni in the dark of the castle chapel vault is described at length, with Domenichino (1581–1641), a painter of the Italian Baroque, brought in for comparison, although others might have been even more appropriate:

4. Nightmare in London with Henry Fuseli

At the moment, in which they let down the body into the earth, the scene was such as only the dark pencil of Domenichino, perhaps could have done justice to. The fierce features and wild dress of the *condottieri*, blending with their torches over the grave, into which the corpse was descending, were contrasted by the venerable figure of the monk, wrapt in long black garments, his cowl thrown back from his pale face, on which the light gleaming strongly showed the lines of affliction softened by piety, and the few grey locks, which time had spared on his temples: while beside him, stood the softer form of Emily, who leaned for support upon Annette; her face half averted, and shaded by a thin veil, that fell over her figure; and her mild and beautiful countenance fixed in grief ... The gleams, thrown between the arches, the vaults, where, here and there, the broken ground marked the spots in which other bodies had been recently interred, and the general obscurity beyond were circumstances, that alone would have been on the imagination of a spectator to scenes more horrible. (III,5)

Radcliffe, however, revealed her architectural preferences clearly in the preface to *The Italian* when commenting on the interior of the church of Santa Maria del Pianto near Naples:

The interior of this edifice had nothing of the showy ornament and general splendour, which distinguish the churches of Italy, and particularly those of Naples; but it exhibited a simplicity and grandeur of design, considerably more interesting to persons of taste, and a solemnity of light and shade much more suitable to promote the sublime elevation of devotion.

In turn, painting is discussed between Cyprian and Ippolito in Maturin's *Fatal Revenge*. Cyprian presses the case for using painting:

to speak to the very soul. Instead of copying the colouring of one artist, the design of another, the trees, and the sun-light, and the ruins, that are handed down from age to age, with mechanical improvement and imitation that excludes originality – I would have the painter look around life, and within himself; I would have him copy from nature in a state of motion, from *existing* life; from those forms and shades of manner and feeling, which are in a perpetual state of animated fluctuation around us, more numerous, more varied, and more vivid than they could have been, from the unimproved state of society, in the time of the elder masters I would make all my figures, *characters*, and all my groups circumstantial and narrative.... I saw a painting ... the interment ... the wretched parent was bowing to the priest, for having performed the last rites; was thanking him with the humility of courteous misery, for having for ever removed from him his last earthy stay and hope. There was something in the expression of the old man, thus trying to work features, convulsed with anguish, into a gentle smile, to blend the duties of the moment with the wrung feelings of the parent, and not forget the decencies of grief, amid its stings and bitterness – I cannot express myself. (6)

That novel later demonstrated how the scale of the imaginative world created for the struggles between Good and Evil was one that was better captured by paintings of a fantastical type. Thus, Ippolito saws through a grating:

> ... a flight of steps at a vast distance, that wound beyond the sight, and of which partial fragments appeared through chasms at a still greater, feebly tinted with the moving rays of the light. And now as it [the light in motion] advanced down the steps, he could see it was borne by a tall, dark figure, who preceded another still more obscure, bearing in his arms something that was enveloped in white. They descended from a vast height at the extremity of a vault, over whose extent the torch as it approached, threw a transient flash without exploring it. As the vast masses of shadow varied with the motion of the torch, Ippolito thought he could discover objects that resembled the

4. Nightmare in London with Henry Fuseli

furniture of a place of sepulture scattered around the vault before him.... (17)

This is an introduction to a cemetery in which a monk tries to murder a woman.

The expression of emotion was both central to evangelicalism and a key element of the Gothic, one taken forward from earlier sentimentalism and etched on a heightened canvas of alarm. That this expression could be overwrought was a product of the conviction of the value of the sublime and an aspect of a theatricality born of a conviction that people were in large part defined by their emotions. The painterly quality was very much an aspect of the posed version of the novels, with characters, major and minor, taking set positions, and this quality combining with a theatricality. Thus, for the night before the execution of Count Montorio in *Fatal Revenge*, with his sons taken to say goodbye:

> The dark habits, the clank of chains, the heavy tread of the armed sentinels, the cheerless and funereal light of the torches, the rush of sudden motion breaking on the silence of night and a prison, and *that* hushed again, hushed by the pause of breathless passion that followed, were impressed for ever on the minds of the witnesses. (24)

So, on a different scale with the description of landscape seen by Ellena from the convent in which she is confined in *The Italian*. This is a word-painting of the sublime:

> ... an horizon, and a landscape spread below, whose grandeur awakened all her heart. The consciousness of her prison as lost, while her eyes ranged over the wide and freely-sublime scene without. She perceived that this chamber was within a small turret, projecting from an angle of the convent over the walls, and suspended, as in air, above the vast precipices of granite, that formed part of the mountain. These precipices were broken into cliffs, which, in some places, impended far above their base, and, in others, rose, in nearly perpendicular lines, to the walls of the monastery, which they supported.

Radcliffe then included a phrase that captured the response sought by readers. So often that response was encouraged by the response described as experienced by the characters in play:

> Ellena, with a dreadful pleasure, looked down them, shagged as they were with larch, and frequently darkened by lines of gigantic pine bending along the rocky ledges, till her eye rested on the thick chestnut woods that extended over their winding base, and which, softening to the plains, seemed to form a gradation between the variegated cultivation there, and the awful wildness of the rocks above. Round these extensive plains were tumbled the mountains.... (I,8)

Later in that novel, there is a specific reference to art, in this case with the view over the Gulf of Naples:

> where the light sails of feluccas, and the spreading canvas of larger vessels, glided upon the scene and passed away, as in a camera obscura. Vesuvius and the city of Naples were on the coast beyond, with many a bay and lofty cape of that long tract of bold and gaily-coloured scenery, which extends toward Cape Campanella, crowded by fading ranges of mountains, lighted up with all the magic of Italian sunshine. (III,3)

That Radcliffe had never been to Italy captured the impact of art, for her vision of Italy was based on paintings and illustrations.

Other writers of Gothic stories were affected by paintings, notably Percy Bysshe Shelley in his play *The Cenci* (1819), a work greatly influenced by his wife Mary. The portrait of Beatrice Cenci (c.1600), attributed to Guido Reni, does not make direct reference to her public execution for the patricide of her incestuous father Count Francesco in 1599, but it provided an arresting image to help fix Shelley's attention on the story. At every stage, there was an overlap between the Gothic and the pictorial that was far more pronounced than in earlier British novels.

Meanwhile, visual dimensions of the Gothic ranged to include caricatures as well as paintings, for example Isaac Cruickshank's 'Raising Evil

4. Nightmare in London with Henry Fuseli

Spirits' (1795),[9] which used *Macbeth* to give a Gothic character to British politics, at once disturbing and thrilling. Whereas women were more commonly vulnerable than villains in Gothic novels, caricatures could present them as predators, harlots, mad, larger than life and threatening, as in depictions of Revolutionary France as overthrowing accepted notions of female morality and linking revolutionary politics with social and sexual upheaval, involving for example Devil-worship. Thus, the connections between the Gothic novel and the art and caricature that reflected and influenced it, ranged in their directness and intensity, just as the Gothic could affect the portrayal of women but did not determine it. This wide usage captured the extent to which the Gothic was far from marginal. It overlapped in addition with traditional religious themes as in the commission to Benjamin West, the President of the Royal Academy, from William Beckford in 1796 to provide scenes from the Book of Revelation for Beckford's home, Fonthill Abbey. That year, West produced a preliminary sketch for his later Death on the Pale Horse (1817), an image of apocalyptic terror.

---

9   British Museum, no. 8777.

5. STAGING THE GOTHIC

With the Regency Crisis of 1788–9, madness and usurpation appeared not to be part of the work of fiction but, instead, a modern-day history staged in public. This was the first of the lurid dynastic dramas of recent British history. Indeed, the bloody battleground of England, which had culminated in the Wars of the Roses of 1455–87, had been followed by Tudor dramas and then Stuart crises. Few Gothic novels could echo the reality and rumours surrounding James, 1st Duke of Monmouth (1649–85), the eldest of Charles II's illegitimate sons and reputedly rightful king, the details of which were mysteriously hidden, who, after an unsuccessful invasion had a grisly execution; or the fate of his nemesis, James II (and VII of Scotland), who was overthrown in 1688–9 by his nephew and son-in-law, William III and then defeated in Ireland in 1690 before living the rest of his life in exile. His only male heir, the 'Warming Pan Baby,' was reportedly the result of subterfuge.

And so also for others. As Electoral Prince of Hanover, the future George I of Britain (r. 1714–27) was married in 1682 to his first cousin, Sophia Dorothea of Celle only for both to turn to affairs. Sophia Dorothea's lover, Count Philip von Königsmarck, was killed in 1694 in the Leineschloss castle in Hanover and probably thrown into the River Leine, with Sophia Dorothea then imprisoned until her death. As part of the route of blood, Königsmarck's brother had allegedly hired the three men who, in 1682, shot dead, in his coach in Pall Mall, Thomas Thynne (a friend of Monmouth) who was married to Lady Elizabeth Percy; Königsmarck had designs on her. Thynne's mock epitaph, which somehow did not make it onto his tomb in Westminster Abbey, captured a related element:

> Here lies Tom Thynne of Longleat Hall
> Who ne'er would have miscarried;

5. Staging the Gothic

Had he married the woman he slept withal
Or slept with the woman he married.

George I's younger grandson, William, Duke of Cumberland (1721–65), the victor of Culloden in 1746, had a sinister political reputation and was criticized by Horace Walpole. The sensitivity of regency arrangements came to the fore after Cumberland's elder brother, Frederick, Prince of Wales, predeceased his father, George II (r. 1727–60), in 1751. Cumberland, the Captain-General of the Army, was presented as a threat to his nephew, George III, and there were references accordingly to Richard III as a sinister royal uncle. In practice, like William IV in the case of Victoria in 1837, George II survived for sufficiently long that there was no regency; while Cumberland, although hostile to Frederick before the latter's death, was a man of integrity and duty, with a keen sense of appropriate behaviour. The fears of the 1750s, however, are a powerful reminder of the dynastic anxieties that played a role in public discussion and proved a background to the publication of, and response to, *The Castle of Otranto*. The role of the usurping uncle was to the fore in much Gothic fiction.

The British press brought news of similar events abroad, some presented in a very lurid fashion. The second half of the century saw the assassination of Gustavus III of Sweden at a ball in Stockholm (1792), an assassination attempt on Louis XV (1757) and the execution of his successor, Louis XVI (1793), an assassination attempt on Joseph I of Portugal (1758), and the apparent madness from 1786 of his successor, Maria I. Tsar Peter III of Russia was murdered in 1762, to the benefit of his wife, Catherine II the Great (r. 1762–96), and this was followed by the assassination of their son, Paul I in 1801.

The 1780s brought particular drama for George III (r. 1760–1820), with his dismissal of the Fox-North ministry in December 1783, the assassination attempt by Margaret Nicholson in August 1786, one where George thanked 'the interposition of Providence,'[1] and the collapse of his health in November 1788 into apparent madness. This touched off the Regency Crisis, with George, Prince of Wales (later George IV, r. 1820–30), the would-be regent,

1 George to Richard Grenville, 29 August 1786, BL. Add. 70956.

linked to the opposition Whigs. Two separate narratives presented Prince and Whigs as seeking to usurp power or, alternatively, William Pitt the Younger's attempts as Prime Minister to restrict the power of the Prince as Regent being a form of usurpation. *Revolutionists*, a caricature published on 30 October but largely describing the situation prior to the Regency Crisis, depicted the followers of the Prince trying to storm a hill marked 'Constitution' on which sat George, was followed, on 25 November, by Thomas Rowlandson's caricature *Filial Piety* which attacked the Prince. On 16 December, James, 2nd Earl of Fife, a supporter of the ministry, asked 'Can anything describe the violence of the present times?'[2]

In the event, George recovered in February 1789. Public celebrations provided an opportunity for a focus on the links between Crown and God, with the service of thanksgiving at St Paul's Cathedral on 23 April, the staging of celebration and devotion. Henry, 2nd Viscount Palmerston presented an image of power and devotion:

> the entering into the church was very magnificent, an avenue all through it being formed by the Guards and Beefeaters [of the Tower of London] in a double row, and in the centre under the dome the astonishing mass of charity children piled up quite round. Their singing as the King came in and went out had a great effect.[3]

Medieval themes were also staged in London theatres, and notably so with Shakespeare's *Macbeth*. The grip of this play on the imagination very much reflected strong interest in the supernatural and in fantastical stories. So also with Shakespeare's *Richard III*. This grip was also in accord with the instinctive response by play audiences, a response that was then increasingly fashionable, in contrast to the earlier, more intellectual response. Drawing on elements of the sublime, this was an aspect of a shift from text to theatrical experience in which emotional atmosphere created by other means,

---

2   Fife to William Rose, 16 December 1788, Aberdeen University Library, Mss. 2226/131; John Derry, *The Regency Crisis and the Whigs, 1788–9* (Cambridge, 1963).
3   Brian Connell (ed.), *Portrait of a Whig Peer Compiled from the Papers of The Second Viscount Palmerston, 1739–1802* (London, 1957), p. 197.

such as the scene-painting was more important than hitherto. The enlargement of Covent Garden in 1792 and Drury Lane in 1794, increased the distance between actors/performers and audience, and led to theatres that were less intimate and, instead, more conducive to the drama of spectacle.

The key designer and painter of sets was the French-born Philip James de Loutherbourg (1740–1812), who settled in London in 1771 and began work at Drury Lane Theatre where his scenic effects owed much to colored lantern-slides as well as the lighting of transparencies. From 1781, he presented the *Eidophusikon*, a mechanical theatre in which the topics included scenes of Satan from Milton's *Paradise Lost*. Loutherbourg's interests included the supernatural and alchemy, and he conducted faith-healing, as well as producing illustrations for an edition of the Bible.[4] The last sentence, which would be easy to omit were I to concentrate simply on the scene-painting, is a reminder of the extent to which many individuals of the period were interested in aspects of the supernatural as well as more conventional Christianity, which provides an instructive context for the response to Gothic fiction.

The Gothic lent itself to the stage, a process encouraged by the popularity of *mélodrame* in France. The sentimental and the Romantic were both presented in terms of horror and the supernatural.[5] The changes in the theatres proved especially conducive to the fashion for Gothic drama. Moreover, some of the Gothic novelists were also dramatists, notably Matthew Lewis, with *The Castle Spectre* and Charles Maturin's *Bertram, Or The Castle of Aldobrand* (1816). Some of the Gothic stories were also translated for the stage, notably Robert Jephson's dramatic adaptation of *The Castle of Otranto*, *The Count of Narbonne* which appeared in November 1781. Its twenty-one nights at the Theatre Royal, Covent Garden in the 1781–2 season was a major triumph, and the play was repeatedly staged during the rest of the century, while there was an edition of the play's text that was printed five times in the 1780s. Other prominent Gothic plays included Francis North's *The Kentish Barons* (1791), J.C. Cross's *Julia of Louvain, or, Monkish Cruelty*

---

4   Rudiger Joppier, *Philippe Jacques de Loutherbourg, R.A., 1740–1812* (London, 1973).
5   Willard Thorp, 'The Stage Adventures of Some Gothic Novels,' *Publications of the Modern Language Association of America*, 43 (1928), pp. 476–86.

(1797), Joanna Baillie's *De Montfort* (1798), and *Presumption; or, the Fate of Frankenstein* (1823), Richard Peake's adaptation of *Frankenstein*.[6]

The interplay between publication and theatre was shown with *The Black Castle* (1800), an inexpensive 48–page novel which had as a full-title *The Black Castle; or the Spectre of the Forest, an Historical Romance. By C.F. Barrett. Founded on the spectacle of that name, performed at the Amph-Theatre of Arts, with unbounded Applause, for Nearly One Hundred Nights*. The castle belongs to Alphar, a Moor who oppresses women, imprisoning, raping and killing Ravia, whose ghost helps Lamora escape her fate. A secret passage is part of the plot, as is a forest, a cave, storms, and the castle bell.

Maturin's *Bertram* begins with a terrifying storm over a monastery, the responses to which capture a major rift which novelists frequently deployed:

1st Monk: O, holy prior, this is no earthly storm.
The strife of fiends is on the battling clouds,
The glare of hell is in these sulphurous lightnings,'
This is no earthly storm.
Prior: peace, peace – thou rash and unadvised man;
Oh! and not to this night of nature's horrors
The darker shadowing of thy wicked fears.
The hand of Heaven, not man, is dealing with us,
And thoughts like thine do make it deal thus sternly (I,1).

The author of *The Kentish Barons*, which was produced at The Haymarket in 1791, was, with Horace Walpole, the most socially exalted of the Gothic writers. Francis North (1761–1817), second son of Frederick, Lord North, later 2nd Earl of Guilford, the Prime Minister from 1770 to 1782, was an army officer who, in 1802, succeeded his elder brother, becoming 4th Earl of Guilford. Described as 'A New Dramatic-Spectacle,' *Julia of Louvain* had a commonplace plot, with St Pierre, a cruel aristocrat, incarcerating a young woman in a convent because she will not marry him, thus setting up the need for a rescue. In the nunnery, presented with the choice of 'Death or St Pierre,' Julia is confined in a sepulchre, but an intervention by townspeople (a scene already occurring in Lewis' novel *The Monk*) leads to the seizure of the

6   Jeffrey Cox (ed.), *Seven Gothic Dramas, 1789–1825* (Athens, Ohio, 1992).

nunnery and, near death, Julia is discovered and freed. Acting-Manager of the Royal Cross theatre in London, J.C. Cross's many plays included *The Apparition!* (1794) and *Joan of Arc* (1798), as well as *Julia of Louvain*.

Joanna Baillie's *De Montfort* (1798 and staged at Drury Lane in 1800) was one of her 'Plays on the Passions,' with the hatred of the arrogant, doom-driven, Marquis De Montfort toward Rezenvelt leading him to breach restraints and to murder. There is a good woman (Montfort's sister, Jane) and a bad one (Countess Freberg), and a Shakespearean intensity to the characterization and action, with the Gothic settings of castle, forests and cathedral. In *Ethwald* (1802), Baillie (1762–1851), a Scot who moved to England in the mid 1780s, borrowed freely from *Macbeth*. Her other Gothic plays included *Orra* (1812). Set in the fourteenth century, this finds Orra exiled from Switzerland to a terrifying haunted castle in the Black Forest for turning down the son of her guardian, Count Hughobert. Instead, she wishes to retain control of her assets. A sinister knight, Rudigere, also desires her. A subterranean passage and a ghost prove part of the action. Orra is driven by fear to madness. Again set in Switzerland, Baillie's *The Dream* (1812), in contrast, has male fear as the issue. Count Osterloo is guilty of murdering a rival in love, the brother of a Prior whose monastery is haunted and from whose vaults a skeleton is exhumed. A secret passage again plays a role, and again in an unsuccessful rescue attempt. Sentenced to death by the vengeful Prior, Osterloo, instead, dies from fear of retribution in Hell.[7] Baillie's religious moralism is brought to the fore.[8]

The first theatrical version of *Frankenstein*, Richard Peake's *Presumption; or, the Fate of Frankenstein*, was staged in London, opening in New York in 1825 and Paris in 1826, at all places with much success, including a run of eighty successive nights in Paris. The addition of an assistant named Fritz was one of the changes from the novel. Mary Shelley was impressed and 'much amused' by the production, and noted 'a breathless eagerness in the audience.' Thomas Cooke, who acted the role of the monster, indicated the

---

7   Thomas Chrochunis (ed.), *Joanna Baillie, Romantic Dramatist* (London, 2004); Diane Hoeveler, 'Joanna Baillie and the Gothic Body: Reading Extremities in *Orra* and *De Montfort*,' *Gothic Studies*, 3, 2 (2001), pp. 117–33.
8   Julie Murray, 'At the Surface of Romantic Interiority: Joanna Baillie's *Orra*,' *Romanticism and Victorianism on the Net*, 56 (2009).

range of Gothic drama. He had already played Almorad in Maturin's *Manuel*, Hans Ketzler in *Castle Spectre* by George Soane (a writer of melodramas), Lord Ruthven in *The Vampyre*, and Dirk Hatteraick in *The Witch of Derncleugh* (1821), a version of Scott's *Guy Mannering* (1815) that takes on the character of Meg Merillies and also Scott's initial, but abandoned, interest in a supernatural approach in this novel.

Peake's *Presumption* was followed by other versions including *The Man And Monster! Or, The Fate of Frankenstein* (1826); *The Monster and the Magician* (1826); *Frankenstein; or, the Model Man* (1849); *The Man and the Monster* (1850); and *Frankenstein; or, The Vampire's Victim* (1887).

Gothic theatre was an important aspect of the Gothic role in culture, and not one that was a footnote to the novels. The Licensing Act of 1737 gave the Lord Chamberlain power to censor plays and made unlicensed theatres illegal, but the Gothic was acceptable, while an Enabling Act of 1788 eased the operation of theatres outside London. Some of the theatres were big, that in Bristol built in 1766 having a capacity of about 1600.[9] Gothic plays offered a way to try to make money, and, as with the range of published novels, from multi-volume heavyweights to shorter chapbooks and bluebooks, ranged considerably. Moreover, for both, there was not a 'fixed' character, but, instead, an overlap, often more than an overlap, with other plot types, notably the sentimental, the historical, and the melodramatic in which the supernatural did not play a role. Recent years have seen more attention to the bluebooks and, to a lesser extent, there is room for more consideration of the plays. They were an aspect of the Gothic as spectacle, because the mental alarm expressed and elicited on the page by the suggestable Gothic of reported sites, sounds, sights and suggestions, had to be depicted. That was far from easy unless the audience was supportive; and the referral of response from readers to theatrical audience, and back again, was part of the way in which the public was important to the Gothic in more ways than simply as purchasing patron.

---

9   I. Mackintosh and G. Ashton (eds), *The Georgian Playhouse: Actors, Artists, Audiences and Architecture, 1730–1830* (London, 1975). For a vivid account of a performance in Falmouth, E. Jaggard, 'James Boswell's Journey through Cornwall, August-September 1792,' *Journal of the Royal Institution of Cornwall* (2004), p. 29.

6. THE TERROR OF REVOLUTION

The French Revolution threw contemporary terror to the fore; and, in doing so, made ironic to a degree a novelistic emphasis on Italy as a seat of terror, because it was France that was now the place of massacre. The young Charles, Earl of Dalkeith, later 4th Duke of Buccleuch, a Tory politician as well as landowner and amateur cricketer, thought that the September Massacres of 1792 in Paris outstripped 'the massacres of [ancient] Rome in its most abandoned style.'[1] Indeed, these were apparently new instances of the fall of Rome to the Goths in 410 and the destruction of the Classical world, a topic that continued to be resonant. The sense captured by Edward Gibbon of a ruined past civilization was differently noted by Radcliffe who, in *The Italian*, presented Vivaldi as crossing Rome en route to imprisonment by the Inquisition. She referred to 'those mighty monuments of Rome's eternal name, those sacred ruins, those gigantic skeletons, which once enclosed a soul, whose energies governed a world!' (II,6).

At the same time, Radcliffe, in this novel, provided a grimmer account of Rome, by reference to an episode held in 52 CE to celebrate the construction of a tunnel:

> "to such a scene as this," said Vivaldi, "a Roman Emperor came, only for the purpose of witnessing the most barbarous exhibition; to indulge the most savage delights! Here, Claudius celebrated the accomplishment of his arduous work ... by a naval fight, in which hundreds of wretched slaves perished for his amusement! Its pure and polished surface was stained with human blood, and roughened by the plunging bodies of the slain, while the gilded gallies of the Emperor floated gaily

---

1   Dalkeith to James, 1st Earl of Malmesbury, 29 September 1792, Winchester, Hampshire Record Office, Malmesbury papers, volume 149.

around, and these beautiful shores were made to echo with applauding yells, worthy of the furies!" (II,2),

the last a diabolical allusion, albeit one that was not too urgent.

The horrors of the French Revolution, anarchic horrors that preceded the full-blown sociopathic Terror of 1793–4, were apparently new instances not only of the fall of Rome, and the vulnerability of civilization, but also indicators of a potential darkness within humans. As such, they introduced a new iteration of the Gothic world that had replaced that of Rome, offering a whole new range of social and cultural settings and references. In one respect, the Gothic novels helped define differing responses to this cultural maelstrom, and as part of a representation of both revolution and counter-revolution.[2]

With reference to events in Paris, the *Leeds Intelligencer* in March 1790 printed a letter from A.B. of Leeds, including: 'I love liberty as well as any man, but not that particular species of it, which allows only seven minutes to prepare for death, before one is hanged up by fish-women at a lamp iron.'

The 1790s saw a revival of a marked ideological partisanship in Britain, notably the consolidation of a new conservatism in reaction to a radical challenge seen at home and abroad, with the latter presented by some writers, including William Radcliffe, the journalist-and-editor husband of the novelist Ann. In reaction, a sense of the precariousness of public order was pushed to the fore, as a result of events in both Britain and France. In the *London Chronicle* of 26 July 1791, 'Quidam' responded to disturbances in Birmingham:

> There are men enough ready at all times and in all countries, ambitious to raise themselves into consequence upon the shoulders of the people ... may God in his mercy give the good people of Britain sense enough to know the due value of a constitution that has long been the admiration of the whole world; and to be warned by the horrors of the perilous experiment of refining

2 Ronald Paulson, *Representations of Revolution 1789–1820* (New Haven, Conn., 1983).

6. The Terror of Revolution

systems of government above the standard of humanity, and then with stern despotism exacting conformity to them!'

The *Westminster Journal* of 26 January 1793 wrote of Louis XVI's execution 'as a murder we are confident it will be felt in the heart of every Englishman.' An item in the newspaper that would have fitted in well with the plotting of many Gothic novels blamed the execution on Louis' cousin, Philip, Duke of Orléans who was described as 'the issue of a criminal connexion between his licentious mother and a coachman.'

Turning republican in 1792 and atheistical, in 1793 Revolutionary France could be seen as anti-Christian, such indeed that in response Catholics could appear as allies for Protestant Britain.[3] In December 1789, the Austrian Chancellor, Count Kaunitz had told the French ambassador that it was not true to say that there was nothing new under the Sun as, in practice, the impiety of some was unprecedented.[4] In the French Revolution, aggressive anti-clericalism was followed by the prohibition of Christian practice and worship, the closing of churches, the replacement of the Christian calendar by a Revolutionary one, and the introduction of new religious cults centred on Reason or the Supreme Being. Even Islamic powers could now be appealed to by Britain for co-operation, on the grounds that the Revolution was a common threat, its murderous trajectory 'unexampled in the history of the most barbarous and savage nations.'[5]

There was a marked lack of agreement, however, over the response to the Revolution, and this provided a context for the reading, and thus writing, of novels. To radicals, a new order, both international and domestic, appeared an imminent prospect, and some were millenarians, including Joseph Priestley in 1793.[6] In contrast, Conservatives saw a need to intervene

---

3   A. Robinson, "Identifying the Beast: Samuel Horsley and the Problem of Papal AntiChrist," *Journal of Ecclesiastical History* 43 (1992), pp. 592–607.
4   Paris, Ministère des Affaires Étrangéres, Correspondence Politique Autriche 358 folio 315.
5   Additional instructions for Robert Liston, envoy in Constantinople, 26 February 1794, London, National Archives, Foreign Office volume, 78/15 folio 47.
6   C. Garrett, 'Joseph Priestley, the Millennium and the French Revolution,' *Journal of the History of Ideas*, 34 (1973) and *Respectable Folly: Millenarians and the French Revolution in France and England* (Baltimore, 1975).

in order to destroy a threatening canker, while ministers sought to define a differently realistic response. Encompassing the range of response, there was a widespread belief in plotting and secret societies as a key aspect of the spread of revolutionary activity,[7] as in William Hamilton Reid's *The Rise and Dissolution of the Infidel Societies in this Metropolis* [London], including the origin of modern deism and atheism (1800), religion being seen as a key to stability. Reid had earlier been a contributor to the *Visits from the World of Spirits* (1791) by Henry Lemoine, a magazine writer, editor and bookseller who in 1792 launched the *Conjurors' Magazine* which, the following year, became the *Astrologer's Magazine*. Rather than being solely to do with a new politics of the revolutionary age, the belief in conspiracy very much went back to earlier prototypes, notably in Britain from the sixteenth century, of Catholic manipulation and conspiracy, including the drama of the Gunpowder Plot of 1605 with its Gothic setting under Westminster Hall.

To Edmund Burke, the danger from the French Revolution was all-encompassing, and space was collapsed, as it were, because the ideological toxin of revolutionary France was revolution, and not solely France. Extremist ideas spread as a result of the influence of the French Revolution, while also drawing on British traditions of revolution. Thus, according to Burke, Britain was at risk irrespective of the precise territorial advance of revolutionary France, and revolution in France was very different to that earlier in the United States or, indeed, in Britain in 1688. In September 1792, he claimed: 'The English assassins of the Jacobin faction are working hard to corrupt the public mind in favour of their brother murderers in France ... these poisons.'[8] In turn, there was a rejection of the 'Jacobins,' the pro-ministerial *Times* informing its readers on 25 November 1790 that:

> Mr Burke, while he has excited the vengeance of the Paris mob by his late publication [the *Reflections*], has gained the reverence and admiration of every thinking man who esteems a well ordered government, which is the best bond of civil society.

7   John Roberts, *The Mythology of the Secret Societies* (London, 1972).
8   Burke to Malmesbury, 10 September 1792, Winchester, Malmesbury papers, vol. 145.

6. The Terror of Revolution

The Revolution did not provide Gothic novelists with any real prequel to Charles Dickens' *A Tale of Two Cities* (1859), which was set in this period. Indeed, Italy, rather than France, was the foreign destination of choice in plots; and certainly not modern France. Yet, there were references, as in *The Old Irish Baronet*, in which the protagonist visits Lyons which had 'not recovered from the effects of revolutionary fury; its magnificent squares were yet strewed with the ruins of its palaces, bearing testimony to the horrid exploits of Collot D'Herbois and his "Comité de Demolition" ... its diabolical activity ... providentially stopped by a new order of things' (II,4). This leads in *The Old Irish Baronet* to a critique of the way in which control over revolution is seized by the vicious:

> ... an ignorant and depraved mob ... popular energy is ever most obedient to the vicious, even ready to destroy rather than to create, to condemn than to absolve; and hence we have seen that, in all countries, nothing is so absurd, nothing so impolitic, unjust, or horribly atrocious, that the dictator of the day can order or invite to, but a blind and furious populace will concur and aid in the perpetration of it. (II,4)

The French Revolution brought to an end the optimism of the Enlightenment which is not usually associated with Gothic writers, but that was definitely shown by Radcliffe in a long passage in *A Sicilian Romance* (1790). Far from making the past romantic, an abbey, 'a large magnificent mass of Gothic architecture,' where Julia takes refuge, provides a 'proud sublimity,' but also 'stood a proud monument of monkish superstition' and offered 'monkish fictions':

> The view of this building revived in the mind of the beholder the memory of past ages. The manners and characters which distinguished them arose to his fancy, and through the long lapse of years he discriminated those customs and manners which formed so striking a contrast to the modes of his own times. The rude manners, the boisterous passions, the daring ambition, and the gross indulgences which formerly characterized the priest, the nobleman, and the sovereign, had now begun

to yield to learning - the charms of refined conversation – political intrigue and private artifices. Thus do the scenes of life vary with the predominant passions of mankind, and with the progress of civilization. The dark clouds of prejudice break away before the sun of science, and gradually dissolving, leave the brightening hemisphere to the influence of his beams.

Radcliffe puts the emphasis on 'reason,' not prejudice; which was a contrast adopted by both reformers and radicals, had been used by both Enlightenment figures and their Revolutionary successors to justify moves against monasteries. This emphasis was certainly not that of counter-revolutionaries. However, before there is a rush to present her as far from conservative, it is worth noting that she called at the close for 'wisdom, simplicity, and pure devotion' (9), an approach that was open to all political tendencies. More generally, it can be all too easy, as well as misleading, to draw political consequences from particular remarks and, linked to that, to seek to discern political consistency.

Although the most obvious Enlightenment theme in Gothic novels was anti-Catholicism, as was very much the case in *The Monk*, other Enlightenment elements were seen in later Gothic novels. Thus, in *The Old Irish Baronet*, there is reference to an improvement in prison conditions. The baronet had helped free a wrongly-accused man:

> The poor man, labouring under anxiety of mind for his own fate, and that of his wife with six helpless children, and deprived, by confinement in a dark and loathsome jail, of air and exercise (for the age of the illustrious [John] Howard had not yet darted like a beam from on high into the drear recesses of Irish prisons), was attacked by a dangerous indisposition. (I,5)

False imprisonment in harsh circumstances was a commonplace in Gothic novels. Later in that novel, there is a brief attack on the slave trade as part of a critique of ideas of the divine underpinning of situations (II,5). This is an argument that speaks to a degree of radicalism, although the slave trade was more generally unpopular by this period.

A Sicilian Romance was written before the brutality of the French Revolution was to become incessantly obvious, and the scene of massacre is

6. The Terror of Revolution

that by rural banditti, but it would have echoed for some the accounts of Revolutionary atrocities already in 1789:

> a dark abyss ... for the murdered bodies of the unfortunate people who had fallen into the hands of the banditti.... The bodies which remained unburied ...exhibited a spectacle too shocking for humanity ... this mansion of the murdered. (13)

Described as a horror, this owed nothing to the supernatural. So also with the account in Matthew Lewis' *The Monk* of a murderous and terrifying popular riot in Madrid directed against an apparently murderous abbess:

> ... the people ... forced a passage through the guards who protected their destined victim, dragged her from her shelter and proceeded to take upon her a most summary and cruel vengeance ... heeded nothing but the gratification of their barbarous vengeance ... loaded her with mud and filth-dragged her through the streets ... trampling her, and treating her with every species of cruelty ... exercised their impotent rage upon her lifeless body. They beat it, trod upon it, and ill-used it, till it became no more than a mass of flesh, unsightly, shapeless, and disgusting. (III,10)

The 'mob' go on to attack the convent, and to kill all the nuns, innocent or guilty. Having thrown in lighted torches, the rioters force a gate, destroy everything, including the relics, and set fire to the convent, the whole presenting 'a scene of devastation and horror,' with falling buildings and flames killing nuns and rioters alone (III,10). The mob was a pointed reference to the French Revolution, rather than the 1766 riots in Madrid, but also brought into play rioting townspeople, a group that had not played a role in earlier Gothic novels. It was however to become more significant thereafter and notably those novels that moved from a ruined or castellated past. In contrast to Lewis, Gibbon's account of the fall of Constantinople to the Turks in 1453 offered a genuine personal horror at the treatment of nuns, combined with a lack of sympathy with the destruction of religious icons.

A sense of the danger of popular fury was also captured by Maturin in *Fatal Revenge* when discussing the suspicion with which Ippolito was viewed as an alleged satanist:

> ... The rage of the vulgar is more deadly and indiscriminating, less liable to be pacified by representations, less assailable by any medium of rational vindication, and more apt to vent itself in sanguinary violence, than that of the higher orders. (17)

There is also an echo of Burke in Maturin's *Fatal Revenge* when a woman whom he has rescued from murder appeals to Ippolito for protection: 'Her appeal was made in a language now little understood – the language of chivalry.... Even at that period [the seventeenth century], this language was much disused' (17).

The Revolution had a wider resonance from the start, notably in Britain. Already, in March 1790, Major-General Richard Grenville, Comptroller and Master of the Household to Frederick, Duke of York, had expressed his (correct) conviction that the elections would go well for the government, adding:

> I hope the example we have before our eyes of the misery and ruin attending a total subversion of all order and government, may check any spirit of that kind which may lay lurking among us.[9]

The political 'location' of Gothic novels is instructive but complex. Although the French Revolutionary period was a serious challenge to the assumptions of the political élite, not least in the creation of a language of class conflict, this challenge was substantially faced using traditional methods. Indeed, the very conservatism of the response to revolution, and the stress on continuity, precedent, privilege, law and religion, the ideological focus of nationhood and counter-revolution encouraged this traditionalism even as economic change, gathered pace while there were in practice also government

9 Grenville to Joseph Ewart, 25 March 1790, Williamwood, Ewart papers, vol. 147.

6. The Terror of Revolution

innovation, from parliamentary union with Ireland to the introduction of a national census. The emphasis on monarchy as an aspect of this continuity and loyalism[10] looked toward the major themes of legitimacy and inheritance in Gothic novels, themes that brought the past into the present. That approach was already apparent prior to the French Revolution, as, very differently, in *Tom Jones, Roderick Random, The Castle of Otranto* and *The Old English Baron*.

Legitimacy could have a profound religious character, as struggles between dynasties were as nothing in significance and across time compared to those between churches. That was a dimension that came to the fore in the 1790s. With the example of France in the foreground, atheism became more urgent as a threat.

Legitimism was also pushed to the fore as republicanism became more of an issue from 1792, with publications such as Richard Lee's *The Death of Despotism, and the Doom of Tyrants* (1795) and his flysheet *King Killing* (1795). Threats to George III's life were a background to the reconsideration of the law of treason.[11] In a scene that could have come from a novel, Queen Charlotte recorded in her diary '… news of a plot being discovered against the life which was to be effected by a poisoned arrow' and reports of a radical plot with the poisoned arrow fired from an airgun circulated.[12] In 1800, George was fired on at Drury Lane Theatre by James Hadfield, a millenarian who believed that his own death would ensure the Second Coming. To that end, he tried to kill George, but then told the uninjured king that he was 'a good fellow.' At least partially deranged, Hadfield was imprisoned until he died in 1841. Millenarians prophesied and desired the overthrow of the monarchy as a prelude to the creation of the New Jerusalem, Richard Brothers in 1794 identifying the Beast of the *Book of Revelations*, a Gothic work, with the British monarchy.[13]

10 Marilyn Morris, *The British Monarchy and the French Revolution* (New Haven, Conn., 1998).
11 John Barrell, *Imagining the King's Death. Figurative Treason, Fantasies of Regicide, 1793–1796* (Oxford, 2000).
12 Queen Charlotte's diary, 29 September 1794, Windsor Castle, Royal Archives, George III papers, GEO/Add. 43/3; M. Thale (ed.), *Selections from the Papers of the London Corresponding Society 1792–1799* (Cambridge, 1983), p. 220.
13 S. Juster, *Doomsayers: Anglo-American Prophecy in the Age of Revolution* (Philadelphia, Penn., 2003).

In 1802, in the Despard Conspiracy, there was an unsuccessful plan to kill George on his way to open Parliament as part of a proposed seizure of power, which was akin to the plots against William III in the 1690s. Although not directed against George, another conspiracy rocked Ireland with rebellion in 1798 while, although their motivation was largely about pay conditions, there were major naval mutinies in 1797. These were prominent instances of a plotting that contributed to a widespread sense of secretive forces challenging order, one that in the Cato Street Conspiracy of 1820 extended to an unsuccessful attempt to kill the entire Cabinet. Conspiracy provided a major plot element in Gothic novels, and one linked to the frequent paranoia of those in charge in the particular story. Plotting was an element, moreover, that could encompass human and diabolical agencies.

At the same time, there was, although Britain was at war with Revolutionary France and providing shelter to Royalist exiles, a presentation in some Gothic novels of the horrors of pre-Revolutionary France. Thus, in Francis Lathom's *The Midnight Bell* (1798), due to a *letter de cachet*, an arbitrary means, Count Biroff is imprisoned in the Bastille, which is presented as a place of torture. That is implicit approval for the Revolution which had led, in 1789, to the storming and destruction of the Bastille. Yet, there is also praise in *The Midnight Bell* for the 'fair trials' and 'mild and free government' of England.

Repeated British failure in war from 1794 helped drive a sense of threat. The *Gloucester Journal* of 22 February 1796 observed: 'there never was a period that called more loudly upon the understanding and prudence of the nation for a suspension of narrow party hostility.' In February 1797, a 1,400 strong French force landed in Pembrokeshire. Seeking to exploit social strains, the French planned to win the support of the local poor and disaffected, and to press on to attack and burn Bristol. Poorly-commanded and vigorously-opposed, the invasion rapidly collapsed. The 1798 Irish rebellion was far more serious, involved large numbers of men and provided a context for the circulation of the Pastorini Prophecies, predicting the imminent end of the Protestant Ascendancy.

War news set the background and tone for both society and culture. If it was offstage in Radcliffe, as in Austen, war was part of the process by which men validated themselves, whether historically, as in *The Mysteries of Udolpho*, or contemporaneously, as with Austen. 'The New Year's Present of the Men who carry *The Dorchester and Sherborne Journal*, and *Taunton*

6. The Terror of Revolution

and Somersetshire Herald, for the Year 1799,' a flysheet commenting on the news of the last year and asking for a tip, stated:

> Much blood, 'tis true, still stains his pages
> But this must be, where battle rages.[14]

Further alarm was excited by support in the British Isles for French examples, support both real and alleged. This sense of alarm and uncertainty provided one context for the Gothic novels. Thus, in 1798, the first issue of the *Weekly Register*, a newly-launched Sunday paper, announced:

> The late rapid and alarming spread of infidelity and even atheism, calls aloud for union of all serious Christians, on the most enlarged scale ... the case of religion, virtue, and social union ... show the harmony subsisting between the dispensations of Divine Providence and Scriptures ... we shall endeavour to strip off the meretricious ornaments of vice, to draw aside the gaudy robe of pleasure and to show the worm that preys within.

In early issues, the paper rejected a contributor's love song as an unsuitable kind of item, printed part of the Bishop of Durham's charge to his clergy against infidelity and, attacking novels as likely to lead people away from the Bible, urged writers to fear divine punishment and to destroy them.[15]

British society was under great pressure, with harvest failures, widespread economic problems, inflation, and monetary pressures. The gold standard, under which paper currency was met by the Bank of England, collapsed in 1797, while there were stagnant, if not falling, real wages and widespread hardship, especially in the 'famine years' of 1795–6 and 1799–1801. The real wages of Lancashire cotton weavers fell by more than a half in 1792–9. Food rioting and trade union agitation were responses.[16]

---

14 BL. L23c4 (45).
15 *Weekly Register*, 11 April, 9, 16, 30 May 1798.
16 John Bohstedt, *Riots and Community Politics in England and Wales, 1790–1810* (Cambridge, Massachusetts, 1983); Roger Wells, *Wretched Faces: Famine in Wartime England, 1793–1801* (Gloucester, 1988).

However, there were other, more positive, responses from the state (the Poor Law), the churches, and private philanthropy, and hardship did not equal famine. There were many local initiatives to mitigate high food prices, such as subscriptions to purchase bread at a high price and sell it to the poor at low, heavily-subsidised prices.[17]

William Blake's 'London' (1794) expressed his concern and anger about the harshness of society:

> I wander through each chartered street,
> Near where the Chartered Thames does flow,
> And mark in every face I meet,
> Marks of weakness, marks of woe.
>
> In every cry of every man,
> In every infant's cry of fear,
> In every voice, in every ban,
> the mind-forged manacles I hear:
>
> How the chimney-sweeper's cry
> Every blackening church appals,
> And the hapless soldier's sigh
> Runs in blood down palace-walls.
>
> But most, through midnight streets I hear
> How the youthful harlot's curse
> Blasts the new-born infant's tear,
> And blights with plagues the marriage-hearse.

The sexual corruption referred to in the last verse was part of the horror of the metropolis, with the emphasis on victims and, unlike many Gothic novels, with no happy ending.

The domestic crisis was less acute in the 1800s, but Britain itself was still under threat. The editorial in the *St James's Chronicle* of 1 January 1801

---

17 For examples in Canterbury, *Kentish Gazette*, 31 Mar. 14 July 1795, 20 May, 10 June, 26 Sept., 31 Oct. 1800.

referred to 'the horrors of revolutionary violence.' Having seized power in France in 1799, Napoleon offered a reason in novels to focus anew on malicious usurpation. That scarcely began with his seizure of power, but the latter helped dramatize both such a seizure and, particularly after he made himself Emperor in 1804, the juxtaposition of good and bad rulers. Napoleon was seen by many not only as a contrast to George III, but also as the Anti-Christ.[18]

Moreover, again presenting a background to the wartime Gothic novels, there was a fresh burst of loyalist activity in 1803–5 in response to the danger of French invasion, which Napoleon indeed prepared for. Newspapers emphasized popular zeal and the extent to which everything held dear was at stake. The *Dorchester and Sherborne Journal* of 22 July 1803 declared:

> It is not a dispute about the possession of a foreign island, but we are to decide whether we shall be free – and *Britons never will be Slaves!* ... what Englishman would basely remain and witness the plundering of his country, his sisters dishonoured, and the murder of his friends?

Separately, Evangelical attitudes were of growing significance in the navy deployed against the French, and not only among the officers. Indeed, Horatio, Lord Nelson was compared to Jesus, saw his captains, the 'Band of Brothers,' in scriptural terms, and, himself the son, grandson and brother of vicars, trusted to God, not least in a command method and style that rejected a carefully-planned, explicitly rational, approach.[19] Nelson was far from alone:

> So now my brave countrymen be not in fear of an invasion for the Lord will prosper your island and will in time restore peace.

18 F.C. Mather, *High Church Prophet. Bishop Samuel Horsley (1733–1806) and the Caroline Tradition in the Later Georgian Church* (Oxford, 1992), pp. 261–8.
19 Michael Palmer, '"The Soul's Right Hand": Command and Control in the Age of Fighting Sail, 1652–1827,' *Journal of Military History*, 61 (1997), pp. 699–702.

> It is the Supreme that fights the battle and whilst we have his help we will defy the world.

Thus, John Jup, an ordinary seaman on board HMS *Orion* was in no doubt that victory at the battle of the Nile in 1798 was providential.[20]

The invasion was thwarted, but Britain's alliance system repeatedly collapsed in defeat in 1805–9, and the sense of threat remained. War meanwhile had encouraged a period of reform designed to enable Britain to meet the challenge from France. Key elements included parliamentary union with Ireland, the establishment of a national census, the extension of the detailed mapping of the country by the Ordnance Survey, the introduction of income tax, and the need to manage the national finances without being on the gold standard.

Papers, such as the *Birmingham Commercial Herald* on 2 January 1809, continued to use the commonplace declaration of intent in the first issue of the year, to declare their loyalty:

> Despising all sneaking attempts to please all parties, we stand forth … the firm advocates of Church and State.

'Church' referred specifically to the issue of opposition to Catholic Emancipation, full civil rights for Catholics, an issue that had helped strongly divide politics from the late 1790s. George III was bitterly opposed to a change. Indeed, ministries fell in 1801 and 1807 largely over this opposition. Providing a means to approach a major theme in Gothic novels, 'No Popery,' and not the war, was the issue that dominated the 1807 general election, which ended with the more radical Whigs in the political wilderness. Led initially by William, Duke of Portland, the new ministry was then replaced, as a result of his ill-health, by another Conservative one under the Evangelical Tory Spencer Perceval that continued on a Pittite base. The revival of the Pittite system after the Whig 'Ministry of All the Talents' of 1806–7 suggested that the basic conservative principles, policies and personnel that had characterized the system were more successful and appropriate for government than those of its rivals. It was indicative that there

---

20   Jup to his parents, 26 Nov. 1798, NMM, AGC/J9.

6. The Terror of Revolution

was scant radicalism even among most of the politicians not seen as Tory. This was partly due to the privileged social context and character of the political system, but also to the extent to which a generally conservative political ideology had become more cautious in response to the radicalism of the French Revolutionary period. In 1810, William, Lord Grenville, who had headed the Ministry of All the Talents, wrote from his seat at Dropmore to Henry Brougham, an energetic Whig MP with a commitment to reform. Grenville's letter was a determined rejection of the horrors of extremes:

> I continue to object strongly to the vague and undefined notions of reforming merely for the sake of reform. That is determining to make some change without previously considering its extent, its principles, or its objects. I hold on the contrary side in equal reprobation the opinions in the other extreme, that on this point alone all change is to be rejected without examination, merely because it is a change. The just sentiment seems to be that in this as in every other matter in which the public interests are concerned the constant and vigilant superintendence of Parliament is required, neither adopting nor rejecting change in the abstract, but weighing each particular proposition in detail by the scale of probable advantage or mischief to the community … all ideas should be disclaimed of extensive and as you justly call them wholesale plans of reform which are at once to strike out for us a new constitution of government and legislation. The idea of introducing separate bills each containing distinct and limited measures is that which entirely meets with my concurrence.[21]

An able financial manager, as well as careful scrutineer of millenarian prophecies, Perceval stood firm against Catholic Emancipation, but was assassinated in 1812 by an embittered merchant. His successor, the Pittite Robert, 2nd Earl of Liverpool, remained Prime Minister until 1827. Indeed, the continuance of the Tory interest seemed foreordained. Byron, who was no friend of the Tories, wrote in *Don Juan* that:

---

21 Grenville to Brougham, 1 May 1810, BL. Add. 58965 folios 10–11.

> Nought's permanent among the human race,
> Except the *Whigs* not getting into place.

In peace and particularly war, this was a system in which the social élite played a key role, and this focused attention on the very landed nobility who dominated Gothic novels. In 1801, Lord Pelham, the Home Secretary, pointed out that 'regiments have been raised by persons having real or supposed influence in the counties they resided in; rank has been given as the price of recruits.'[22] Yet, in Gothic novels, many of these figures were sinister, albeit frequently because they had seized inheritances from the rightful owners. Thus, the imagination was menaced, rather as Britain was.

More generally, a nationalistic perspective that owed much to Protestant zeal and hostility toward foreign developments was widely combined with a strong interest in history. Thus, in 1828 Edward Nares, Professor of Modern History at Oxford from 1813 until 1841 and a friend of Liverpool, produced a major three-volume life of Elizabeth's leading minister, William Cecil, Lord Burghley. In the preface, Nares declared 'he prides himself upon being an Englishman, an English Protestant, a Church of England man, a Divine [clergyman].'[23]

Separately, novelists joined most historians in a hostile treatment of the French Revolution as violent, terrifying, and un-English.[24] This was an important context for Gothic fiction, one that was far more present and urgent than medieval imaginings. The lack of detail generally given to the medieval background provided an opportunity to use Gothic fiction to record wider concerns.

---

22 Pelham to Addington, First Lord of the Treasury, 23 September 1801, BL. Add. 33120 folio 59.
23 Edward Nares, *Burghley* (London, 1828), pp. xx-xxii; J.M. Black, 'A Regency Regius: The Historian Edward Nares,' *Oxoniensia*, 52 (1987), pp. 173–8.
24 B Melman, *The Culture of History: English Uses of the Past, 1800–1953* (Cambridge, 1968).

7. ANN RADCLIFFE, THE QUEEN OF THE GENRE

Robert Martin is shamed in Jane Austen's *Emma* because he had never heard of either Ann Radcliffe's highly popular *The Romance of the Forest* (1791) or Regina Maria Roche's *The Children of the Abbey* (1798), a Radcliffe imitation, before his fiancée, Harriet Smith, had mentioned them. Robert Martin at once determines to obtain copies of them.[1] Albeit fictional, such demand helped explain Radcliffe's commercial success. She sold the publication rights to *The Mysteries of Udolpho* for £500 and those to *The Italian* for £800, extraordinary sums for the period.

Like the paintings of Fuseli discussed earlier, the plots of Gothic literature tested conventional notions of probability, not least the established patterns of expressing and moulding experience with reference to the interior and natural world. Gothic fiction reworked many of the images of landscape poetry: monastic stonework and trees became ruined abbeys and sinister woods that both served as malign settings for the plot and also represented the psychological strains of the psyche. This fiction, which in part was a Reformation throwback with its echoes of malign and corrupt monks and nuns, was different to the metropolitan settings that had dominated the culture of print at the start of the eighteenth century and the country houses that had followed.

An emphasis on the wilful protagonist was located in the Romantic fascination with the ego. To be a hero, however, the Romantic hero required a brooding quality, a dignified melancholy and mysterious introspection, that separated him from the more easily driven and readily explained villains of most Gothic novels. Nevertheless, Schedoni, the complex, troubled, austere, monkish villain of Radcliffe's *The Italian, or The Confessional of the Black Penitents* (1797) showed signs of being such a presence, but not really a hero: '…His air and countenance were something also terrific in the silent

---

1   *Emma*, I, 4.

stalk of so gigantic a form; it announced both power and treachery' (II,8). More positively, that chapter shows Schedoni 'sensible to some pity' as well as in pursuit of 'lofty plans' cruelly implemented: 'Is one spark of the fire, which has so long smouldered within my bosom, and consumed my peace, alive.... Shall the spirit of my family yield for ever to circumstances?' In the event, despite having 'an assassin's heart,' he does not murder her.

Rather than developing the character of her central figures in an original fashion to test notions of the hero or heroine, Radcliffe was successfully conventional. Instead, her settings were part of the heroism, or at least drama, for they very much captured the sublime. In *The Mysteries of Udolpho*, Emily crosses the Alps into Italy:

> often as she travelled among the clouds, watched in silent awe their billowy surges rolling below; sometimes, wholly closing upon the scene, they appeared like a world of chaos, and, at others, spreading thinly, they opened and admitted partial catches of the landscape – the torrent, whose astounding roar had never failed, tumbling down the rocky chasm, huge cliffs white with snow, or the dark summits of the pine forests, that stretched mid-way down the mountains. (II,i)

In Radcliffe's *The Italian* (1797), the captured Ellena Rosalba, another woman given limited physical agency by her role as a captive, offered an appropriate response to the darkening forcefulness of the landscape that she was thrust into with all the attention of an enraptured spectator of an awesome painting. Indeed, as an instance of the movement between genres, there are references to illustrations:

> It was when the heat and the light were declining that the carriage entered a rocky defile, which shewed, as through a telescope reversed, distant plains, and mountains opening beyond, lighted up with all the purple splendor of the setting sun. Along this deep and shadowy perspective a river, which was seen descending among the cliffs of a mountain, rolled with impetuous force, fretting and foaming amidst the dark rocks in its descent, and then flowing in a limpid lapse to the brink of other

7. Ann Radcliffe, the Queen of the Genre

precipices, whence again it fell with thundering strength to the abyss, throwing its misty clouds of spray high in the air, and seeming to claim the sole empire of this solitary wild. Its bed took up the whole breadth of the chasm, which some strong convulsion of the earth seemed to have formed, not leaving space even for a road along its margin. The road, therefore, was carried high among the cliffs, that impended over the river, and seemed as if suspended in air; while the gloom and vastness of the precipices, which towered above and sunk below it, together with the amazing force and uproar of the falling waters, combined to render the pass more terrific than the pencil could describe, or language can express. Ellena ascended it, not with indifference but with calmness; she experienced somewhat of a dreadful pleasure in looking down upon the irresistible flood; but this emotion was heightened into awe, when she perceived that the road led to a slight bridge, which, thrown across the chasm at an immense height, united two opposite cliffs, between which the whole cataract of the river descended. The bridge, which was defended only by a slender railing, appeared as if hung amidst the clouds. Ellena, while she was crossing it, almost forgot her misfortunes.

Born in London in 1764, Ann Ward came from a mercantile background, and moved quietly in educated circles, marrying, in 1787, William Radcliffe, an Oxford graduate and journalist who was editor and part-owner of the *English Chronicle*. Although many details of her life are obscure, William apparently encouraged her to write. Ann's first novel offered two characteristics of much of the developing genre, a setting at once medieval and castellated. Furthermore, her own writings helped fix much of the genre in a way that Walpole did not, in part because his lack of repetition helped limit his formulaic role.

Set in Scotland, Radcliffe's *The Castles of Athlin and Dunbayne. A Highland Story* (1789) had what were becoming familiar Gothic features, including a past murderous usurpation, the resulting threat to the heroine, and a rightful heir who has been brought up as a peasant. There is no real horror, but a lot of danger, notably with the villain's capture of the heroes and the repeated threats to the female characters, from imprisonment to abduction. In the event, the rightful heir rescues the heroine. This novel had scant success, and the limited attention it receives is due to her later writing. However, the setting was a reflection of contemporary interest in Highland Scotland.

Following in 1790, *A Sicilian Romance* moved the setting to Italy, which proved appropriate for an emphasis on the sublime in, and through, landscape, and put the stress on the women, thus prefiguring her approach in *The Romance of the Forest* (1791) and *The Mysteries of Udolpho* (1794). Chases and unexpected meetings serve to underline unpredictability and thereby challenges to control, both self-control and control of and by others.

Radcliffe's placing of Sicily differs from that of Otranto by Walpole. Whereas the latter was beyond the bounds of the well-known, and was more exotic due to its brief conquest by the Turks in 1480–1, Sicily had received tourists during the century and greater public attention in recent years. Neville, 6th Lord Lovelace (*c.* 1708–36) and John King (1706–40) sailed there from Naples in 1728 on an English merchantman, while John Frederick (1704–77) and Roger Kynaston (*c.* 1710–88) sailed round the island in 1749, taking Richard Dalton (*c* 1713–91) with them as a travelling draughtsman. Sir William Stanhope MP (1702–72) went from Naples to Sicily in 1754, while Sir Thomas Worsley (1728–68) made a six-week visit in 1766, although he left his family in Naples. On his second trip to Italy, Richard Payne Knight (1750–1824) visited Sicily in 1777. He sailed from Naples, stopped at Paestum and the Lipari islands, landed at Milazzo, toured the Classical remains at Segesta, Selinus, Agrigento, Syracuse and Taormina, climbed Etna, and sailed back to Naples from Messina. His companions, the German painter Jacob Philipp Hackert and Charles Gore, made sketches from which copies were commissioned from John Robert Cozens and Thomas Hearne. Later an MP, Knight was a Herefordshire gentleman whose family had become rich through the Shropshire iron industry, as well as a prominent Classical scholar, numismatist, and connoisseur. Gore (1729–1807) was a Lincolnshire landowner and an amateur artist who had sailed to Italy in 1773 with his wife Mary and three daughters after spending the winter of 1772–3 in Lisbon in an effort to repair her health. Charles Cadogan toured Sicily and climbed Etna in 1785, reaching the crater at dawn, having walked eight miles over the snow, while Sir James Hall (1761–1832) was also in Sicily in 1785, although he was 'stormstay'd' a week in Stromboli on the way there.[2] This probably did not bother him as he was very interested in geology, particularly the formation of volcanoes, which led him to study rocks in Italy and Sicily. Active volcanoes were not found in Britain, and were a great curiosity.

The Classical remains in Sicily received attention from artists, tourists and government alike in the late eighteenth century. The first excavations on the theatre at Syracuse were carried out in 1756, while the temple there was restored in 1781, and those of Juno and Concord at Agrigento in 1787 and 1788 respectively.

Greater interest in southern Italy in the second half of the eighteenth century produced a limited number of guidebooks and journals. The most important was Henry Swinburne's *Travels in the Two Sicilies in the Years 1777, 1778, 1779, and 1780*, a work published in 1783–5 that described Sicily and southern Italy. Swinburne (1743–1803), the fourth son of Sir John Swinburne of Capheaton Hall, Northumberland, was a Catholic, educated in a monastic seminary in France, who was well-received at the courts of Paris and Vienna. Also author of *Travels through Spain in the Years 1775 and 1776* (1779), he played an important role in spreading information about travel in southern Europe. A different perspective was offered by Patrick Brydone (1736–1818), the bearleader (travelling tutor) who accompanied William Fullarton in 1769–70, who, in 1773, published his *Tour through Sicily and Malta*. Three years later, *A Voyage to Sicily and Malta* by John Dryden (*c.* 1667–1703) was published; this journey had actually been made by the famous poet's second son, accompanying William Cecil, second son of the 5th Earl of Exeter, in 1700–1. In 1792, Brian Hill's *Observations and Remarks in a Journey through Sicily and Calabria in the Year 1791* appeared.

Drawing on this widespread interest, Radcliffe's *A Sicilian Romance* begins with a ruined shoreline castle. The theme in the preface is one of grandeur and awe, rather than terror. The sublimity of the scene is dominant until a friar provides relevant judgment:

2   House of Lords RO. Cadogan papers, 4/6; Thomas Brand to Robert Wharton, 13 July 1785, Durham, University Library, Wharton papers, nos. 198–9.

> These walls were once the seat of luxury and vice. They exhibited a singular instance of the retribution of Heaven, and were from that period forsaken, and abandoned to decay.

This launches what ostensibly becomes a history, one based on conversation with the abbot as well as access to documents. This bridging of history and literature was commonplace in eighteenth-century British novels, particularly the Gothic ones, providing a grounding in verisimilitude as well as a suggestion of importance.

As later with *The Mysteries of Udolpho*, Radcliffe went for a late-sixteenth century setting. Mystery again is brought to the fore:

> they were surprised by the appearance of a light through the broken window-shutters of an apartment, belonging to a division of the castle which had for many years been shut up.

An attempt to discover the cause leads to a deserted courtyard and a door that cannot be opened. The latter is a frequent theme in Gothic fiction, one often linked to rusty keys or locks. Some critics might seek a sexual metaphor, or one about the blockade to fruition. In terms of the plots, doors that are not opened for years lose their openness. The idea of a haunting presence gathers pace during the action, as in:

> They were engaged in interesting discourse, when madame, who was then speaking, was interrupted by a low hollow sound, which arose from beneath the apartment, and seemed like the closing of a door. Chilled into a silence, they listened and distinctly heard it repeated. Deadly ideas crowded upon their imaginations, and inspired a terror which scarcely allowed them to breathe. (2)

It is feared that 'disembodied spirits' are responsible. A door hidden by a tapestry, a potent image, is found, but initially defies efforts at opening. When the door is prised open, we enter a pursuit by Ferdinand through a vaulted hall, a narrow passage and a winding stair-case, and being plunged into a terrifying darkness. The ruinous stair-case partially collapses, forming:

7. Ann Radcliffe, the Queen of the Genre

a chasm in the stair-case that terrified even Ferdinand, who was left tottering on the suspended half of the steps, in momentary expectation of falling to the bottom with the stone on which he rested. In the terror which this occasioned, he attempted to save himself by catching at a kind of beam which projected over the stairs, when the lamp dropped from his hand, and he was left in total darkness. Terror now usurped the place of every other interest. (3)

Surviving the ordeal, and returning to the quest the following night, Ferdinand finds the tower again invulnerable, but he focused on the hall:

An air of proud sublimity, united with singular wildness, characterized the place, at the extremity of which arose several gothic arches, whose dark shade veiled in obscurity the extent beyond ... his imagination, affected by the surrounding scene, often multiplied the echoes of his footsteps into uncertain sounds of strange and fearful import ... a sullen groan arose from beneath the spot where he stood. (3)

Hauntings by the ghost of a murdered rival of Ferdinand's grandfather is revealed as the cause of the 'horror ... the walls were still the haunt of an unquiet spirit, which seemed to call aloud for retribution on the posterity of him who had disturbed its eternal rest' (3). This is a frequent theme in Gothic novels, one that highlights the lack of any clear boundary between past and present, the living and the dead and, indeed, a fascination with that interaction. Moreover, time travel of a form is central: spirits and the fear of them both travel through time, and the past can only be rectified through action in the present.

In contrast, a white magic is revealed to Julia from the window of her castle apartment:

The night was still, and not a breath disturbed the surface of the waters. The moon shed a mild radiance over the waves, which in gentle undulations flowed upon the sands. The scene insensibly tranquilized her spirits. A tender and pleasing melancholy diffused itself over her mind; and as she mused, she heard the dashing of distant oars. Presently she perceived upon the light surface of the sea a small boat. The sound of the oars ceased, and a solemn strain of harmony (such as fancy wafts from the abodes of the blessed) stole upon the silence of night. A chorus of voices now swelled upon the air, and died away at a distance. In the strain Julia recollected the midnight hymn to the virgin, and holy enthusiasm filled her heart. (3)

This shoreline bliss is the positive background to Julia's subsequent travails and serves to underline the degree to which Radcliffe repeatedly offers the positive as well as the threatening. Indeed, as such, she provides another instance of the dichotomy more general to eighteenth-century novelists, while introducing particular emphases of her own, notably in this one, the stress on foreign settings. Shoreline bliss was also seen in *The Italian*, although with significant variations. Fearful of murder, Ellena looks from the window of her room:

The moon, rising over the ocean, showed its restless surface spreading to the wide horizon; and the waves, which broke in foam upon the rocky beach below, retiring in long white lines far upon the waters. She listened to their measured and solemn sound, and, somewhat soothed by the solitary grandeur of the view, remained at the lattice till the moon had risen high into the heavens; and even till morning began to dawn upon the sea, and purple the eastern clouds. (II,7)

As with earlier novelists writing about heroines under risk in Britain, there was in Radcliffe the threat to vulnerable women and notably so from men, especially older men. Imprisonment in one form or other is repeatedly a theme, with physical imprisonment a clear metaphor for sexual and emotional control. Thus, Julia is intended by her father for the Duke of Luovo who shares 'the love of power' of the father as a 'ruling passion': Luovo 'delighted in simple undisguised tyranny.' Similarly, Ellena in *The Italian*, another designated victim, is described as a 'poor insect' (II,8).

7. Ann Radcliffe, the Queen of the Genre

Eloping, Julia escapes her fate, while the suspicion of a ghost is eased by a natural expression, which was to be the norm for Radcliffe:

> ... A part of the decayed roof was fallen in, and the stones and rubbish of the ruin falling against the gallery door, obstructed the passage. It was evident, too, whence the noise which occasioned their terror had arisen; the loose stones which were piled against the door being shook by the effort made to open it, had given way, and rolled to the floor. (4)

Julia's mysterious escape from imprisonment is explained by the theft of keys. What Radcliffe terms superstition does not attract her praise:

> The mind of Ferdinand was highly superior to the general influence of superstition ... a variety of terrific circumstances, which existed only in the heated imaginations of his fellow-servants, but which were still admitted by them as facts.... His absurd fear did not suffer him to recognize the voice of Ferdinand. (6)

There is a social dimension to such criticism, with servants, on a more general pattern, seen for example with Fielding, being especially superstitious or prone to fear. Radcliffe finds the fault as primarily in the imagination: She at once uses her imagination to paint scenes, yet also provides criticism of the apparently unbalanced imagination of others. This lack of balance, a key feature of eighteenth-century thought, is not limited to those who are of humble social origin. Thus, for Emilia:

> Wild and terrific images arose to her imagination. Fancy drew the scene; – she deepened the shades; and the terrific aspect of the objects she presented was heightened by the obscurity which involved them. (6)

Other heroines display the same feature.

The Romance of the Forest (1791) referred to the 'cause of morality' in the dedication to Catherine, Duchess of Leeds. While capturing a general goal of the period, this was an instructive remark as Catherine's husband, Francis, the 5th Duke, had divorced his first wife in 1779 after she ran off with Captain John Byron, later father, by his second wife, of the poet George, Lord Byron. This was a reminder that the complex familial relationships that helped provide the plot background and dynamics of so many Gothic novels were also a reflection of life.

Set in seventeenth-century France, *The Romance of the Forest* (1791) begins with Pierre de la Motte, the protagonist, lost on a 'wild heath' on a 'tempestuous' night, and seeking refuge in a house where he is received by a mysterious stranger who locks him in a room. As with many Gothic novels, there are strange sounds – 'the sobs and moaning of a female.'[3] La Motte is made to take the unknown young and attractive woman, Adeline, away with him, and readers are speedily made aware of the jeopardy of circumstances:

> Such elegance and apparent refinement, contrasted with the desolation of the house, and the savage manners of its inhabitants, seemed to him like a romance of imagination, rather than an occurrence of real life. (1)

Travelling on while fearful of pursuit leads to an account of a journey disordered by anxiety, which was very much the case with Radcliffe's novels. There is a reiterated attempt to communicate suspense:

> … the evening twilight … diffused a solemnity that vibrated in thrilling sensations upon the hearts of the travellers. Expectation kept them silent. The present scene recalled to Adeline a remembrance of the late terrific circumstances, and her mind responded but too easily to the apprehension of new misfortunes. (1)

Not great writing, but an attempt to create a continuous sense of crisis.

The La Motte party end up in a ruined monastery at night, which Radcliffe uses to play on the emotions both of that party and of the readers:

3   *Romance* 1.

7. Ann Radcliffe, the Queen of the Genre

> The partial gleams thrown across the fabric seemed to make its desolation more solemn, while the obscurity of the greater part of the pile heightened its sublimity, and led fancy on to scenes of horror. Adeline, who had hitherto remained silent, now uttered an exclamation of mingled admiration and fear. A kind of pleasing dread thrilled her bosom, and filled all her soul. (2)

This is very much the emotional range that Radcliffe sought, and her use of words is fascinating. 'Pleasing dread' that both thrilled and filled the soul was a description of both end and means. The sexual consequences are brought out as a tearful Adeline then:

> hung upon the arm of La Motte. The atmosphere soon becomes tenser: 'They were all silent – it was the silence of terror.... A tremendous gleam ... many nameless objects were seen imperfectly through the dusk.'

In an instructive female undermining of the male protagonist, one that was to be seen in a number of Gothic novels:

> Adeline with a smile, inquired of La Motte, if he believed in spirits. The question was ill-timed, for the present scene impressed its terrors upon La Motte, and, in spite of endeavour, he felt a superstitious dread stealing upon him. He was now, perhaps, standing over the ashes of the dead. If spirits were ever permitted to revisit the earth, this seemed the hour and the place most suitable for their appearance. (2)

Such an idea of a gap in time was a troubling one in many of the novels, and was to be developed in science fiction. The idea had an older genesis, looking back to the interventionist role on Earth of sacral and ancestor figures, a notion repeatedly at play in Gothic novels with their dynastic themes.

Radcliffe challenged the very rationale of her novels by suggesting that fear was a matter of foolish ignorance, notably on the part of the poor. Thus, in *The Romance of the Forest*:

> it was said, that strange appearances had been observed at the abbey, and uncommon noises heard; and thought his report had been ridiculed by sensible persons, as the idle superstition of ignorance, it had fastened so strongly upon the minds of the common people, that for the last seventeen years none of the peasantry had ventured to approach the spot. (2)

Later came the observation 'the marvellous is the delight of the vulgar' (5). This social placing left the path open for heroism on the part of valorous members of the élite. Fear was a product of a lack of social rank, with those, in contrast, who were brave peasants in fact changelings and thus rightfully members of the social élite, as in Reeve's *The Old English Baron*.

Alongside a social contrast, there was, for Radcliffe, that between passion and reason, an eighteenth-century commonplace and one also seen in Austen's novels. Thus, in *The Romance of the Forest*, Radcliffe observed: 'The operation of a strong passion confuses the powers of reason, and warps them to its own particular direction ... so much did passion win upon her judgment' (4). This was a pre-Romantic sentiment, and that was the essential setting for Radcliffe's moral compass.

At the same time, there is in Radcliffe an understanding of emotions that are not readily included in the duality of reason and passion. In the same chapter, La Motte, after going down stairs opened up by a concealed trap door, crossing a long narrow passage, and breaking through a locked door, finds himself in a closed underground room in which there is a large chest containing a human skeleton:

> Horror stuck upon his heart, and he involuntarily stepped back. During a pause of some moments, his first emotions subsided. That thrilling curiosity which objects of terror often excite in the human mind, impelled him to take a second view of this dismal spectacle. (4)

Yet, reason plays a role, and he interprets the skeleton as proof of murder in the abbey.

Radcliffe moves in the novel between, on the one hand, a pervasive atmosphere of threat and oppression, notably to women, alongside intimations of horror, and, on the other, more commonplace discussions of relations between her principals, most of which relate to the standard tropes of sentimental fiction, albeit in a different context. The narrative provides opportunities for suggesting alarm, as when Louis secretly follows his father, La Motte, 'through the most gloomy part of the forest' to 'the ruins of a small building' where, amidst the shadows, he sees a mysterious figure. This, however, does not have any alarming consequences (5). Drama built-up is thus assuaged, a smaller-scale instance of the wider structure of her novels, each reinforcing the other. So also in the next chapter when there is a night-time assault on the abbey:

> … the violence of the assailants seeming to increase with every gust of the tempest: the gate, which was old and decayed, burst from its hinges, and admitted them to the hall … a scream from Madame La Motte … Adeline had fainted. (6)

All turns out alright in this case, but, in the next chapter, there is the more disturbing intimation of a nightmare, one experienced by Adeline, that adds the sexual dimension found in the dreams in a number of Gothic novels. Adeline sees the features of a dying man in an ancient part of the abbey she has not hitherto visited, a man calling to her who seemingly 'in the agonies of death' grasps her hand violently:

> she struggled in terror to disengage herself and again looking on his face, saw a man, who appeared to be about thirty, with the same features, but in full health, and of a most benign countenance. He smiled tenderly upon her, and moved her lips, as if to speak, when the floor of the chamber suddenly opened, and he sunk from her view. (7)

The disciplines of time appear forsaken in dreams and, with that, alarm is foregrounded.

In another dream, lost in the abbey passages at twilight, and with a bell tolling and a distant light glimmering, a mysterious man clad in funeral garb appears and leads her to the foot of a staircase: 'Here she feared to proceed, and was running back, when the man suddenly turned to pursue her.' The resulting terror wakes her but, falling asleep, she, in a new dream, follows the man into very ancient apartments prepared for a funeral, before seeing in a coffin the young man in the first dream: 'While she looked at him a stream of blood gushed from his side, and descending to the floor, the whole chamber was overflowed … the horror of the scene so entirely overcame her' (7). There are some elements of *Dracula* in the story. Such a stream of blood from the side had a New Testament connotation.

In reality, Adeline is threatened by the risk of a bigamous marriage with Phillippe, Marquis de Montalt, who wants her as wife or mistress and, thwarted, sets out to kill her. He had murdered her father, who was his half-brother, and stolen the inheritance; but villainy cannot triumph. Montalt is thwarted in his incestuous plan, confesses, and commits suicide, an end that robs him of any hope of redemption or mercy from God. Sin is fully punished. This very popular novel went through four editions in 1791–4, and was Radcliffe's first major success.

Although critical remarks are made in the novel by and about positive characters, such as Blanche (III,10–11), *The Mysteries of Udolpho* was to a degree pro-Catholic by the standards of the period. While set chronologically in the period of the French Wars of Religion, the novel starting in 1584, Radcliffe avoided any discussion of these conflicts and, instead, preferred to focus its limited politics on Italy. This meant that it was unnecessary to take sides between the Huguenots (French Protestants), Henry III of France, and the Catholic League. In Italian politics, in contrast, Catholicism was not an issue, and the discussion of Venice, which, in reality, could be anti-Papal in policy, did not extend to that factor. Instead, Catholicism was present in the novel largely in the shape of monastic foundations, with elderly clerics seen as figures of wise authority, notably the abbess but also the father confessor.

This positive character was a counterpart of the more general benign account of the Gothic offered by the novel, as with the descriptions of the monasteries of St Claire and St Clair (III,11, IV,15).[4] Gothic buildings, as part of a pattern of repetition decried by the *Critical Review* in its review of *The Mysteries of Udolpho*, might be the setting for responses of horror and terror; but, in an important distinction, they were not the cause. Indeed,

---

4   See also *The Italian* II,4.

7. Ann Radcliffe, the Queen of the Genre

much of the resolve of the novel became the revelation as explicable of Emily's repeated sense of horror and terror.

The reader earlier was invited also to misread the castle of Udolpho, a process encouraged by pushing Emily's perspective to the fore. *The Mysteries of Udolpho* indeed became somewhat like Mervyn Peake's surreal *Gormenghast* series (1946–60); both depicting partly-ruined castles that spread through apparently innumerable rooms and passages. This was a more fantastical account of the castle of Udolpho than any suggestion of strange sounds and sights. The unrealistically extensive character of the castle provided a counterpart to the sublime character of the landscape. Indeed, however plausible, a more modest size would have seemed totally out-of-place. So also with the scale of the Inquisition's prison in *The Italian*. In the case of *Gormenghast*, however, the very enormity of the castle is an apt setting for a plotting and characterization that knows no bounds of reason, and with the evil Steerpike as a human of satanic character who, in a Gothic image, at one time, in *Titus Groan*, dresses as a ghost. In *Gormenghast*, Steerpike, both holds women captive in a deserted section of the castle and, eventually revealed as a murderer, hides in the recesses of the castle, another Gothic note.

Reverting to Radcliffe, against the background of clouds entirely concealing the moon and assuming 'a red sulphureous tinge,' and with 'vivid lighting,' the troubled Emily 'frequently addressed herself to Heaven for support and protection, and her pious prayers, we may believe, were accepted of the God, that giveth comfort' (III,4). Radcliffe was in no doubt of the cause of virtue, and Emily was far from alone: 'Blanche's thoughts arose involuntarily to the Great Author of the sublime objects she contemplated' (III,10). At times, the resulting writing seems uncertain. Thus, in *The Italian*, in a passage on the impressive scenery of the Apennines, Radcliffe writes: 'the plane, the oak, and the chestnut still threw a pomp of foliage round these smiling spots, and seemed to consecrate the mountain streams that descended beneath their solemn shade' (II,10).

The suggestion of religious truth as somehow greater than that of mere rationality, a generally-established view, was part of the equation of meaning in *The Mysteries of Udolpho*. With the aura of age being part of the prestige of what in effect was the book's 'white magic,' then the Catholic Church appeared the obvious choice. Moreover, the French noble family selected for discussion also breathed conservative values. For all those reasons, *The Mysteries of Udolpho* could be seen as a legitimist novel in which the good French are the heroes; while the cold rationalist who seeks power through exploiting aristocratic weakness is the Italian Montoni, who operates both in France and in Italy. He can be regarded as a product of a sour Enlightenment that had turned Revolutionary; and not least so in terms of his determination to calculate everything as well as his concern for power rather than right and legitimacy. Montoni was almost an object lesson in the character flaws mentioned by Burke in his dismissal of modern values in his *Reflections on the Revolution in France* (1790).[5]

At the same time, alongside his calculation and villainy, there is an element of the dark Romantic hero in Montoni's will, a man who has no principle of action *but* his will (III,6):

> ... unprincipled, dauntless, cruel and enterprising.... Delighting in the tumult and in the struggles of life, he was equally a stranger to pity and to fear; his very courage was a sort of animal ferocity; not the noble impulse of a principle, such as inspirits [sic] the mind against the oppressor, in the cause of the oppressed; but a constitutional hardiness of nerve, that cannot feel, and that, therefore, cannot fear. (III,3)

There is something inhuman about such an individual and, to a degree, supernatural; but Radcliffe keeps her villains human, and thus provides a secular explanation for their motivation. This indeed was a characteristic of her work, and one that many authors took from her. The will was to be heroic for many Romantic writers, for example Percy Bysshe Shelley, but was not so for their predecessors, unless linked to moral purpose. The emphasis on the rational reflected her interest in national religion, in the hand of the Creator operating behind the veil of nature, an approach that both led her to see the sublime and poetry in nature, and also to be less than interested in revealed religion.

Part of the appeal of *The Mysteries of Udolpho* is that it does not need to be read as a political work, but that element was also present. Indeed, this was more so in 1794 than in 1790, the year of the publication of

---

5   See chapter of this book.

7. Ann Radcliffe, the Queen of the Genre

Burke's *Reflections*, because the attack on Christianity in France was at fulltilt by 1794, and with, in particular, the destructive force of the Jacobin Terror. In Britain, this attack in France encouraged a sympathetic interest in Catholicism as part of a Christianity that was under assault. This was very much the attitude of the British government, and Radcliffe's book can be seen as in line with a society in which there were collections for refugee French nobles and clerics. Vaulaincourt, the hero, is a French army officer, as are several other positive characters, and that at a time when Britain supported Royalist French plots against the Revolutionary government. In the book, there was the hope for a happy ending, a hope that helped make *The Mysteries of Udolpho* a romance.

The Italian setting reflected in part the greater interest in its history stemming from William Robertson's highly-successful (both in esteem and commercially) *The History of the Reign of the Emperor Charles the Fifth* (1769), with its argument that modern international relations dated from the outbreak of the Italian Wars in 1494. In *The Italian*, moreover, Radcliffe refers to 'a volume or two of Guicciardini's history' being made available to Ellena in the convent (I,8). Rather than the situation in Italy in the 1580s itself, the impression created by Robertson (and, previously, Guicciardini) for an earlier period is captured by Radcliffe in *The Mysteries of Udolpho*:

> The prospect of going to Italy was still rendered darker, when she considered the tumultuous situation of that country, then torn by civil commotion, where every petty state was at war with its neighbour, and even every castle liable to the attack of an invader. (I,13)

Radcliffe explains at length that times of peace then were violent due to the bellicose role of disbanded troops, and Montoni is described in terms of the resulting *condottieri* (hired soldiers, III,3). The intrigues and violence of that period was a theme of English Renaissance fiction, as in Gothic-style plays such as John Webster's *The Duchess of Malfi* (1614) and Thomas Middleton's *The Revenger's Tragedy* (1606), a true Dance of Death ('No power is angry when the lustful die,' V,3). They are present again not only with Radcliffe but also with Lewis' *Abaellino* and Charlotte Dacre's *Zofloya*, which were both set in Venice.

Terror and horror are terms very frequently employed in *The Mysteries of Udolpho* (as in other Gothic novels), and they contribute to the 'disturbed fancy' (II,4) of both Emily and the reader. This 'fancy' offers a route in for the supernatural. A belief in it builds not only on the 'reveries of superstition' (I,10), but also on the extent to which settings and events work on wrought nerves and those under pressure. Radcliffe works with this, but also makes fun of it, as when Mademoiselle Bearn tells Blanche:

I had begun to think some wonderful adventure had befallen you, and that the giant of this enchanted castle, or the ghost, which, no doubt, haunts it, had conveyed you through a trap-door into some subterranean vault, whence you was never to return.

Blanche replies 'laughingly' and Henri soon after gets Mademoiselle Bearn to laugh with his:

> no ghost of these days would be so savage as to impose silence on you. Our ghosts are more civilized than to condemn a lady to a purgatory severer even, than their own, be it what it may. (II,x)

False sentiment, a guide to hypocrisy, also attracts Radcliffe's attention, and, in the person of the Countess de Villefort, and on the model of many other novelists, of all types, it is an aristocrat that receives criticism, and counterpoint is the means of deflation and criticism:

> She had dismissed the grace of modesty, but then she knew perfectly well how to manage the stare of assurance; her manners had little of the tempered sweetness, which is necessary to render the female character interesting, but she could occasionally throw into them an affectation of spirits, which seemed to triumph over every person, who approached her. In the country, however, she generally affected an elegant languor, that persuaded her almost to faint, when her favourite read to her a story of fictious sorrow; but her countenance suffered no change, when living objects of distress solicited her charity, and her heart beat with no transport to the thought of giving them instant relief; - she was a stronger to the highest luxury, of

which, perhaps, the human mind can be sensible, for her benevolence had never yet called smiles upon the face of misery. (III,13)

Radcliffe followed up *The Mysteries of Udolpho*, not with the last of her novels published during her lifetime, but with an account of her sole tour abroad, *A Journey made in the Summer of 1794, through Holland and the Western Frontier of Germany* (1796). Far from serving as a seedbed for future novels, or as a record of a changing Gothic landscape or, indeed, an opportunity to study a region succumbing to war, this was an essentially conventional work, with such observations as the cost of travelling on Dutch rivers and canals, including tax, being 1d per mile, and a trifle more to sit on the roof of the cabin, which provided a better view. Radcliffe also commented on the impact of the war, as with the 'heaving trampling of feet… [and] … the sound of martial music' as troops moved, as well as the large number of hospital wagons near Cologne.[6] Radcliffe opposed British intervention in the war, and thus took a position very different to that of Burke.

Radcliffe was not alone. In his *Gleanings through Wales, Holland and Westphalia* (1795), Samuel Pratt remarked on:

> the general history, alas, of almost every other nation in the habitable globe; a picture of battles lost and gained, cities sacked or besieged, villages buried, burned, or desolated, the fury of men contending with man, and the disasters of human nature aggravated by the ambition and weakness of human creatures.[7]

After *A Journey* came the last of her novels published during her lifetime, *The Italian or The Confessional of the Black Penitents. A Romance* (1797). In part, this novel was a continuation of a pattern Radcliffe had established in her earlier novels, and should be seen in that light; but there was also a more specific context, that of a response to Matthew Lewis' far more lurid *The Monk*. Possibly as a result, the apparent supernatural played

6   Radcliffe, *Journey*, pp. 17, 271, 329.
7   S.J. Pratt, *Gleanings*, II, 532.

a far smaller role than in her previous novels, for as it were, she underlined the contrast with *The Monk*.

The literary continuity that was offered, instead, was that with Walpole. His *Mysterious Mother* was cited at the start of the first chapter:

> What is this secret sin; this untold tale,
> That art cannot extract, nor penance cleanse?

There was also the standard conceit of an account produced from the past, one 'written ... soon after the affair became public' (preface); although, in this case, the story was allegedly set in very recent times, in Naples in 1758, the account having being handed over in 'about the year 1764.' That year, ironically, was the one in which Edward Gibbon had his revelation in the Roman Forum, as reported in his autobiography, a revelation across time that led to his great work of history:

> It was at Rome, on the 15th of October 1764, as I sat musing amidst the ruins of the Capitol, while the barefoot friars were singing vespers in the Temple of Jupiter, that the idea of writing the decline and fall of the city first started to my mind.

In both cases, Italy was the setting for the imagination, with Radcliffe in this case taking that up to very near the present, and thus presenting the society being challenged by the advance of French forces, rather as Giacomo Puccini was to do with his opera *Tosca* (1900), with its story set in 1800.

There was a clear linkage between Gibbon and the Gothic novel in that both addressed the precariousness of civilization, the nature of 'barbarian' sway, the character of Christianity, and the possibility of a new Fall of some type. The last was to be given vivid demonstration in the apocalyptic paintings of John Martin (1789–1854), paintings that brought him great success, notably *The Fall of Babylon* (1819), *Belshazzar's Feast* (1820), *The Destruction of Pompei and Herculaneum* (1821), and *The Deluge* (1834). Martin also painted a *Macbeth* (c.1820) showing the witches confronting Macbeth and Banquo.[8]

8 Michael Campbell, *John Martin, 1789–1854. Creation of Light* (Madrid, 2006).

His was an approach wider in scope than Fuseli's, and with a more spectral but less intense image.

The Italian is much tighter in structure, setting and action than *The Mysteries of Udolpho*, the latter a work often adrift in its subplots, even by the standards of a genre that proved particularly prone to this fault. The entry in *The Italian* of mystery and a sinister figure is prompt, as is the sketching of the family dynamics and role of the villain. After a building of menace, the heroine, Ellena di Rosalba, is seized from near Naples and taken to a mountainous convent. This novel is far more critical of the Catholic Church than its predecessor. Monasteries, a particular characteristic of Catholicism, come in for much obloquy, one that extends to the aesthetic of 'sacred gloom' (I,9). There is extended praise of the *Santa della Pietà*, but it is presented as unusual:

> The society of *Our Lady of Pity*, was such as a convent does not often shroud; to the wisdom and virtue of the Superior, the sisterhood was principally indebted for the harmony and happiness which distinguished them.... Her religion was neither gloomy, nor bigoted; it was the sentiment of a grateful heart offering itself up to a Deity, who delights in the happiness of his creatures; and she conformed to the customs of the Roman church, without supposing a faith in all of them to be necessary to salvation. This opinion, however, she was obliged to conceal, lest her very virtue should draw upon her the punishment of a crime, from some fierce ecclesiastics, who contradicted in their practice the very essential principles, which the Christianity they professed would have taught them. (III,4)

The control the Church exercised was dramatized in *The Italian* both by incarceration in a convent and by the Inquisition:

> the nun, still silent, conducted her through many solitary passages, where not even a distant foot-fall echoed, and whose walls were roughly painted with subjects indicatory of the severe superstitions of the place, tending to inspire melancholy awe.

> Ellena's hope of pity vanished as her eyes glanced over these symbols of the disposition of the inhabitants, and on the countenance of the nun characterized by a gloomy malignity, which seemed ready to inflict upon others some portion of the unhappiness she herself suffered … hearts, which even the offices of hourly devotion had not purified from the malignant envy, that taught them to exalt themselves upon the humiliation of others. (I,6)

While holding others prisoner, the Church treats them as a threat, not least by trying to make them incriminate themselves, as does the Inquisition with Vivaldi. Moreover, the clerical protagonist, Schedoni, sees women themselves as a threat, presenting Ellena in terms of the female entrapper who the Devil uses to lead Ambrosio astray in Lewis' *The Monk*. In the case of *The Italian*, in contrast, the accusation is wrong:

> What do those deserve, who deliberately utter falsehoods … who deceive, and flatter young men to their destruction … Who disturb the peace of families – who trepan, with wanton arts, the heirs of noble houses. (II,8)

The Inquisition, a threat not hitherto used by Radcliffe, is to be taken up by other writers,[9] for example Charlotte Dacre in *Zofloya* (1806), in which it is feared by the evil Victoria: 'The terrible Inquisition! – its horrid torments, its lynx-eyed scrutiny, pressed upon her brain' (25). An aspect of the past, the Inquisition still resonated for modern readers. It played a significant role in the denouement of Lewis' *The Monk* and was cited through the nineteenth century. Thus, the first leader [editorial] in the *Western Times* of 18 January 1851 declared that, behind Catholic pretensions, there was 'an Inquisition, and a staff of goalers.'

The Italian sees much moving around in the dark and encountering sinister individuals and settings, as when Vivaldi finds himself trapped in a

---

9   Peter Herman, '"Terror in Inquisition": Terrorists and Inquisition in the British Gothic Literature of the 1790s,' in Herman (ed.), *Terrorism and Literature* (Cambridge, 2018), pp. 196–211.

7. Ann Radcliffe, the Queen of the Genre

vault by a door of 'unconquerable strength,' finding then 'a garment covered with blood … while even the floor below was stained with gore' (I,7). The depiction of the Inquisition, which seizes Vivaldi, is harsh; and their very appearance is used to provide a clearly sinister indication:

> … their countenances expressed a darker cruelty, mingled with a sly demureness, and a solemn self-importance, that announced them at once as belonging to the Inquisition … the principles of cunning and cruelty, which seemed particularly to characterize Inquisitors … a tribunal, whose mysterious and terrible proceedings appalled even the bravest spirits.… Their visages, with few exceptions, seemed stamped with the characters of demons … as if their very looks possessed some supernatural power, and could have struck death.… Dante's inscription on the entrance of the infernal regions, would have been suitable to a place, where every circumstance and feature seemed to say, "Hope, that comes to all, comes not here!" … demons like these … the most diabolical cruelties. (II,6)

In the criticism of the Inquisition, Radcliffe brought together Enlightenment values, with the violent policies not only of the French Revolution but also of their foreign supporters, including in Italy, the area in which they are most prominent. It can be a serious mistake to see all texts as political, but there was a degree to which the focus on the Inquisition and on recent decades might have been a statement of commitment on Radcliffe's part, but also one that was safe. So also in the novel with giving Schedoni the reactionary comment, 'Fools are always wondering at the actions of those above them' (II,1); while an arrogant and malicious aristocrat, the Marchesa di Vivaldi, callous mother to the hero and controlling patron to Schedoni, is the cause of most of the problems faced by the good characters. Radcliffe, in her discussion of the Marchesa, clearly distinguishes between evil as a description and evil as a comparison:

> Her heart was possessed by evil passions, and all her perceptions were distorted and discoloured by them, which, like a dark magician, had power to change the fairest scenes into those of gloom and desolation. (III,iii)

The Age of Nightmare

After *The Italian*, Radcliffe published no other novels in her lifetime. There were reports that she was mad or dead, but it is possible that an inheritance from her father or a dislike of criticism were key causes. In the meanwhile, she had left a major legacy of key Gothic novels, and a profitable genre that others were to take on.

8. IN ANN'S SHADOWS

Radcliffe's novels appeared against a background of a range of Gothic works that helped make her books appear as impressive literature. For example, the popular *The Cavern of Death* (1794), a series of anonymous periodical pieces, has aristocratic rivalry over Constance, as well as a haunted cavern, a ghost, a skeleton, and a murderous past. The same year, Stephen Cullen's *The Haunted Priory; or, The Fortunes of the House of Rayo* used medieval Castile as the setting, with a cowled spectre, a ruined chapel, and the mysteries of an overthrown aristocratic house. As so often with the Gothic, the unknown enemy beyond the mental stockade is a root fear – although, when revealed, marked differences emerged between novels. In this case, and on the pattern of *The Castle of Otranto*, a gigantic figure provided a guide to a past murder. The plot includes the ghost of a father, a Midnight Mass, a mysterious key, a ruined convent, and an underground burial vault. An Irish writer, Cullen also wrote *The Castle of Inchvally: A Tale – Alas! Too True* (1796), the title itself having a somewhat 1930s feel to it.

1794 saw evidence of the potential range of the Gothic. Karl Friedrich Kahlert's *The Necromancer; or, The Tale of the Black Forest*, a translation from the German by Peter Teuthold, (lampooned by Jane Austen in *Northanger Abbey*) emphasized superstition, notably the raising of ghosts, but the supernatural is revealed to be a series of tricks that serve a gang of robbers, and this approach led to some approval by critics. On a pattern that was to be ably developed in a number of Gothic novels, there is a frame story that serves to organize the number of narratives on offer. This method was to be ably used by Mary Shelley in *Frankenstein*.

Rather differently, *Things as They Are; or The Adventures of Caleb Williams* (1794) provided William Godwin, the father of Mary Shelley, with an opportunity to attack abuses of power. Barnabas Tyrrel, an oppressive landowner, imprisons his niece, Emily, when she falls in love against his wishes, and she dies in imprisonment. Tyrrel's murderer, Emily's beloved

Ferdinando Falkland, a neighboring wealthy landowner, frames Caleb Williams because the latter discovers his guilt. Escaping prison, Caleb is pursued by Falkland and eventually brought to trial, although in the published ending, unlike the original version, he is vindicated. Instead of a storyline fleeing with protagonist and reader through passages and vaults, the emphasis is on power as the issue, but power shorn of its usual Gothic evils, and focused on personal convenience rather than dynastic ambition.[1]

Radcliffe's influence was seen in providing a powerful degree of sensibility for the Gothic novel, and that influenced the works of others, for example Eleanor Sleath's *The Orphan of the Rhine* (1798). In a relatively short work, this fits in a convoluted plot of aristocratic villainy and seduction centered on the murderous Marchese de Montferrat who turns Julie de Rubine, the aristocratic orphan who is the heroine, into his cheated mistress. Abduction, imprisonment, castles, double-crosses, women shut up in convents, and a happy ending are all part of the mix. Sleath (1770–1847), a young widow driven to authorship by debt,[2] followed up *The Orphan of the Rhine* with *Who's the Murderer?* (1802), another Minerva Press work, as were her next three.

Some of the other novels had an energy and pace Radcliffe often lacked. Thus, the anonymous *Count Roderic's Castle; or Gothic Times, a Tale* (1794), was a popular Minerva Press novel set in medieval Lombardy. As so often, usurpation was a key element, with Astolpho murdering Count Roderic and seizing his territory, while imprisoning Isabel the beloved of Roderick's son Rhinaldo, who has to overturn the tyranny. Dungeons, castles, and a ghost keen on revenge – 'A deadly paleness overspread the countenance – the eyes were hollow, and sunk – the hair was clotted with blood – with which his garments were also stained' – were all part of the mix in a fast-paced adventure.

The rush of Gothic novels from 1795–9 was particularly notable in entrenching the genre. There is no space to summarize all the novels, but the commonalities were those of setting and challenge. In order both for ghosts to play a role as well as to provide the Gothic sensibility, the most frequent settings were medieval abbeys, as in Isabella Kelly's *The Abbey of St Asaph*

---

1   Kenneth Graham, *The Politics of Narrative: Ideology and Social Change in William Godwin's 'Caleb Williams'* (New York, 1990).
2   Rebecca Czlapinski and Eric Wheeler, 'The Real Eleanor Sleath,' *Studies in Gothic Fiction*, 2 (2011), pp. 5–12.

(1795), George Moore's *Grasville Abbey* (1797), and two anonymous works, *Almagro and Claude; or Monastic Murder; Exemplified in the Dreadful Doom of an Unfortunate Nun* (1803) and *The Midnight Groan; or, the Spectre of the Chapel: Involving an Exposure of the Horrible Secrets of the Nocturnal Assembly* (1808); and castles as, very variously, in, for example, Anna Maria Bennett's *Ellen, Countess of Castle Howel* (1794), a Minerva Press Book, John Bird's *The Castle of Hardayne* (1795) and the anonymous *The Mysterious Penitent; or, the Norman Chateau* (1800) and *The Castle of Eridan* (1800).

Isabella Kelly (1759–1857), Scottish-born exponent of the Gothic novel, was typical of the large number of female writers who were driven in part by financial need to socially acceptable authorship and, in her case, as with that of others, led to an appeal for grants to the Royal Literary Fund, appeals that provide insights on their situations. She began with *Madeline, or The Castle of Montgomery* (1794), which was an aspect of her focus on British settings. Kelly sought the support of Matthew Lewis, a homosexual who became infatuated with her son William, who was a beneficiary in his will. Her second novel, *The Abbey of St Asaph* (1795) was attacked in *The Critical Review* for being formulaic - 'horrid cavern ... fiery spectre ... moving and shrieking skeleton.' Alongside the usual haunted ruined castle and established subterranean crypt, there was certainly novelty in the terror:

> a figure ascended, which slow and gradual rose to a stupendous height, the extended arms lengthened in proportion, and forming a circle, totally inclosed her. The head was large, and almost shapeless; something like a countenance appeared in front, but horrible beyond imagination; the eyes seemed globes of fire; and the gaping jaws emitted sulphurous flames; the bristled hair stood erect; and a vesture which floated loosely around the spectre, represented by pale gleams of light, the forms of every noxious reptile. (II)

However demonic this vision might appear, it is revealed to be the consequence of disguise by means of phosphorous. So also with the skull that moves as a result of a rat inside.[3]

3   Tenille Nowak, 'Isabella Kelly's Twist on the Standard Radcliffean Romance,' *Studies in Gothic Fiction*, II,2 (2012), pp. 4–12.

The Age of Nightmare

The Castle of Hardayne (1795), unusual in being published in a British provincial centre, Liverpool, was prefaced by a quotation from Homer:

> Distracted in his mind,
> Forsook by Heaven—forsaking human kind;
> Wide o'er the Aleian field he chose to stray,
> A long, forborn, uncomfortable way.

The quotation captured the idea of a lonely quest by a marginal figure and the character of a strand of fiction, although not so much that of the domestic victim. Introduced at the outset, Giraldus crosses a barren terrain in bleak weather, with 'black and heavy clouds' obscuring 'the face of heaven.' Lightning reveals the ruins of a substantial castle, and we are on the case: 'an extensive hall ... with ... awful gloom and silence,' a mysterious door, a totally dark passage, and the protagonist is given the response that the reader should have:

> he began to feel a secret horror stealing over his mind, and impressing it with a superstitious dread, which the lonely desolation of the place seemed formed for inspiring. (1)

Attempting to sleep, Giraldus saw: 'a glittering light in an opposite corner ... he thought he saw the figure of a man, though faintly and imperfectly shadowed out,' but it disappeared without any visible means of entrance or retreat, a frequent occurrence in such stories. Offering different approaches to nightmare, Giraldus:

> began to think he must have been mistaken, and that the appearance was only one of those illusions of fancy that the disturbed imagination will at times seem to represent; the thought somewhat satisfied him, he endeavoured to calm his perturbed mind,

only for 'a deep and hollow groan, that seemed to proceed from a place immediately under him' to lead him to fall through an opening into an old well (1) and find a newly-bludgeoned body. Falling through the floor both echoed, and was different from, an episode in *The Castle of Otranto* where weight was the key element.

Caverns provided a natural equivalent to castles and abbeys, sharing with buildings the sense of underground menace and control, notably dungeons, as in any number of references to caves and caverns, most notably Laetitia Pilkington's *The Subterranean Cavern; or Memoirs of Antoinette de Monflorance*, a Minerva Press publication of 1798, and the anonymous *Labyrinth of Corcira* (1804). Pilkington also produced *Delia, a pathetic and interesting tale* (1790), *Rosina; a novel* (1793), and *The Accusing Spirit, or De Courcy and Eglantine. A Romance* (1802). Another cavern of alarm appeared in the anonymous *The Black Forest; or the Cavern of Horrors! A Gothic Romance* (1802), in which the frontispiece showed 'The terror of Henry and the appearance of a Skeleton waving a Bloody Sword.'

Short works of the period included the anonymous, 48–page long *Barbastal, or, The Magician of the Forest of Bloody Ash* (c.1795), which was published by Ann Lemoine, a chapbook that proved popular and was reprinted. Incorporating imprisonment, the subterranean, the aristocracy, inventiveness, and Providence, the 24–page *The Affecting History of the Duchess of C——, who was confined nine years in a horrid dungeon under ground, where light never entered; a straw mattress being her only resting-place, and bread and water her only support, conveyed to her by means of a turning box by her inhuman husband; with the manner she was providentially discovered and released by her parents* (1799), indicated the extent to which the Gothic novel could be a catch-all.

Lurid, but lacking the Satanic dimension of *The Monk*, *The Haunted Cavern* (1795), the opening novel by John Palmer, Junior (1776–1809), was set in early-fifteenth-century Aberdeenshire. This tale of abduction and imprisonment in order to thwart true love, begins with 'a gothic castle' in the first sentence, and included the cavern with its skeletons, ghosts, murders, and a grisly back-story that is revealed in the usual pattern of the Gothic detective novel. For example, for the hero imprisoned in the cavern:

> During the whole night, he was disturbed by a repetition of sighs and melancholy noises ... which kept him in a state of racking uneasiness and anxiety.... While sleeping, his dreams

presented the figure of an aged man … immured in a thick vaporous cloud, from which his utmost efforts were vainly put in force to disengage himself, till casting an eye on Eldred, the mist he was involved in vanished, his silver beard and hair were converted into jetty locks, while the feeble limbs of age grew renovated, and formed an hero in the prime of manhood, cased in steel: full he gazed on Eldred and uttering these words "Heaven guard you!" disappeared. (11)

Albeit of a different period, the comments on Highland Scotland make an interesting contrast with those of Scott. The son of an actor, Palmer was an actor himself. His first novel was reprinted in Dublin, New York and Baltimore in 1796, and was followed by his other Gothic novels, *The Mystery of the Black Tower* (1796) and *The Mystic Sepulchre; or, Such Things Have Been* (1806).

Another 1795 debut was *The Castle of Ollada* (1795), by Francis Lathom (1774–1832), who used Radcliffe's device of explaining the apparent supernatural. Lathom published a number of Gothic novels, including *The Midnight Bell* (1798), *Astonishment!!!* (1802), *The Impenetrable Secret, Find it Out!* (1805), *The Fatal Vow; or, St Michael's Monastery* (1807), and *The Unknown* (1808), but, like most of those who wrote such novels, he did so as part of a wider portfolio which, in his case, included (non-Gothic) plays, life-and-times novels, and historical novels, notably *The Mysterious Freebooter; or, The Days of Queen Bess* (1806), which showed that historical novels did not have to be Gothic.

Elizabeth Bonhôte's *Bungay Castle* (1796) used medieval England as a setting, and was inspired by her husband's purchase of the ruins of that castle in 1791. Dedicated to the Duke of Norfolk, the novel reflected her more general royalism, although the book has been presented as also showing a degree of proto-feminism. Strange sounds in the depths of the castle, a familiar theme, lead from mystery to terror. A castle is also in the fore of Anne Ker's *The Heiress di Montalde; or, the Castle of Bezanto* (1799).

So also with monasteries. *The Abbey of Clugny* (1796), by the productive Mary Meeke,[4] was another work from the Minerva Press, and one that

---

4   Roberta Magnani, 'The Mysterious Mrs Meeke: A Biographical and Bibliographical Study,' *Cardiff Corvey: Reading the Romantic Text*, 9 (December

made much of a ghost. Gothic themes and devices were frequent in her work, not least uncertainty over origins and identity, as in *The Veiled Protectress, or the Mysterious Mother* (1819). She published under her own name and that of 'Gabrielli' (possibly a tribute to the significance of Italy in Gothic fiction) as well as anonymously. Her novels included *The Sicilian* (1798), *Mysterious Husband* (1801), *Something Strange* (1806), and *Langhton Priory* (1809), and she also translated works from French and German. Regina Maria Roche's *The Children of the Abbey* (1796) was an instance of the application of Gothic methods to sentimental fiction, and, looked at differently, the extent to which Gothic fiction should be seen as part of a continuum rather than a separate sub-genre. This novel offered sinister settings, notably the haunted Dunreath Abbey where Lady Dunreath is imprisoned, as well as a brother and sister defrauded of their inheritance. Abduction and attempted seduction are threats to the heroine, but, after the travails of a sentimental novel, she marries Lord Mortimer.

The Horrors of Oakendale Abbey (1797) by Mrs Carver, possibly Anthony Carlisle, a surgeon, was a successful work set in an apparently haunted Cumberland abbey used by body snatchers, those who sold corpses for dissecting purposes. If Carlisle was the author, the use of a female pseudonym was instructive. Although far from solely a female form, women often were the writers of Gothic novels—a parallel with the major role of women in Methodism. The resolute heroine, Laura, a refugee from revolutionary France who is not put off by apparent horrors, was also at risk from the local aristocrat, the libertine Lord Oakendale. Body-snatching was a crime of the present-day, one found in Britain, and not restricted by history, geography or religion. Moreover, the details of decaying bodies in this novel were graphic, and ensured that the resolve or revelation of the apparent supernatural still induced horror. Elizabeth Hervey's *The Church of St Siffrid* also came out in 1797, as did Joseph Fox's *Santa-Maria: Or, The Mysterious Pregnancy*, which involves villainous Carthusian monks willing to poison and rape the aristocratic heroine. Promising to 'make the sensitive soul thrill with horror,' the plot of this was more implausible than most, and the book accordingly was harshly reviewed. Fox had already published two medieval

2002): http://www.romtext.org.uk/reports/ cc09_n04/, accessed 24 December 2021.

Gothic works, *Tancred, A Tale of Ancient Times* (1791) and *The Bastard of Normandy, A Tale on the Seine* (1793), but did not write any more, at least under his own name. In the first, there is the villainous Lady Marguerita, who murders two husbands and has her son, Tancred, exposed in the forest, only for him to survive and gain his inheritance. Marguerita stabs herself to death. The Catholic clergy often remained in the fore, as in the anonymous, 40–page, *Almagro and Clause; or Monastic Murder; Exemplified in the Dreadful Doom of an Unfortunate Nun* (undated).

The vogue for Gothic novels, a demand for new titles that drove the pace of publication, was satirized in F.C. Patrick's *More Ghosts!!!* (1798) which, published by the Minerva Press, had its joke at the supernatural surfeit of such novels. Patrick was the author herself of *The Irish Heiress* (1797). She went on to write an historical novel of conspiracy, *The Jesuit; or, the History of Anthony Babington, Esq. An Historical Novel* (1799), which brought together anti-Catholicism, English history and a setting in the sixteenth century. At the same time, Mrs Patrick, who may have been a pen name, illustrated the range of the Gothic, and how it could illuminate other genres.

Satire of a different form came in William Beckford's *Azemia* (1797), which made fun of sensationalist writing and the Minerva Press. This included in its sub-story that of *Another Blue Beard*, the harsh Mr Grimshaw killing his first wife, Gertrude, and her brother. He also imprisons in a dungeon his second wife, who, however, eventually escapes with the help of the ghosts of Gertrude and her brother. Justice is thereby served. In the main plot, Azemia, the protagonist, faints when she enters a dark mausoleum, and a form appears. It is Lord Scudabout who has scared her on purpose. Later in the novel, Azemia is captured by bandits while taking a walk, only to be rescued and marry her rescuer when money is provided.

The range of the Gothic was also the case with the type of publication. That has been particularly, and profitably, discussed of late with reference to the 'bluebooks,' shorter, less expensive works of the early nineteenth century, but was also seen by the use of serial publication. The very first serial novel had been the non-threatening Gothic of Tobias Smollett's *Lancelot Greaves*, in which a modern gentleman acts like a medieval knight. Others followed, notably Sophia Lee's popular *The Recess*, published from 1783 to 1785, and George Moore's *Grasville Abbey* which appeared from March

1793 until August 1797 in a monthly, *The Lady's Magazine*. Published by G.G. and J. Robinson, the publisher of *The Mysteries of Udolpho*, this was a magazine that proved particularly welcoming to the Gothic, which, in turn, lent itself, in its structure and dynamics of a wavelike series of alarms, to serial publication. The heroine, Matilda, is observant of a buildup of alarm, and Moore presents this as differentiating her and, by extension, her generation from that of her mother:

> … the light in the west tower. The strange circumstances which seemed to encompass this abbey with a mist of doubtful horror, every day became more uncomfortable and disagreeable. It was true, the good sense and instructions of her mother had brought her up to despise superstition, and laugh at the folly of those who listened to uncommon reports. But the occurrences she had lately been witness to gave her strong reasons to believe in supernatural existences…. such strange and mysterious events staggered all the fortitude she had derived form the lessons of her parent.…

Father Peter warns her about the risk of 'tales of horror, and terrific recitals, which curiosity prompts us to listen to, and which so far win on our fancy, as to make us anxious after such entertainment,' and also counsels against visiting the abbey. The fearful Agnes, Matilda's servant, is fearful of 'some hobgoblin' entering from the mysterious room next door.[5] Matilda's father has been murdered by her uncle, Count D'Ollifont, who has usurped the family inheritance. Set in the reign of Louis XIV of France, the action included young women forced into convents.

Grasville Abbey, which proved popular in Britain, and was rapidly translated into French and German, contained the habitual ensemble of family mysteries, murders and sinister foreigners. The obscure Moore also produced the strongly anti-Catholic *Theodosius De Zulvin: The Monk of Madrid* (1802), *Montbar; or The Buccanneer* (1804), and *Tales of the Passions* (1808).

---

5   George Moore, 'Grasville Abbey,' *The Lady's Magazine*, 26 (September 1795), pp. 402–7. This is one of a number of items made more accessible by being reproduced in Rictor Norton's *Gothic Readings 1764–1840* (2000).

Another part-work, published in *The Lady's Magazine*, was the anonymous *The Monks and the Robbers: a Tale of the Fifteenth Century*, which was begun by one contributor, possibly Mary Meeke, in 1794, but left, essentially as a stub, to be finished by another author in parts published in 1798–1805 and then published as a book in 1808. Set in Sicily, this is a story with a confused plot and many jumps. As so often, characterization is poor, but, looked at differently, this is a matter of a structured approach in which plot episodes are prioritized, rather than credible characterisation. There are bandits, an evil monk, villainous (as well as good) aristocrats, catacombs under a gloomy castle where murder takes place with a poisoned dagger, abductions, a lost heir, and a happy ending.

1798 also saw *The Animated Skeleton*, *The New Monk*, a satire on *The Monk*, and Richard Sicklemore's *Edgar; or, The Phantom of the Castle*. In turn, 1799's appearances included T.J. Horsley Curteis' *Ethelwina, or, The House of Fitz-Auburne* and a republication of William Ireland's *The Abbess*, which was first published in 1796.

With its brilliant title, *The Animated Skeleton*, was a highly successful anonymous work published by the Minerva Press, that was unusual in the degree of dark comedy alongside the horror. As per normal, there was mysterious disappearance, usurpation, and a setting amidst the medieval élite. The preface reflected on the relationship between the Gothic and other fiction as part of a discussion of that between facts and fiction. This included the observation that, in contrast with the norm:

> I pretend not here to produce facts for my foundation: through the regions of imagination only have I strayed to gather those materials which arose spontaneously, whichever way I moved. To me it has ever appeared, that turning truth into romance was divesting it of its real charms.... If my story has any merit, it consists in its brevity, in its being entirely invention, and without a sentiment intended to corrupt the heart.
>
> The reign of Hugh Capet [of France, 987–996] presented to my mind the overgrown power of the nobles; and there alone have I glanced at reality, except in attempting to adapt my story to the manners of the times.

8. In Ann's Shadows

The first chapter of *The Animated Skeleton* began with a sinister account of Duke Albert, 'a great enemy to all the poor vassals in his territories, who have any handsome females belonging to them.' This captured the sexual menace that was so important in Gothic novels of whatever type, a menace especially to heroines, but not only to them. Aside from Albert, there are Brunchilda, his cruel and tyrannical wife, and 'those terrible ghosts in the castle' who 'are all caused by his great wickedness.' Albert had replaced Count Richard, a benign ruler who had disappeared. It is no surprise that Brunchilda's favourite, Conrad, who is killed at the hands of a valiant peasant repelling an unprovoked attack, dies 'uttering blasphemous execrations.' Villainy, however, is checked, the plot tempered, and the tone lightened somewhat, with the animated skeleton that haunt a castle.

Richard Sicklemore, author of the favorably-received *Edgar; or, The Phantom of the Castle* (1798) similarly included a castle, a usurper, and a skeleton. Armine Fitz-Elmar overthrows the benign Baron Fitz-Elmar, and set out to kill the latter's son, Edgar; leading Edgar to flee on a stormy night to an atmospheric ruined priory. On his return, Edgar terrifies the killers by wearing his father's armour, being seen as his ghost. The terror is of the Radcliffe-type and not supernatural, and there is a major debt to *Hamlet*. The first chapter began with a quote from the Scottish poet Robert Blair's *The Grave*:

—Strange things,
the neighbours say, have happen'd here;
Wild shrieks have issu'd from the hollow tombs:
Dead men have come again, and walk's about:
And the great bell has toll'd, unrung, untouch'd.

In the priory, Edgar, unsurprisingly, forces open a door which creaks on its rusty hinges, only for the door to then close with a crash such that Edgar cannot open it. By the light of lightning flashes, he descends a staircase, and then goes through a passage in 'impenetrable darkness,' past an iron door, into an underground room poorly lit by a lamp which 'spread a tremulous gleam, more horrible than darkness itself' (1). With a reminder that fear was not necessarily of the supernatural, a point that was more generally true, Edgar is concerned that the abbey might be a bandit lair, which was a frequent trope. After a winding passage, and a door only just forced open, the light is extinguished, while Edgar, 'alarmed by a violent and uncommon noise,' is 'absorbed in silent terror.' Both of these are habitual occurrences in Gothic novels, indeed almost formulaic. Most commonly the case for female characters, they also, as here, affected men.

After a series of further mishaps, Edgar falls through a floor that gives way (a repetition of that theme), only to stumble on a body. 'The wayward gales of outrageous fortune' certainly buffet Edgar (16), but his character is proof from any earthly fall, not least because he relies on divine support. The first volume ends on a very strong religious affirmation, one that made much sense in the culture of the time:

> trust in that most benignant and adorable Being, the supreme Creator of all things; and you may confidently rest assured that your hope will not fall to the ground: his aid never fails: he will with safety deliver thee out of the power of thine enemies; and remember, when once thou hast sullied they good name, by suffering thy principles to degenerate, the sting of remorse will probe thy breast in the hours of retirement. An honest heart is a jewel not to be purchased by the wealth of nations; be careful then to govern thy passions, and preserve thine from the destructive contamination of guilt; persevere in virtue, and merit the commendation of Heaven. (16)

Thomas Curties' *Ethelwina; or, The House of Fitz-Auburne* (1799) offered a beautiful aristocratic heroine, Ethelwina, Countess of Auburne, whose wooing by the harsh Leopold, Lord of St Iver, involves her seizure and incarceration in a mountain-girt castle. Set in the reign of Edward III (1327–77), usurpation by enforced matrimony is the intention, as in many other Gothic novels the use of potions, imprisonment in a dungeon, and the threat of rape are all means employed, and the scenario includes an armour-clad ghost bearing a bloody sword and signs of a past murder in the dungeon. Treason is held up for obloquy, and honor identified with loyalty.[6]

6   Dale Townshend, 'Royalist Historiography in T.J. Hosley Curtie's *Ethelwina, Or The House of Fitz-Auburne* (1799), *Gothic Studies*, 14 (2018), pp. 57–73.

8. In Ann's Shadows

Clandestine marriage was important in *The Heiress di Montalde; or, the Castle of Bezanto* (1799) and *Adeline St Julian; or, the Midnight Hour* (1800), both by Anne Ker, the wife of a probably illegitimate son of John, 3rd Duke of Roxburgh.[7] The first was described in the *Critical Review* as an 'imitation in Mrs Radcliffe's manner,' and followed her in an Italian setting, an oppressed heroine, a castle, dungeons, secret marriages, and an eventually rational explanation of the supernatural events. The plot included inheritance, manipulation, incarceration, suicide, a dungeon gate, 'a most desperate-looking wretch, whose ruffian aspect chilled my very heart' (11), an escape plot, ghosts, secret doors, and some pretty dreary conversation, and was dedicated to a daughter of George III.

In contrast, *Adeline St Julian*, set in France in the 1630s, was more violent and anti-Catholic, with Elinor, who has secretly married and become pregnant by Henry de Castelle, a cleric, harshly imprisoned. Torture is used and the supernatural plays a modest role with Castelle tried and executed for using supernatural powers to seduce women, and Cardinal Richelieu, the first minister of Louis XIII, a villain. There is no happy ending.

Curties also produced the plagiaristic *The Monk of Udolpho* (1807), of which, like some of the other Gothic novels, the title is the best feature. He also wrote *Ancient Records, Or, The Abbey of Saint Oswythe* (1801); *The Scottish Legend, Or The Isle of Saint Clothair* (1802), *The Watch Tower; Or, The Sons of Ulthona* (1804) and *St Botolph's Priory; Or, The Sable Mask* (1806).

Set in Florence, William Henry Ireland's *The Abbess* (1799) drew heavily on the model of *The Monk*, with Catholicism, a nunnery, and sexual drives to the fore. There is sleepwalking, self-flagellation, secret oaths, mysterious meetings, nightmares, and a sinister Abbess. A committed pursuer of profit, as shown by his forging of Shakespeare plays, Ireland (1775–1835) went on to publish other Gothic novels, notably *Rimualdo: Or, The Castle of Badajos* (1800) and *Gondez the Monk: A Romance of the Thirteenth Century* (1805). Bringing forward Gothic patterns and setting the story in medieval Spain, Ireland in *Rimualdo* offers the poor lighting that

7   Rachel Howard, 'Anne Ker: A Biographical and Bibliographical Survey,' John Steele, 'Anne and John Ker: New Soundings,' *Cardiff Corvey*, 11, 12 (2003, 2004).

communicates frightening impressions, as well as nightmares, murders, hauntings, the subterranean, caverns, and a sinister monk, Sebastiano. Deception is brought to the fore. In 1801, *The Monthly Review* mentioned the novel's 'winding sheets, and winding stair-cases.' In *Gondez*, a medieval monastery is revealed to be a prison with magic, demonic figures, torture chambers and sexual slavery.

The tropes still played well with the audience. They had been summarized in an anonymous piece of 1797, 'Terrorist Novel Writing,' which was published in *The Spirit of the Public Journals for 1797*. Drawing on the borrowing from French of 'terrorisme,' this was the author's term for what is now called Gothic novels, a term that was not employed at the time. The author referred to the 'great quantity of novels … in which it has been the fashion to make terror the order of the day, by confining the heroes and heroines in old gloomy castles; full of spectres, apparitions, ghosts, and dead men's bones.' A recipe was offered:

> Take – An old castle, half of it ruinous.
> A long gallery, with a great many doors, some secret ones.
> Three murdered bodies, quite fresh.
> As many skeletons, in chests and presses.
> An old woman hanging by the neck; with her throat cut.
> Assassins and desperados quant, suff.
> Noises, whispers and groans, three score at least.
> Mix them together, in the form of three volumes, to be taken at any of the watering-places before going to bed.

The recipe certainly worked in this period.

9. MONK LEWIS

Ambrosio, the protagonist of Matthew Lewis's lurid novel *The Monk* (1796), is presented as a victim of his own irrational impulses, specifically lustful self-destructive drives, which are, at the end of the novel, unconvincingly attributed to diabolical forces. He was more frightening than the creations of Walpole and Radcliffe, and was a threat to all, notably women. More generally, their victimhood was a theme in the fiction of the period, as in Mary Wollstonecraft's *Wrongs of Woman: or Maria* (1798), which is overwhelmingly a tale of male cruelty and the oppression of women. Lewis, who may have been an homosexual, a theme developed in Ambrosio falling for Rosario only for the latter to be revealed to be Matilda, expressed misogynistic comments: '…she was wise enough to hold her tongue. As this is the only instance known of a woman's ever having done so, it was judged worthy to be recorded here' (I,1). Or, again, 'Look with indulgence on a woman's weakness' (I,2), and, if Matilda is given some good lines (I,2), she is revealed as a deceiver. There is also in *The Monk* a reference to the interacting dangers of female sensibility and fiction, as Rousseau's *La Nouvelle Heloise* plays a role in an unfortunate love affair.

While not as well-connected socially or politically as Horace Walpole, Lewis (1775–1818) was from the higher echelons of society. The eldest son of a senior civil servant, he received an élite education at Westminster and Christ Church, Oxford. In 1791–4, partly in preparation for a diplomatic career, Lewis became absorbed in Continental society, notably that of Germany, where he visited Weimar, met key literary figures, acquired a fascination for *schauerronman* or spine-chillers, translated Wieland's *Oberon* (1780), an epic poem in which a magic horn, a magic ring, and the spirit world all play a role, and became acquainted with Goethe.

Germany was an important source of ideas for Lewis, and the notion of Gothic novels as somehow arising from English conditions, notably an English theological tradition, is less than fair to the major significance of German parallels and influences. German literature proved exceptionally popular in Britain in the late 1790s,[1] leading Charles Maturin, in *Fatal Revenge* (1807), to refer to 'German horrors,' 'the *plague ship* of German letters,' and the 'figures of a German magic lanthorn.' Lewis also drew on French libertine literature.[2]

Traditional astrological and occult beliefs and practices continued to play a large role in Germany, looking forward to Carl Maria von Weber's brilliant opera *Der Freischütz* (1821) which was based on a story from Johann August Apel's *Das Gespensterbuch* (1811–15), with Samiel, the Black Huntsman, magic bullets, the selling of souls, and eerie orchestration. These beliefs affected many, including those far from the humble ranks of society. Thus, growing up in a Calvinist home in Nassau, the enlightened Baden bureaucrat Johann Reinhard (1714–72) encountered a world peopled largely by witches and ghosts, where the devil was omnipresent. Vampires and the supernatural played a role in Gottfried Bürger's influential ballad *Lenore* (1773).

Robert Southey's 1799 ballad 'The Old Woman of Berkeley' provides a vampiric witch who sucks the breath of sleeping babes as well as the Devil. The poem was reproduced in Lewis's anthology *Tales of Wonder* (1801). Southey's other ballads include his 'Rudiger,' in which a German knight who has won the promise of happiness from the Devil at the cost of his first-born child is dragged into 'the dark profound' by giant arms. In 'Lord William' and 'The Inchcape Rock,' murderers die in the same way that they have inflicted death. The Devil turns up in the last, in 'Cornelius Agrippa' and in 'The Old Woman of Berkeley.'

Lewis became an MP in 1796, succeeding William Beckford in the Wiltshire 'pocket borough' of Hindon, although he only served one term and lost interest in politics after standing down in 1802. As a further instance of the overlap between politics and Gothic novels, George Porter MP was the dedicatee of Richard Sicklemore's *Raymond* (1801). Lewis subsequently became interested in the theatre, publishing numerous plays from 1796, only to die having caught yellow fever while visiting the Jamaican estates he had inherited.

---

1 Patrick Bridgwater, *The German Gothic Novel in Anglo-German Perspective* (Leiden, 2013), pp. 439–40.
2 Valentina Bortoluzzi, *Matthew Gregory Lewis's 'The Monk': A Literary Patchwork* (thesis, University Ca' Foscari Venice, 2011–12).

9. Monk Lewis

Begun in 1792 as 'a Romance in the style of *The Castle of Otranto*,' Lewis was encouraged to press on by reading, soon after its appearance, *The Mysteries of Udolpho*, which impressed him. *The Monk* should be considered in part as a response to Radcliffe, to which she in turn responded in *The Italian*; but also with reference to the stylistic sequels by others. Indeed, in February 1796, the *Critical Review* observed:

> Since Mrs Radcliffe's justly admired and successful romances, the press has teemed with stories of haunted castles and visionary terrors; the incidents of which are so little diversified, that criticism is at a loss to vary its remarks.[3]

Drawing on the *Santon Barisa*, a Persian tale, Lewis rapidly finished. *The Monk*, which was published in 1795 to favorable reviews. The book was reissued in 1796, equipped with a new title page giving 1796 as the year of publication. Another edition swiftly followed, and, to this, Lewis put his name on the title page. As with other writers, including Walpole, he was not tempted into public authorship with the first edition.

At the outset, *The Monk* offers its lurid action of sexual temptation and fall, and a nightmare in Madrid in which dreams of marriage to Antonia are interrupted by the dramatic struggle between good and evil:

> ... before he had time to receive her, an unknown rushed between them: his form was gigantic; his complexion was swarthy, his eye fierce and terrible; his mouth breathed out volumes of fire, and on his forehead was written in legible characters – "Pride! Lust! Inhumanity!" Antonia shrieked. The monster clasped her in his arms, and, springing with her upon the altar, tortured her with his odious caresses. She endeavoured in vain to escape from his embrace. Lorenzo flew to her succour; but, ere he had time to reach her, a loud burst of thunder was heard. Instantly the cathedral seemed crumbling into pieces; the monks betook themselves to flight, shrieking fearfully; the lamps were extinguished, the altar sunk down, and in its place

---

3   *Critical Review*, 16 (1796), p. 222.

appeared an abyss vomiting forth clouds of flame. Uttering a loud and terrible cry the monster plunged into the gulph, and in his fall attempted to drag Antonia with him. He strove in vain. Animated by supernatural powers, she disengaged herself. (I,1)

The supernatural and the seductive character of horror were both present from the first chapter, and the prose was as if 'touched by the rod of some magician' (I,2). As a background, a gypsy fortuneteller provides a curse and a warning about 'Lustful man and crafty devil' (I,1), in a prediction that proves true. As with *Macbeth*, this raised the issues of human agency versus predestination. The nature of free will was at issue up to the close of the novel.

There was a pornographic character to some of the writing:

> She had torn open her habit, and her bosom was half exposed. The weapon's point rested upon her left breast. And, oh! That was such a breast! The moon-beams darting full upon it enabled the monk to observe its dazzling whiteness: his eye dwelt with insatiable avidity upon the beauteous orb: a sensation will then unknown filled his heart with a mixture of anxiety and delight; a raging fire shot through every limb; the blood boiled in his veins, and a thousand wild wishes bewildered his imagination. (I,2)

Matilda tempts Ambrosio's dreams, merging with the image of the Madonna so that he 'rioted in joys till then unknown to him,' and she becomes a succubus leaving him exhausted by 'his provoking dreams' (I,2). They become lovers soon after, and sex rapidly becomes a theme in the novel. The following chapter introduces a woman who describes how 'my passions overpowered my virtues.' Later, Ambrosio assaults Antonia:

> ... wild with desire, he clasped the blushing trembler in his arms. He fastened his lips greedily upon hers, sucked in her pure delicious breath, violated with his bold hand the treasures of her bosom, and wound around him her soft and yielding limbs. Startled, alarmed, and confused at his action, surprise at first

> deprived her of the power of resistance. At length, recovering herself, she strove to escape from his embrace.... But the licentious monk heeded not her prayers: he persisted in his design, and proceeded to take still greater liberties. Antonia prayed, wept, and struggled.... (II,7)

The sucking reference possibly hints at the ideas of the incubus/succubus and the vampire. Thwarted by the arrival of her mother, Elvira, Ambrosio swears that 'cost what it would, he still would possess Antonia,' and is tempted by Matilda's offer of the use of diabolical means.

Matilda tempts him first with a magic mirror which provides another pornographic image, that of a naked Antonia preparing for her bath. Aware that he was making his breach with Heaven 'irreparable,' Ambrosio still turns to temptation and is led by Matilda, who now carries a golden wand, through narrow passages, past 'sculls, bones, graves...,' before she calls on a demon with an incantation involving the burning of fingers and an *agnus dei*. The demon comes as a beautiful, naked youth, and Ambrosio gains the power to rape Antonia in her sleep. His attempt is interrupted by Elvira who he kills in order to protect his reputation, before fleeing without raping Antonia. This takes Ambrosio back into the need for diabolical assistance, which leads to his hoodwinking by Satan who takes his soul.

Praised in reviews in the *Monthly Mirror* and the *Analytical Review* in 1796, *The Monk* was savaged by Samuel Taylor Coleridge in the *Critical Review* of February 1797.[4] Held up as corrupting, irreligious, and inappropriate for an MP, this attack was followed by others, notably Thomas James Matthias in *The Pursuits of Literature* (1797) which attacked *The Monk* for diablerie, pornography and blasphemy. The comments on the Bible caused particular comment, while there was concern that the novel was improper for a young woman:

> Many of the narratives can only tend to excite ideas the worst calculated for a female breast: everything is called plainly and roundly by its name; and the annals of a brothel would scarcely furnish a greater choice of indecent expressions. Yet this is the

4   Coleridge, review of *The Monk, Critical Review*, 19 (1797), pp. 194–200.

book which young women are recommended to study, which is put into the hands of children, able to comprehend little more than those passages of which they had better remain ignorant, and which but too frequently inculcates the first rudiments of vice, and gives the first alarm to the still sleeping passions. (II,7)

Alongside criticism in the reviews, there was also praise, for example in the *Monthly Mirror* of April 1797 in which *The Monk* is presented as moral.

Nevertheless, as a result of the attacks, Lewis withdrew the third edition, that of 1797, and replaced it with a much changed fourth edition in 1798. At the same time, the furore helped sales and contributed to the production of other versions, including chapbook and stage ones. By 1800, there were five London and two Dublin editions aside from chapbook versions. *The Monk* was adapted for the stage into *Raymond and Agnes; or The Bleeding Nun of Lindenberg*. There was also satire, of varied form, from *The Monk of Udolpho* to James Gilray's 1802 caricature *Tales of Wonder!* which shows four genteel women reading *The Monk*. It carried the note 'This attempt to describe the effects of the Sublime and Wonderful is dedicated to M.G. Lewis Esq. MP.' The decorative items on the mantelpiece included the model of a skeleton.

Its reception was a literary event,[5] with Byron and Scott being among the admirers of *The Monk*. More recently, the play has been treated as the acme of a supposedly male Gothic, one that was more violent and prone to use the supernatural than the supposedly female Gothic represented by Radcliffe. In reality, there was a considerable overlap in devices between male and female writers. Yet, the two authors were contrasted by contemporaries, the Marquis de Sade, in his *Idée sur les Romans* (1800), preferring Lewis and linking *The Monk to* the tensions and violence of a revolutionary cataclysm and an 'age de fer' [iron].[6]

Lewis's Gothic energies led him to the theatre, notably the highly successful play *The Castle Spectre* (1797), and his inherent theatricality proved

5   André Parreaux, *The Publication of 'The Monk.' A Literary Event 1796–1798* (Paris, 1960).
6   Octave Uzanne edition of Sade's *Idée sur les Romans* (Geneva, 1967), pp. 31–3.

well-suited to the stage machinery and audience of the period. Set in the Middle Ages around 'Castle Conway,' *The Castle Spectre* offered spectacle and atmosphere. Inherently dramatic, and with a strong supernatural element, the play was criticized for radicalism as a result of its attacks on slavery and feudal oppression. Lewis produced plays in a number of styles and tones. His Gothic plays included *Adelmorn the Outlaw* (1801) and his melodrama *The Wood Daemon, or, The Clock has Struck* (1807) which depicts a pact between the villain and the wood daemon. Lewis' poem *Isle of Devils* was published in Kingston, Jamaica in 1827. It presents the rape by a devil of the heroine Izra, which is possibly a reference to fears of a slave rising.

Duty and desire, themes in *The Castle of Otranto*, are brought to the fore in *The Monk*. However, the church, rather than the dynastic claims of *The Castle of Otranto*, provides the context, and, as such, offers a very varied and stressful milieu for control and sexuality. The traditional fascination with the supposed sensuality of nuns comes to the fore. There is both anti-Catholicism and yet also a location of this in terms of contemporary debates about female drives.

Lewis produced only one other novel, *Abaellino. The Bravo of Venice* (1805), a version of a German work, Zschokkie's *Abalino* (1794). Lewis' version had an overwritten quality:

> "Fate," he at length exclaimed in a paroxysm of despair, "Fate has condemned me t be either the wildest of adventurers or one, at the relation of whose crimes. The world must shudder! To astonish is my destiny." (I,2)

Abaellino is presented as so inhuman in his look that "'Satan must certainly have appeared to his mother while she was big with him,'" with reference subsequently made to the ugliness of the fallen angels, and to Abaellino's strength, suggesting that "'he must have made a compact with the devil'," although that is a remark rather than the product of a horrific scene suggesting such an event (I,3). So also when Abaellino is described as an 'outcast of hell' and as 'Satan himself in a human form' (III,4). A lethal criminal network of great power is depicted, a network treating virtue and vice simply as names, indeed in a reversal of ordinary perception, as 'phantoms created by ... imagination' (I,4). Catholicism is held up as at fault, with Contarino, one of the conspirators, remarking:

> Flatter the pride of these insolent friars; paint for them upon the blank leaf of futurity, bishops' mitres, patriarchal missions, the hats of cardinals, and the keys of St Peter; my life upon it, they will spring at the bait, and you will have them completely at your disposal. These hypocrites, who govern the consciences of the bigoted Venetians, hold man and woman, the noble and the mendicant, the Doge and the gondolier, bound fast in the chains of superstition, by which they can lead them wheresoever it best suits their pleasure ... the confessors, whose blessings and curses pass with the multitude for current coin. (II,8)

Lewis plays with the audience's expectations, entitling the key and penultimate chapter 'Apparitions' (III,6) and having Abaellino ask in that: 'If you have once pledged your word, you ought to keep it, though given to the Prince of darkness' and again 'hear the ghosts of your victims!' In the plot, a villainous Cardinal seeks to use assassination in order to destabilize Venice. Thus, the anti-clericalism that had focused in *The Monk* on the convent was reprised. In *The Monk*, there had also been an account of questioning by the Inquisition, notably torture in order to obtain an admission of guilt, including of crimes not committed:

> Ambrosio suffered the most excruciating pangs that ever were invented by human cruelty.... fainting from excess of pain, insensibility rescued him from the hands of his tormentors.... his dislocated limbs, the nails torn from his hands and feet, and his fingers mashed and broken by the pressure of screws ... guilty or innocent his judges were bent upon condemning him. (III,12)

Lewis was not alone in introducing the challenge of Spanish Catholicism. It also occurred in *The Old Irish Baronet*, with the description of capture in battle leading to imprisonment by the Inquisition:

9. Monk Lewis

> two of the most diabolical-looking imps my eyes ever beheld under the human shape, dressed in long black wrappers, or cloaks, that completely enveloped them, frightfully ornamented with glaring red, and caps of the same colours, that, together with their black faces, gave them an appearance of devils ... led, by ascents and descents, through creaky doors and vaulted passages ... during the term of eighteen years, I was not to be seen beyond the walls of the Inquisition ... never had the consolation of hearing myself addressed by a human voice ... the distant groans of misery ... the shriek of agonizing torture ... gesture of such diabolical meaning ... perpetually apprehensive. (II,9)

George Moore's *Theodosius de Zulvin, the Monk of Madrid* (1802) was modelled on Lewis.

Lewis was clear on the struggle between good and evil, and *The Monk* very much took on board traditional presentations of Satan and of diabolical purposes and means:

> borne upon sulphurous whirlwinds, Lucifer stood before him [Ambrosio] a second time.... He appeared in all that ugliness which since his fall from heaven had been his portion. He blasted limbs still bore marks of the Almighty's thunder. A swarthy darkness spread itself over his gigantic form: his hands and feet were armed with long talons. Fury glared in his eyes, which might have struck the bravest heart with terror. Over his huge shoulders waved two enormous sable wings: and his hair was supplied by living snakes, which twined themselves round his brows with frightful hissings. In one hand he held a roll of parchment, and in the other an iron pen. Still the lightning flashed around him, and the thunder with repeated bursts seemed to announce the dissolution of Nature. (III,12)

Moreover, the denouement of the book focused on the struggle for Ambrosio's soul. Satan has a 'look of mingled malice, exultation, and contempt.' Improbably, he revealed that Ambrosio had been pardoned by the Inquisition and had thus sold his soul without need. Ambrosio is told that he was a fool 'to confide yourself to a devil!' To stop Ambrosio from seeking the divine mercy that is always offered as part of redemption, Satan seizes him and soars aloft to a great height before releasing him so that he falls and is badly injured. Ambrosio then suffers an earthly hell:

> The sun now rose above the horizon; its scorching beams darted full upon the head of the expiring sinner. Myriads of insects were called forth by the warmth; they drank the blood which trickled from Ambrosio's wounds; he had no power to drive them from him, and they fastened upon his sores, darted their stings into his body, covered him with their multitudes, and inflicted on him tortures the most exquisite and insupportable. The eagles of the rock tore his flesh piecemeal, and dug out his eye-balls with their crooked beaks. A burning thirst tormented him; he heard the river's murmur as it rolled beside him, but strove in vain to drag himself towards the sound. Blind, maimed, helpless, and despairing, venting his rage in blasphemy and curses, execrating his existence, yet dreading the arrival of death destined to yield him up to greater torments, six miserable days did the villain languish. On the seventh a violent storm arose: the winds in fury rent up rocks and forests: the sky was now black with clouds, now sheeted with fire: the rain fell in torrents; it swelled the stream; the waves overflowed their banks; they reached the spot where Ambrosio lay, and, when they abated, carried with them into the river the corse [corpse] of the despairing monk. (III,12)

The end of the book was scarcely an affirmation of self or a discussion of theological novelty. This is a death of the sinner, indeed a Judas, in a setting that is timeless. The theme is Gothic in the sense of medieval, pre-Reformation Christianity, rather than the contrasting ornate Romantic exoticism of a chaotic end impassively orchestrated by the protagonist in Eugène Delacroix's dramatic painting *The Death of Sardanapalus* (1827). Lewis had provided a back-story for Ambrosio that involves a measure of sentimentality and understanding:

...his parents had beheld his dawning virtues with the fondest delight and admiration. Unfortunately, while yet a child, he was deprived of those parents. He fell into the power of a relation whose only wish about him was never to hear of him more.... His instructors carefully repressed those virtues, whose grandeur and disinterestedness were ill suited to the cloister... While the monks were busied in rooting out his virtues, and narrowing his sentiments, they allowed every vice which had fallen to his share to arrive at full perfection. He was suffered to be proud, vain, ambitious, and disdainful. (II,6)

The anti-clericalism of the book focused not so much on Catholic clergy as a whole, as specifically as on monks and nuns, who lived in cut-off communities bound by separate rules. Thus, Ambrosio had 'never saw, much less conversed with the other sex' (II,6), while the account of the nunnery is of brutal tyranny. The freeing of Agnes from her subterranean imprisonment bears comparison with Beethoven's opera *Fidelio* (1805), which was also set in Spain, but the rescue from the Underworld looks to Christoph Willibald Gluck's opera *Orfeo ed Euridice* (1762), as well as to a long tradition of works about imprisonment in nunneries. The travails of nuns were a major theme in the novel, notably Agnes who, confined in Germany, observes 'Flight is my only resource from the horrors of a convent' (II,4) and who seeks to escape by using the story of the spectre or 'the bleeding nun' of Lindenberg which Lewis took from Johann August Musäus' *Die Volksmärchen der Deutschen* (1782–6). In *The Monk*, Agnes brings up the perversion of good and evil that is so frequent in a work in which hypocrisy plays a major role:

> they are God's servants who make me suffer thus! – They think themselves holy, while they torture me like fiends! – They are cruel and unfeeling; and 'tis they who bid me repent; and 'tis they who threaten me with eternal perdition! Saviour, Saviour! you think not so ... how dreadful are the abodes so falsely termed religious. (III,10)

The arrival of Satan, a potent figure, in *The Monk* very much captured the continuation of a belief in the real presence of Evil. That continuation represented an element of the Enlightenment and the post-Enlightenment that it is all-too-easy to underplay. Gothic fiction was not simply about this, and the novelists did not take a uniform position; but, alongside the interest in a story, there was the concern about saving souls, winning redemption, and achieving salvation. Predestination played only a limited role in these novels, for there was justification by faith and action with the ability to thwart evil intentions, notably by resisting temptation. The context varied, as did the course of events; but the need for constancy and salvation was the same, and novelists captured this.

10. MISS AUSTEN RESPONDS

On a 'cold and stormy' night, with the wind roaring round the house, Elinor starts 'back with a look of horror' when she sees the 'flaring lamps of a carriage' drawn by four horses (instead of two) and therefore moving fast. Jane Austen could certainly do drama, but, in this case, Elinor Dashwood's visitor in *Sense and Sensibility* turns out to be far from sinister, in a passage in which the author is clearly having much fun.[1] Indeed, far from being tempted to adopt the Gothic, Austen's novels were praised for not being Gothic by some. These included the critic and satirist William Gifford, editor of the *Quarterly Review*, who recommended to the latter's publisher, John Murray, that he accept *Emma* precisely because Austen kept Gothic excesses away or mocked them. In the March 1816 issue of the *Quarterly Review*, Sir Walter Scott favoured Austen's novels for the same reason. An even more extreme contrast with the Gothic was offered by Hannah More (1745–1833), a conservative religious writer whose *Cheap Repository for Moral and Religious Tracts* produced instructive moral works from 1795 to 1817, the majority written by More, and with great commercial success. Her longer moralistic novels included the popular *Coelebs in Search of a Wife* (1809).

In practice, alongside obvious differences between Austen and Radcliffe, and those coming from Austen because Radcliffe did not need to respond to her, there were similarities. Key ones were the place of a Christian moral universe, although Catholic settings made Radcliffe more wary of the Church in her novels. For both Austen and Radcliffe, there was also the question of the relationship between experience and reality, an issue, probed in *Northanger Abbey*, that was of particular concern for novelists, seeking, as they did, to build on the capacity for imagination.[2]

1   *Sense and Sensibility* (III, 7–8).
2   J. Lamb, 'Imagination, Conjecture, and Disorder,' *Eighteenth*-Century *Studies* 45 (2011), pp. 53–69.

As individuals, Radcliffe might seem very different from Austen, not least in being married, but there were instructive similarities, especially in their being very private: While the destruction of much of Austen's correspondence was far from helpful, less indeed is known of Radcliffe's life. Moreover, both were very much professionals in their writing, not least in carefully considering reviews and trying to develop their style, which underlines the limitations of pushing genre as a classifying model, and, still more, as the basis for judgement. Each depicted female characters who matured under (very different) adversity.

Begun in 1798, but not published until 1818, Austen's *Northanger Abbey* finds the protagonist, Catherine Morland, 'left to the luxury of a raised, restless, and frightened imagination over the pages of *Udolph* [*The Mysteries of Udolpho*], lost from all worldly concerns of dressing and dinner,' although she discovers that the abbey where she is staying is not only not a ruin, but also not a setting from the pages of Gothic fiction. Ironically, in *Northanger Abbey*, real life turns out to be worse in some respects than the imagined perils of Gothic fiction. The cruelty to women seen in Radcliffe's novels, notably to wives in *A Sicilian Romance* and *The Mysteries of Udolpho*, affects Catherine Morland in her response to Northanger Abbey.

In Bath, Catherine and Isabella discuss *Udolpho*, focusing on the mystery of what is behind the black veil. Catherine is wrongly convinced 'it must be a skeleton.' Isabella then proposed that they read Radcliffe's *The Italian* together followed by 'a list of ten or twelve more of the same kind.' These were novels published between 1793 and 1798, and therefore evidence of what had just been published when Austen was writing. Eliza Parsons is the author of two, *The Castle of Wolfenbach* (1793) and *The Mysterious Warning* (1796), Regina Maria Roche of *Clermont* (1798), Francis Lathom of *The Midnight Bell* (1798), and Eleanor Sleath of *The Orphan of the Rhine* (1798), and two are translated from German, *The Necromancer: or The Tale of the Black Forest* (1794) and *Horrid Mysteries* (1796).[3] The

---

[3] Michael Sadleir, *The Northanger Novels: A Footnote to Jane Austen* (Oxford, 1927); Eleanor Ty, 'Catherine's Real and Imagined Fears: What Happens to Female Bodies in Gothic Castles,' *Persuasions*, 20 (1998), pp. 248–69; Anthony Mandal, 'Revising the Radcliffean Model: Jane Austen's *Northanger Abbey* and Regina Maria Roche's *Clermont*,' *Cardiff Corvey*, 3 (1999).

10. Miss Austen Responds

seizure of land and women, notably young women, are key goals in these novels, and abduction and murder frequent means. The Minerva Press, which William Lane (1745–1814) established in about 1790, published these books, seeking to appeal to a growing public, and doing particularly well from Gothic fiction, which it dominated until the 1820s.

The Midnight Bell, which Austen noted in October 1798 was being read by her father who had borrowed it from the library, provides an instance of the novels cited by Austen. There was a formulaic character with the hero, Alphonsus Cohenburg, seeking to reverse crime in the shape of an uncle apparently murdering Alphonsus's father and seizing the estates. Moreover, Alphonsus's wife is later kidnapped by other villains. There is a Gothic castle, lightning, a mysterious midnight bell, hermits, lust, disappearances, forests, torture, a cavern, and ghostly black figures who, in the event, are sinister Catholic priests.

Eliza Parsons (1739–1811) fell on hard times due to the business failure of her husband and his strokes, and as a result she wrote 19 novels from 1790, the year of his death, until 1807. Gothic writing was her choice because it was a way to make money, although, in the event, she faced frequent financial problems. *The Castle of Wolfenbach* (1793) provided the anti-Catholicism that was characteristic of Parsons' novels. The heroine, Matilda Weimar, is under threat from her uncle who has killed Count Berniti, his brother, her father (not that Matilda knows that), and has designs on Matilda. The other villain, Count Wolfenbach, imprisons his wife, Victoria, in his castle, takes away their son, and is a murderer, not least of Victoria's first true love (whose body is locked into a closet with Victoria) and of Victoria's servants. The castle of Wolfenbach is apparently haunted, but the chains and groans heard are in fact from those whom Count Wolfenbach has imprisoned. After many travails, Matilda discovers her aristocratic identity and can therefore marry Count de Bouville without loss of status. This discovery represents the overcoming of successive attempts to maintain secrets and keep people hidden. Murder and arson are ready plot devices, because frequent villainy is easy for villains, even if they may repent. There is a happy ending, but the work has its limitations.

So also with her *The Mysterious Warning* (1790) which was subtitled *A German Tale*. Family secrets and apparitions are part of the setting and action. Her later novels, including her two last, *Murray House* (1804) and *The*

The Age of Nightmare

Convict, or Navy Lieutenant (1807), abandon these Gothic settings for the problems of women in contemporary Britain.

As with Radcliffe, but still more clearly, Austen provided a rational explanation to what had seemed supernatural. Radcliffe might refer to a 'demon in the garb of a monk,'[4] but there were none such in any of Austen's novels. No one was going to see the ridiculously oleaginous Mr Collins in Austen's *Pride and Prejudice* in this light. Moreover, in *Northanger Abbey*, Catherine Morland is totally disabused and also reminded by Henry Tilney, an exemplary cleric, that she is a 'Christian' (II,9). This, more generally, is a critique of the willful imagination at play in Gothic fantasies, as with Catherine's fear that she will be abducted by villains and forced into a carriage that speeds off.

Rebuked by Henry Tilney, Catherine Morland comes to realize that she has been misled by Gothic novels:

> Charming as were all Mrs Radcliffe's works, and charming even as were the works of all her imitators, it was not in them perhaps that human nature, at least in the midland counties of England, was to be looked for … there was surely some security for the existence even of a wife not beloved, in the laws of the land, and the manners of the age. Murder was not tolerated, servants were not slaves…. Among the Alps and Pyrenees, perhaps, there were no mixed characters…. But in England it was not so; among the English, she believed, in their hearts and habits, there was a general though unequal mixture of good and bad.[5]

Austen thereby suggests a contrast between a reality of complexity, that she associates with Englishness, and an extremity of character. The latter is portrayed both as foreign and as an integral part of the Gothic novel. If paternal tyranny are found in both, General Tilney's in *Northanger Abbey* is not that of abduction and murder, but, rather, of social exclusion. That is hurtful and harmful, but not lethal.

The settings were very different from those of Radcliffe, and the tone

4   *The Italian*, I,1.
5   *Northanger Abbey*, II,10.

10. Miss Austen Responds

far less melodramatic, but yet there was a common context. Austen was in no doubt about good and evil being mediated by punishment. Elinor in *Sense and Sensibility* reflects 'Each faulty propensity in leading him to evil, had led him likewise to punishment,' while Marianne Dashwood wishes to have time 'for atonement to my God.'[6]

The loss of meaning with which Austen humorously plays in *Northanger Abbey* was more clearly, dramatically and worryingly the case in Radcliffe's novels. She deals with the errors of her female protagonists, errors that helped to lead them into danger. The villains are separately faced by a loss of meaning, as in *The Italian*:

> The callous Schedoni, by a mistake not uncommon, especially to a mind of his character, substituted words for truths; not only confounding the limits of neighbouring qualities, but mistaking their very principles. Incapable of perceiving their nice distinctions, he called the persons who saw them, merely fanciful; thus making his very incapacity an argument for his superior wisdom. And while he confounded delicacy of feeling with fatuity of mind, taste with caprice, and imagination with error, he yielded, when he most congratulated himself on his sagacity, to illusions not less egregious because they were less than brilliant, than those which are incident to sentiment and feeling. (III,2)

Radcliffe shared in Austen's conviction of a divine providence. Thus, pursued into a cavern, Julia, in *A Sicilian Romance*, 'endeavored to resign herself to her fate, and to compose her distracted thoughts. The remembrance of her former wonderful escape inspired her with confidence in the mercy of God' (14). This mercy is much in evidence and essentially effective in Radcliffe's novels, which was not the case in either respect in Lewis' *The Monk*.

Soon after, Julia finds her imprisoned mother who says 'my prayer is granted. I am permitted to embrace one of my children before I die.' Told that her son is dead, the Marchioness 'raising her eyes to heaven, endeavoured to assume a look of pious resignation' (14). Religion is presented as

---

6   *Sense and Sensibility*, III, 8, 10.

the support of reason; with the Marchioness explaining that solitary imprisonment 'would certainly have subdued my reason, had not those firm principles of religious faith, which I imbibed in early youth, enabled me to withstand the still, but forceful pressure of my calamity' (14). Julia urges her mother to trust in God:

> Surely, the providence on whom you have so firmly relied, and whose inflictions you have supported with a fortitude so noble, has conducted me through a labyrinth of misfortunes to this spot, for the purpose of delivering you! (14)

The Marchioness accordingly commits 'herself to the protection of God.' This is a reversal of the proud and vicious conduct seen with most of the aristocracy, but the Marchioness has 'that affecting eloquence which true piety inspires' (14). In turn, the guilty are punished:

> "The retribution of heaven is upon me," resumed the marquis. "My punishment is the immediate consequence of my guilt. Heaven has made that woman the instrument of its justice, whom I made the instrument of my crimes; - that woman, for whose sake I forgot conscience, and braved vice." (14)

Suicide and murder are part of the outcome in *A Sicilian Romance*, demonstrating 'divine vengeance' (14), which was in accordance with established views. Thus, the *Weekly Register* of 25 April 1798 noted:

> To form an accurate and sublime view of the dispensations of Providence, we should at the same time consider the sovereignty of the Supreme Governor, and the free-agency of the instruments which he employs.

Again, the items in the 'Sunday Monitor section' of the first three issues of *E. Johnson's British Gazette and Sunday Monitor* of 1798 were headed: 'Goodness proved to be a Divine Perfection,' 'Moral evil consistent with the Divine Goodness,' and 'The Creation of Mankind a Proof the Divine Goodness.'

10. Miss Austen Responds

Austen was far from alone in being able to find fun in the Gothic. In contrast, in his *Nightmare Abbey* (1818), Percy Bysshe Shelley's friend Thomas Love Peacock made fun of the interest in the Gothic and macabre. Published in the same year as *Northanger Abbey*, the humour is different, with, for example, a servant with the name of Graves, a secret room, and reports of a ghost (which turns out to be a sleepwalker). Unlike in much of Gothic fiction, love is unfortunate. A millenarian, Mr Toobad, who believes in the struggle between Good and Evil, is one of the characters, most of whom are caricatures of literary figures of the period, notably Coleridge. So also with Sarah Scudgell Wilkinson's humorous *The Eve of St Mark; or, the Mysterious Spectre* (1820), in which the protagonist, Margaret, has read all the Gothic novels in the local library and is able to deploy Gothic tropes such as the animated portrait, only to find it difficult to discern fancy from truth. The wide resonance of horror included its easy use for humour, for the points of reference were well understood. There were to be a series of humorous works mocking Gothic fiction, works that took on their appeal and character thanks to the widespread popularity and familiarity of the genre and its readily recognisable settings and images, one seen, thereafter, as in the film *Young Frankenstein* (1974). This familiarity reflected the extent to which a formulaic character worked in order to ground the genre in the popular consciousness.

11. FORGOTTEN DECADE

The ease of leaping from Radcliffe and Lewis to the evening on Lake Geneva whence sprung Frankenstein and Byron's vampirish fragment is compounded by Walter Scott's suggestion in 1814 that the influence of the former novelists was long gone. This is ironic. It was not so much that both Radcliffe and Lewis were still alive, but rather that others were publishing Gothic novels in the meanwhile.

The first decade of the nineteenth century had seen the publication of many more Gothic novels, including Richard Sicklemore's popular and grizzly *Mary-Jane* (1800), *Rashleigh Abbey: Or, the Ruin on the Roch* (1805), and *Osrick: or, Modern Horrors* (1809), Henry Summersett's *Martyn Fenrose; or, The Wizard and the Sword* (1801), *The Impenetrable Secret* (1805) and *The Castle of Berry Pomeroy* (1806). Some authors, such as Summersett, also produced plays. Writers clearly regarded Gothic novels as a source of profit, as did publishers, notably William Lane, the key entrepreneur in the field whose publications were also the most actively reviewed.[1] This was a period of 'bluebooks' – cheap Gothic novels covered with blue paper,[2] that contrasted most clearly with the multi-volume novels. Short chapbooks summarized longer novels, *Rayland Hall* (1810) for example being a far shorter adaptation of Charlotte Smith's *The Old Manor House* (1793). Flexibility was increased by publishing stories separately, as well as in collections such as *Wild Roses; or, Cottage Tales* (1808) which included popular titles such as *The Mysterious Spaniard; or, the Ruins of St Luke's Abbey* (1808).

Criticism was not always favourable. His *The Offspring of Russell* (1794),

---

1 Megan Peiser, 'Review Periodicals and the Visibility of William Lane's Minerva Press,' *Research Society for Victorian Periodicals*, 4 March 2016.
2 Angela Koch, '"The Absolute Horror of Horrors" Revised. A Bibliographical Checklist of Early-Nineteenth-Century Gothic Bluebooks,' *Cardiff Corvey*, 9 (December 2002).

11. Forgotten Decade

The Fate of Sedley (1795), *Probable Incidents; or, Scenes in Life* (1797), *Mad Man of the Mountain* (1799), and *Jaqueline of Olzeburg; or Final Retribution* (1800) were each fairly innocuous, but Summersett's *Martyn of Fenrose*, a novel that included damnation and murder, was attacked as blasphemous. It was followed by his melodramatic *The Worst of Stains* (1804), which began with seduction, insanity and suicide, and became a slow-burn of corrosive jealousy and would-be adultery, reflecting his interest in Shakespeare.

Irish-born Henrietta Rouviere (?–834, after her marriage in 1806 Henrietta Mosse), moved to London in 1802 and 1803, publishing novels from 1804 beginning with *Lussington Abbey*. Her *The Old Irish Baronet* (1808) was based on Clara Reeve's *The Old English Baron*. It begins with a tale of bones rising from graves, but that is given to a butler of 'absurd credulity' (1). The landowner, Sir Thomas O'Callaghan, doubts tales of fairies. His daughter, Ellen, is presented as natural, but that is seen not as a route to edginess of some type, but, rather, as a positive critique of fashionability. Moreover, Ellen is devout:

> … she commenced her repast, with the appetite, not of a fine lady, labouring under the distinguishing traits of vapour and spleen, a martyr to the fashionable overthrow of rational hours, but with a degree of hunger perfectly *roturier* with the zest of a vulgar healthy country lass, who could boast of seeing the sun shine every day it was visible, and ever – O disgraceful reflection on a young lady of quality! even behold its majestic appearance in the east, and watch its western decline from her bed-room windows, as she prayed to its great Author [God], and retired to her peaceful pillow without once dreaming of illuminated halls, nightly dinners, thronged assemblies, or morning suppers! (1)

Ellen tells her father that it is said that the gigantic bones will not rest in peace till the lawful heirs of these dead are discovered. The butler thinks them the bones of Lord Duncarty and his Spanish wife, and that their son was carried off by the fairies, and there is talk of the old castle and the old chapel. A pro-Catholic theme continues in that the baronet is happy to meet Father Dunlavie, the French-speaking priest:

> It is not a man's religion that will send him to Heaven, or keep him out of it – It is his deeds here that will determine his fate hereafter; and a good man, of whatever sect, is acceptable in the sight of God. (I,1)

However, the heir, Edward Newburgh from England, enunciates a very different doctrine, that of absentee landownership, which is presented by Rouviere/Mosse as very unattractive (I,8). As part of the challenge of the new, the baronet has lost his long-held seat in Parliament due to the Acts of Union of 1800, as a result of which the Dublin Parliament merged with the Westminster one in 1801; and all is volatile. In this context, Rouviere/Mosse quotes Edmund Burke, giving Doctor Clayfield the lines:

> The spirit of prying analysis that now stalks abroad, searching to spy into all things, nay, even into the hidden things of God, is, I fear, equally pernicious in politics as in religion. If men were wise, they would content themselves, as the illustrious Burke advises, "to understand it according to their measure, and to venerate where they are not able to understand." (I,9)

He presses on to praise a constitution that goes back to the Magna Carta (1215), but that leads to a riposte that, instead, (rightly but anachronistically) criticizes the Magna Carta as not benefiting 'the mass of the people,' and focuses, instead, on the Glorious Revolution of 1688, with the argument that England had no proper constitution till then:

> Let us not evoke the bugbear of antiquity to oppose the practical amelioration.... The present degree of perfection to which the structure of public weal has attained, is the result of successive improvements, and the farther we trace back our steps ... the nearer we come to those times when barbarism and servitude went hand in hand.

The first volume ends with a rational explanation of the bones appearing above the ground: They had been disinterred in the search for treasure. However, the second volume leads in a new direction with the translation of documents found in a casket revealing that the late Spanish-born Lady Duncarty had been led by her confessor and was terrified by the 'White Boys,' Irish 'banditti,' whom she feared had abducted her infant boy (II,2). This is no defence of medievalism.

> A medieval setting was the case with Jane Harvey's *The Castle of Tynemouth: a Tale* (1806), which has an evil Countess in control of a castle where her victims are imprisoned. Set in England, and not on the Continent, there are charges of sorcery and a presence of the supernatural, albeit an indistinct one as in 'what appeared to be a phantom'; alongside the subterranean passages and vaults that are part of a system of imprisonment. The resolution explains the apparent supernatural, and a character is revealed to be a Marquis; both customary features of such novels. This was an aspect of the repeated settings of Gothic novels in castles or abbeys, but yet very different to much of the medievalism of the following decades, for example the novels of Catherine Ward published from 1810, notably *The Castle of Villeroy* (1827) and *The Knight of the White Banner* (1827).

The standard repertoire of images is seen anew in George Brewer's *The Witch of Ravensworth* (1808). This provided readers with the villainous Baron de La Braunch who, in order to marry Lady Alwena, wishes to remove his wife and son and, to that end and to secure his wife's inheritance, recruits a witch who has sold her soul. As with *The Monk*, the Baron plunges into evil, including murder. He is persuaded by the witch into making a satanic pledge that brings immediate success, but no happiness. *Macbeth* is clearly in the background, not least with demonic rituals on show. A miscellaneous writer, Brewer did not produce other Gothic works.

The most dramatic writer of the 1800s was the somewhat mysterious Charlotte Dacre (c. 1772 – 1825), who published four novels from 1805 to 1811: *Confessions of the Nun of St Omer* (1805); *Zofloya; or, The Moor: A Romance of the Fifteenth Century* (1806); *The Libertine* (1807); and *The Passions* (1811). The titles themselves captured what authors and booksellers thought likely to appeal, and *Zofloya* certainly did, being translated into French and German, as well as appearing, in a shorter form, as *The Daemon of Venice* (1810), one of the chapbooks that further helped disseminate Gothic titles. Percy Bysshe Shelley was a fan of *Zofloya*, and Dacre's work also influenced Byron. There is an edginess in all Dacre's novels, in none of which the female protagonists end well, for example the seduction in her *Confessions of the Nun of St Omer*, one combining libertine energy, convent titillation, and a Gothic reworking; and this edginess helps keep the reader interested.

Zofloya, however, was the wildest of her novels, in that it presents a murderously lustful female protagonist and a trans-racial dynamic toward the close; although the latter element is less to the fore than the former. Nightmare provides a lengthy and vivid explanation in *Zofloya*. Shaken by violent sensations and believing 'herself under the influence of some superior and unknown power,' Victoria, in a 'disturbed slump,' finds 'dreams of mysterious tendency.' Sexual envy of Lilla and Henriquez leads 'the most horrible and raging pains' to shoot through her heart, and she discerns 'a group of shadowy features … of a deadly paleness' hovering in mid-air, amongst whom is Zofloya, a majestic Moor, who extends his arms to her, filling her with terror. Her horror at the imminent marriage of Lilla and Henriquez leads Victoria to accept the Moor's promise to stop it in return for being his:

> In an instance *she* occupied the place of Lilla; and Lilla, no longer the blooming maid, but a pallid spectre, fled shrieking through the aisles of the church, while Berenza [Victoria's unwanted husband], suddenly wounded by an invisible hand, sunk covered with blood at the foot of the altar! Exaltation filled the bosom of Victoria; she attempted to take the hand of Henriques; but casting her eyes upon him, she beheld him changed to a frightful skeleton, and in terror awoke! (17)

The seductive Zofloya is very different to Shakespeare's Othello. 'Towering as a demi-god' (22), Zofloya provides Victoria with poisons to remove the unwanted. He is ready to follow up with further violence, as in the vivid killing of an elderly woman not yet dead from the poison that has been administered: 'stooping over the struggling unfortunate, he compressed her withered throat with his dark hand, and the sounds, half-formed, rattled within it' (23).

11. Forgotten Decade

Victoria's descent from spoilt childhood to an insane willfulness is captured in what becomes a living nightmare for her and others:

> the wild gloom seemed to suit the dark and ferocious passions of her soul. She gave way to the chain of thought that came pressing on her mind, her heart was anarchy and lust of crime, and regretted that she had suffered till now, the existence of aught between her and her desired happiness ... buoying herself up to frenzy, she admitted no reflection of danger.

To a contemporary critic, Victoria's evil descent might appear an affirmation of agency, but the moral span was clear in the tale, and it becomes more so as the crisis accelerates. More generally, a moral approach is offered by Dacre, who frames the book in terms of 'causes' and 'effects,' with sin the common element, an element that provides both plot and interest. The first paragraph begins with a conventional rejection of chronology:

> The historian who would wish his lessons to sink deep into the heart, thereby essaying to render mankind virtuous and more happy, must not content himself with simply detailing a series of events – he must ascertain causes, and follow progressively their effects.

The last paragraph of the book offered a reprise, not least with the direct address:

> Reader – consider not this as a romance merely. – Over their passions and their weaknesses, mortals cannot keep a curb too strong. The progress of vice is gradual and imperceptible, and the arch enemy ever to take advantage of the failings of mankind, whose destruction is his glory! That his seductions may prevail, we dare not doubt; for can we otherwise account for those crimes, dreadful and repugnant to nature, which human beings are sometimes tempted to commit? Either we must suppose that the love of evil is born with us (which would be an insult to the Deity), or we must attribute them (as appears

more consonant with reason) to the suggestions of infernal influence. (33)

The last consideration, on the source of evil, was a traditional one, and, aside from the narrative energy, helped explain the struggle over sin in the novel, and the role in it of Providence as well as Satan. Moreover, the digression from the fate of Victoria toward the close, so as to cover the deaths of earlier characters – her mother, Laurina, Megalina Strozzi, and her brother, Leonardo, served to underline the theme of choices causing a descent. These choices owed much to over-indulgence and related sinfulness, an approach also seen in *The Monk*. This again was an approach that might seem conservative, Dacre writing:

> lavish and imprudent was the fondness bestowed by the parents upon their idolized off-spring – boundless and weak was the indulgence for ever shown to them. The youthful parents little comprehended the extent of the mischief they were doing: to see their wayward children happy, their infantine and lovely faces undisfigured by tears or vexation, was a pleasure too great to be resigned, from the distant reflection of future evil possible to accrue from the indulgence (1).

Edmund Burke had already captured the sense of values as under challenge in the *Reflections*, in a much-cited passage that set the tone for much Gothic fiction:

> the age of chivalry is gone. – that of sophisters, economists, and calculators, has succeeded; and the glory of Europe is extinguished forever. Never, never more, shall we behold that generous loyalty to rank and sex, that proud submission, that dignified obedience, that subordination of the heart, which kept alive, even in servitude itself, the spirit of an exalted freedom. The unbought grace of life, the nurse of manly sentiment and heroic enterprise is gone!

Similar arguments were frequently repeated. Thus, the Reverend Edward Nares, in a sermon preached in 1797, on a day of public thanksgivings for

11. Forgotten Decade

British naval victories, contrasted the correct use of information with what he presented as the destructive secular philosophy of present-mindedness:

> From the first invention of letters, by means of which the history of past ages has been transmitted to us, and the actions of our forefathers preserved, it has ever been the wisdom of man, under all circumstances of public and general concern, to refer to these valuable records, as the faithful depositaries of past experience, and to deduce from thence by comparison of situations, whatever might conduce to his instruction, consolidation, or hope. Thither the statesman of the present day frequently recurs for the conduct and support of the commonwealth.... Thither ... the religious man ... bent upon tracing the finger of God in all concerns of importance to the good and welfare of man, is pleased to discover, in the course of human events, a direction marvellously conducive to the final purposes of Heaven, the constant and eternal will of God, and continually illustrative of his irresistible supremacy, his over-ruling Providence ... the enemy begin their operations on the pretended principle of giving perfect freedom to the mind of man ... the first step to be taken in vindication of such a principle is to discard all ancient opinions as prejudices.[3]

Another impressive Gothic novel of the first decade of the nineteenth century was *Fatal Revenge or The Family of Montorio* (1807) by Charles Maturin (1782–1824), an Irish (Protestant) curate who taught and wrote as ways to raise additional funds, mostly famously producing *Melmoth the Wanderer* (1820), a classic account of an outsider. *The Albigenses* (1824) brought in werewolves. Aside from anti-Catholic sermons, Maturin produced plays, notably the highly successful *Bertram, or The Castle of St Aldobrand* (1816), which involved a monastery, a storm and Satan.

Maturin's preface to *Fatal Revenge* suggested that the subjects of contemporary novels and romances 'are calculated to unlock every store of

---

3   Edward Nares, *A Sermon, Preached at Parish Church of Shobdon in the County of Hereford, December 19, 1797*.

fancy and of feeling,' and that he had founded 'the interest of a Romance on the passion of supernatural fear.' The story, set near Naples in the late seventeenth century, contained the range of secrets, family rivalry, usurpation, a ruined chapel, a deserted part of a castle, ghosts, a strange light, a mysterious, empty tomb, a tolling bell, 'livid streaks of blood' (3), a vampire, a monk with a great secret who had disappeared (5), homosexuality (9), and mysteries. Visiting a chamber where murder had taken place, always a place of foreboding, Annibal sees:

> the figure of an armed man in the tapestry, whose bold and prominent outlines rendered it even strongly visible in that dim light. A weapon which it held, was pointed in the direction I was about to explore; the head was thrown back, and the features of a strong profile were fixed on the same direction. As I gazed on it, the large eye appeared to live; it moved; it looked at me; it turned to the spot, to which the arm pointed, and the arm vibrated with a slow and palpable motion ... I became inflamed, impelled, exalted; a certain supernatural dignity mingled with my feelings, I felt myself the summoned agent of destiny, yet not the less did I feel that I was surrounded by horrors; that I was treading where the living inhabited not; that I was called by voices nature shudders to hear. But they appeared to me the instruments by which I was appointed to work out some great purpose, and I grasped them with a convulsed but daring hand (10).

Tapestries were frequently troubling. In this case, a fracture in the wall yields to pressure, reveals a door, thence a cavity, and a chest that contains a skeleton: 'Murder hurtled in mine ears' (10), that of his uncle. Uncles were a frequent presence in Gothic novels, and often as figures of menace. The isolation Annibal then feels is one of so many in these novels. Not only is there a physical threat, but also a challenge of scale and ability, and one that is carefully linked to the pace of the novel:

> That momentary courage, which the emergency had invested me with, seemed suddenly to desert me. I looked around me: two lonely beings, shuddering over a discovery which conveyed

11. Forgotten Decade

nothing but terror to them, by the dim evening light, in the remote and long-deserted towers of an ancient castle, far from the comfort of human aid or presence.... The confidence of the delegate of heaven was over: I felt myself a timid human being, encompassed by things, and the fear of things, which nature shrinks from.... In our hurried passage through the cabinets and chamber, we walked with silent and breathless fear. (10)

The next night, Annibal sets out for the supposed tomb of Count Orazio. We are soon in the world of a mysterious light, a 'dark gigantic figure,' and 'a strange motion in the air ... like a charnel-stream.' The novel provided very different accounts of time, with a monk who is vampirish and 'cannot walk in the light of noon... "I have a darker tale to tell than the owl that sits on the desolate ruin; than the raven that beats heavily at the window of the dying."' When asked where his soul had gone, the monk replies with reference to the omnipotence of evil:

I must not tell, nor could you hear the secrets of the world of shadows; my taskers, who are ever around me, would flash upon your sight, and sweep me away before you, if I told their employment. The bare sight of them would shrivel you to dust, and heap this massy tower in fragments over your head.

In a rejection of previous accounts, he continues:

no visions of moon-struck fancy; no paintings of the dying murderer; no imaginings of religious horror have touched upon the confines of the world of woe.

In the meanwhile, Nelson's victory over the Franco-Spanish fleet at Trafalgar in 1805 did not end anxiety about national security. Indeed coalitions constructed with British help to fight Napoleon collapsed into defeat in 1807 and 1809. In the former year, Commodore Sir Home Popham of the navy worried that the French could invade Ireland from Lisbon.[4] More

---

4   Popham to Viscount Melville, 23 November 1807, BL. Loan 57/108 folio 19.

seriously, fear of invasion from France and the French-occupied Low Countries led to the unsuccessful and very costly attack on Walcheren in 1809, as part of an attempt to destroy the dockyards at Antwerp. Separately, the number of Gothic novels set in Spain, during the period of British warfare against, or in, Spain from 1796 to 1813, indicated contemporary interest in Spain, but also the continued resonance of the moral and social threats and interest apparently posed by the Inquisition and by bandits. Anti-Catholicism remained significant in British thought.[5]

A decline in the number and significance of Gothic novels in the 1810s has since been discerned. Then, the historical novel offered a different approach, not least to the Middle Ages, as in Jane Porter's *The Scottish Chiefs* (1810), about William Wallace (1270–1305), a key figure in the struggle for Scottish independence. Nevertheless, the decade began with more Gothic novels, including George Lipscomb's *The Grey Friar, and the Black Spirit of the Wye* (1810), and Augustus Jacob Crandolph's *The Mysterious Hand; Or, Subterranean Horrors* (1811). The former, by a doctor and local historian, offered an account of medieval England in which the benign Bolebec family are good aristocrats, but 'tyranny and despotism were too generally the sinews of power,' while 'the habitations of the nobles afforded, in general, a dreary or melancholy scene of gloomy pomp or revengeful cruelty … suggesting to all who approached it the horrid ideas of chains, imprisonment, and torture' (1). Sir Hugh de Bolebec was 'among those patriotic nobles who laid the foundation of English liberty' by obtaining Magna Carta from King John in 1215. However, there is condemnation of 'the turbulent Barons' who opposed Henry III (r. 1216–72), as well as praise for his son, the future Edward I, who Hugh de Bolebec is implausibly still alive to serve. The medieval essence of English Gothicism comes in for criticism:

> The feudal times were alike unfavourable to the cultivation of science, and dangerous to domestic conduct. Wealth and power have been, in every age, almost synonymous; – in those times

[5] Angela Wright, 'Spain in Gothic Fiction,' in Diego Saglia and Ian Haywood (eds),, *Spain in British Romanticism 1800–1840* (Basingstoke, 2018), pp. 177–94.

11. Forgotten Decade

they were truly so. Power constituted riches, and the plunder of the defenceless or unprotected was considered a kind of prowess, which, however barbarous, was far from disgraceful. There was no idea of virtue attached to compassion or humanity; and even the severest cruelties were overlooked, in the boldness of the enterprises which led to them. (1)

There is also hostility toward the Church:

devotion was insisted upon as a mystic rite, to be performed with awful and submissive exactness, without one word of inquiry into those sublime mysteries, of which the priests represented themselves to be the sacred depositaries. (1)

In contrast to Lipscomb's *The Grey Friar*, Crandolph presented a full-throated Gothic horror novel set in France in which improbability was to the fore. The ruthless Count Egfryd, a libertine and villain who, nevertheless, has many qualities, including being brilliant and handsome, seeks to wreak vengeance on Theodore Dalbert and his beloved, Julia Bolton. The plot sees classic themes, such as a skeleton, a mysterious corpse, and incest, but also more original, indeed ridiculous, sites for villainy including a balloon and a booby-trapped island. In Crandolph's words, and offering a classical image of horror, one that was to attract J.M.W. Turner in his painting *Ulysses Deriding Polyphemus* (1829), there is 'a cavern more horrible than that of the Cyclops.' As in a number of eighteenth-century novels, the hero, Theodore, is framed for murder.

The religious context of *The Mysterious Hand* was very clear, and the Gothic was presented as a positive aspect of this, with the identity brought out clearly in the reference to:

the Gothic chapel ... a place to inspire sentiments of religious fervour, to humble the pretensions of human pride, to extinguish frivolity, and to dissipate the clouds of arrogance and selfishness. A venerable and awful gloom prevailed in every part of it.... The dim rays of coloured light that entered it through the variegated casements partook of the austerity of the building.

The symbols of revelation, the hallowed signs of Christian mysteries, and the sufferings of the martyrs and of their God, that every where met the eye in this consecrated spot, might awaken sentiments of piety in an apostate, or fill the atheist with terror (II,1).

The idea of terror, like horror, as being specific in its impact on individuals in this fashion was one that was more generally valid for the religious context. In this particular case, the varied implications and links of places were taken further by noting that the chapel both 'communicated with heaven' and 'threatened hell.' The altar is 'sublime.' At the same time, evil threatened:

Man of faith, beneath those hallowed vaults our enemy is hidden, gnashing his teeth with agony at their happiness, and seeking to seduce thee from righteousness and heaven to the path of utter and everlasting torment ... it is Satan that invites, and if thou hearken to him, damnation will be thy lot. (II,1)

There is praise from Crandolph for Catholicism, not least the link with saints, and criticism for the 'Reformation, if properly so called' (II,1), as well as for the secular Enlightenment: 'the ignorant Sceptick with all his vanity, or the empty Philosophist with all his petulance' (II,1). This is very much Crandolph following Henry Fielding in commenting directly on the novel. This was a process that the Gothic story made readily easy, but it was at the cost of breaching the dynamics of the story, and the claustrophobic atmosphere which the novelist sought to create. For example:

It is not my wish to dwell on minute or unimportant facts. If I ever err in this respect, I err unintentionally, and I would now land my personages in England, without further delay, impatient as I am to enter on the principal event of my history, but for an incident that occurred aboard their ship, not less terrible than it was singular. (II,3)

Or, again,

11. Forgotten Decade

Here might I pause! I have already passed over many leagues of land and water, my personages have suffered sundry misfortunes. Scenes of horror and events of mystery have employed me. I have travelled through France .... but the most difficult part of my performance is not yet begun.... I narrate nothing but what may be proved ... I have to record a true history.... . (II,3)

Crandolph certainly shows a characteristic of all Gothic fiction, namely that of finding meaning beyond the materialist. Indeed, he criticizes those who 'see in man and nature matter alone, dull and sluggish matter' (II,1). This is totally different from the later 'Condition of England' novels, notably those from the 1840s by Charles Dickens, Elizabeth Gaskell and Charlotte Brontë with their engagement with inequality.

Like many heroines, Julia faces nightmares, dreaming for example of approaches by the Count Egfryd:

Against the presumption of his manner she tried to frown, to shriek, but her muscles refused their office, her rebellious organ denied a sound, and she seemed to suffer a total revolt of her limbs and senses. (II,1)

This is not assault by Dracula, but Julia, poisoned by the Count, had raved. This raving leads her in the direction of Dracula:

She had heard of the vampire and the hag of night, and she had read of incubus and incantation. Witchcraft and drugs, the philtres of vitious love, and the imps of perdition, opiates, charms, and conjurations, passed in a rapid and revolting series through her thoughts. (II,1)

As with Van Helsing in *Dracula*, Julia turns to a crucifix, though, like a heroine of the eighteenth century, she also relies on 'sentiment' and 'sensibility.' The fears of night seen in other Gothic novels also assail Julia, who therefore secures her door carefully, and scrutinize her chamber, establishing that there was no place of concealment nor secret door, and that the tapestry does not conceal any entry. However, Julia finds a hollow space above part of the ceiling, a space linked to devilry in the past:

> The subject painted on it was the apparition evoked by the hag of Endor for Saul. The ground was black, and along the edge of the witch's drapery, she, at length, by dint of examination, discovered something like a crevice

which turns out to be part of a secret door. Despite suspicious sounds, Julia survives the night, but is left contemplating: 'what evil was there that might not be dreaded from the courage, the arts, and the villainy of the Count?' (II,1). The 'hag of Endor' is not a happy reference, as, in the Old Testament, she had castigated King Saul for disobeying God and accurately predicted his defeat and death at the hands of the Philistines. The story, which included the ghost of Samuel, led to some glosses about diabolical role. Much quoted by John Wesley, both Benjamin West and William Blake depicted the episode on canvas, although it did not have the power and theatricality of Macbeth and the witches.

In *The Mysterious Hand*, Theodore meanwhile, imprisoned in a cavern, faces the challenge of possible seduction by Marie de Solase, who is a murderess: 'The deformity of her character was legible in every feature of her face.... He felt remorse at his own immorality. His seducer was ... unfeminine' (II,2). Theodore tries to escape by following an underground river in the dark, an episode that reflects the growing geological exploration and interest of the period. The account offers an unfamiliar 'sublime':

> ... he hears a noise of a thousand cataracts, louder than the loudest thunders of the torrid zone, tumbling impetuously, and roaring with infernal violence among the rocky passages below. A spray like a heavy shower of rain falls upon him. Torrent against torrent, gulph within gulph, horror on horror, blackness and solitude, despair and death, interminable extent, incalculable ruin, and a depth to the very bowels of the earth; all that experience can furnish of most perilous, all that the imagination supply of most dreadful, what man avoids, and what nature hides, were there. (II,2)

11. Forgotten Decade

In a classic instance of what in Britain and America was to be called the 'Boy's own style' of children's adventure fiction, the slate on which Theodore is resting collapses under his weight, and both fall into the abyss, only for Theodore, after recommending his soul to mercy, catching 'most providentially' a remaining part of the ledge, from which he reaches safety. From there, he takes refuge in a recess, only, due to a collapse, to be buried 'alive in a untimely and abhorred sepulchre.' Yet he escapes 'by a sudden and powerful exertion' (II,2). Rescued, Theodore takes a boat to England, only to be thrown into the Bay of Biscay by an agent of the Count who hooks a leaden weight to his coat. However, as we subsequently discover, the heaviness of the weight leads to it being detached from the coat, and Theodore is able to catch onto a coop that has been thrown overboard, and is then rescued by a British vessel. His rescue is attributed to Heaven's protection.

In England, Theodore is wrongly accused of murder, which provides Crandolph with an opportunity to launch a bitter attack on capital punishment, 'a bloody code found on cruelty, supported by ignorance, and extended by tyranny!,' and then, more generally, to proclaim a call for reform:

> Alas! How weakly do reason and virtue oppose, how slowly do they conquer prejudice and violence? If we look into the page [sic] of history, what does it disclose? A tissue of craft, rapine, slaughter and imbecility. Each revolution has discovered, and published, and derided the errors and the absurdities of the age preceding it: and we, at this day and in this kingdom, wonder at the laws of Draco, the existence of slavery, the institution of the Holy Office, at the use of the rack, at the trials by ordeal and by battle, at the acquittal by compurgation, and at the mortal penalty of witchcraft. We wonder at these excesses of superstition, at these mistakes of polity; and we deplore their evil effects; but we are blind to the barbarism, and savageness of our own institution. (II,5)

The anonymous *Allan the Freebooter, or, The Witch of Glenross* (no date, c.1810) had a castle as well as a witch, who demands worship: 'tear that brilliant cross from thy bosom, trample it under thy feet – then kneel and worship me!," and screams in a demonic fashion.

The decade continued with more Gothic novels, not least *Barozzi; or, The Venetian Sorceress* (1815), *Theresa; or, The Wizard's Fate* (1815), Jane Harvey's *Brougham Castle* (1816) and Selina Davenport's, *An Angel's Form and a Devil's Heart* (1818), and these were recognizably different in type to historical romances of a melodramatic character, such as Alicia LeFanu's *Strathaldan* (1816), which shares a concern with inheritance and family strains, but not in such a lurid fashion.[6]

Isaac Crookenden (1779–1809) was very interested in Italian settings, as in *The Skeleton; or, Mysterious Discovery* (1805), *Fatal Secrets; or, Etherlinda de Salmoni. A Sicilian Story* (1806); *Horrible Revenge or The Monster of Italy!! A Romance of the Sixteenth Century* (1806); *Dalmanutha; or, The Monster of Venice*; *The Mysterious Murder; or, The Usurper of Naples* (1827); and *Spectre of the Turret: or Guolto Castle* (1815). Sceloni, a monk who imprisons the hero (typically a foundling) in a dungeon, gives the title to Crookenden's *The Vindictive Monk; or, The Fatal Ring* (1802), the last in *Romantic Tales*, a book of his work that included *The Revengeful Turk; or, Mystic Cavern* and *The Distressed Nun*. Morality was central to his fiction, and there was particular concern about incest.

A title that aimed to cover several bases, *The Spectre of Lanmere Abbey* (1820), was the work of Sarah Scudgell Wilkinson (1779–1831), who produced many chapbooks and children's fiction, as well as running a circulating library and being a teacher. A precarious existence saw her receiving financial support from the Royal Literary Fund from 1818, but only just avoiding debtors' prison and dying in a workhouse. Wilkinson's works included a number of Gothic tales, not least *The Subterraneous Passage; or, Gothic Cell* (1803), *The Spectre; or, the Ruins of Belfont Priory* (1806), *The Fugitive Countess; or, Convent of St Ursula* (1807), *The Castle of Montabino; or, the Orphan Sisters* (1809), *The Convent of Grey Penitients: or, the Apostate Nun* (1810), *The Priory of St Clair: or, Spectre of the Murdered Nun, a Gothic Tale* (1811), and *The Eve of St Mark; or, the Mysterious Spectre* (1820). In *The Subterraneous Passage*, a sinister governess and her ally, a bandit leader, kidnap an aristocratic girl and force her into marriage. In *Priory of St Clair*, Lewis, Count de Valvé, having failed to persuade Julietta, a nun, to elope with him, gives her

---

6 Anna Fitzer, 'Fashionable Connections: Alicia LeFanu and Writing from the Edge,' *Romanticism*, 24 (2018), pp. 179–90.

a drink that, unbeknownst to her, simulates death, takes her coffin, and, when she awakens and refuses him, forces himself on her. Julietta later tries to flee her new role as mistress, only for Lewis to stop her in the castle chapel and kill her at the altar, a particular site for sacrilegious horror. He is then haunted by her ghost, which helps lead to his eventual exposure. Repeatedly in Wilkinson's novels, there are harsh husbands and selfishly neglectful fathers, and it is wives and daughters who are victims. Women are often imprisoned, as in *The Fugitive Countess*, in which the Count's first wife and their daughter are held prisoner in an underground prison.[7]

Gothic chapbooks, bluebooks, and ballads, with the shorter and more streamlined stories they offered, represented a way to make money and an offering that provided a way to extend literature to an expanding readership provided by the growth in population, disposable income, and literacy. This readership matched the expansion from the 1810s of an unstamped newspaper press,[8] as well as the legitimate press. Excluding Ireland, the population rose from 10.5 million in 1801 to 20.8 million in 1851, while, aside from this major aggregate growth, the per capita readership of newspapers rose from the later 1830s.[9] Meanwhile, entrepreneurial publishers, such as Ann Lemoine[10] and Thomas Tegg, played a major role in developing the chapbook industry, which testified, like so much of the industrialisation and culture of the period, to both supply and demand, and provided the basis for the subsequent growth of popular fiction.

---

[7]   Franz Potter, 'Writing for the Spectre of Poverty. Exhuming Sarah Wilkinson's Bluebooks and Novels,' *Cardiff Corvey: Reading the Romantic Text*, 11 (2003).

[8]   Joel Wiener, *Unstamped British Periodicals 1830–1836* (Ithaca, New York, 1969); Patricia Hollis, *The Pauper Press* (Oxford, 1970).

[9]   David Mitch, *The Rise of Popular Literature in Victorian England. The Influence of Private Choice and Public Policy* (Philadelphia, Penn., 1992); John Jordan and Robert Patten (eds), *Literature in the Marketplace. Nineteenth-Century Publishing and Reading Practices* (Cambridge, 1995).

[10] Roy Bearden-White, *How the Wind Sits: The History of Henry and Ann Lemoine, Chapbook Writers and Publishers of the Late Eighteenth Century* (2017).

12. AND SO TO FRANKENSTEIN

For Sir Walter Scott, it was Radcliffe's *The Mysteries of Udolpho* that was the obvious point of reference and comparison when assessing Gothic novels. Alongside this sense of change from the 1790s (for *Waverley* was published in 1814) *Frankenstein* (1818), very differently, also registered change. Scott began his book with a process of reflection:

> Had I, for example, announced in my frontispiece, "Waverley, a Tale of Other Days," must not every novel-reader have anticipated a castle scarce less than that of Udolpho, of which the eastern wing had long been uninhabited, and the keys either lost, or consigned to the care of some aged butler or housekeeper, whose trembling steps, about the middle of the second volume, were doomed to guide the hero, or heroine, to the ruinous precincts? Would not the owl have shrieked and cricket cried in my very title-page? (1)

Scott's first novel, *Waverley* (1814), was one he could have taken in any direction, and was set in recent history, at the time of the '45. This was the Highlands without any spooky mystery, and a more powerful novel because of its well-etched setting. In part, there is an element of the strength of the Scottish Enlightenment. It is certainly noteworthy that Scotland did not have many troubling, indeed macabre, Gothic novels parallel to those of England and Ireland. The poet James Hogg drew on Border superstitions, notably spirits that are able to abduct people, and the particular hazard of Halloween, for his *The Brownie of Bodsbeck* (1818), his first novel, again an historical one. However, most of his works did not take this direction.

Border superstitions in the shape of fairy people play a role in Jane Harvey's *Brougham Castle: a Novel* (1816). This English work had similarities with other Gothic novels, being set in the past, in this case 1636, and in a (fictional) castle, and involves issues of paternity, mysterious relationships, and malign Catholic clerics. At the same time, the historical background was modest in its impact, and the supernatural slight and unthreatening, there was scant physical threat, and the novel's focus on Anglo-Irish family links and tensions really looks toward standard themes in the Victorian novel. And far more so than *Frankenstein*.

Waverley helped popularize the historical novel as a major form, not least in terms of the apparent authority of male authors.[1] In turn, this process had an impact on the representation and reputation of Gothic novels. With *Ivanhoe* (1819), which had a very different setting to *Waverley*, Scott also turned the medieval away from its standard Gothic presentation. At the same time, the development of historicism and historical consciousness helped establish a boundary athwart the easy Gothic reading from past crimes to present discontents. Yet fiction and formal historical work sought in part differently to bridge the divide, in part employing plotting and imagination to those ends.[2]

Historical novels located in British history became increasingly common in the 1810s, with *Ivanhoe* published as part of an upsurge in medievalism, which was to include the word *medieval* replacing *Gothic* in many contexts.[3] This element also ensured that romance sat alongside the Gothic, as in Anne Ker's *Edric, the Forester: Or, the Mysteries of the Haunted Chamber. An Historical Romance* (1817), a work that includes the villainous Lord Fitzosric whose Castle St Egbert contains the ghost of his first wife, Lady Jane, imprisoned women whom he seeks to seduce, the real Lady Jane, who pretends to be a ghost in order to haunt Fitzosric, and Edric, who is the true heir to Castle St Egbert, which he gains at the close, also marrying one of the women Fitzosric has tried to seduce. This was an example of the Gothic Romance novels that were so significant in the 1810s.

---

1   Ina Ferris, *The Achievement of Literary Authority: Gender, History and the Waverley Novels* (1991).
2   Porscha Fermanis and John Regan (eds), *Rethinking British Romantic History, 1770–1845* (Oxford, 2014).
3   Michael Alexander, *Medievalism: The Middle Ages in Modern England* (New Haven, Conn., 2007).

In contrast, and typically set on the Continent, *Barozzi; or the Venetian Sorceress* (1815) by Catherine Smith introduced a mysterious sorceress, with much of the action set in sixteenth-century Venice. Demon-conjuring plays a role, but, on the Radcliffe pattern, the supernatural is held at bay in a moral close. Set in Naples, George Soane's *The Eve of St Marco* (1813) had the habitually evil monks, the Inquisition, and, oppressed by a tyrannical father, a young aristocrat who becomes a bandit, an occupation that can cover the gamut from villainy to the hero pursuing freedom. The characterization and dialogue are scarcely subtle, and clichés come apace.

In contrast, *An Angel's Form and a Devil's Heart* (1818) by Selina Davenport (1779–1859) offered more. A prolific novelist, her eleven novels, published between 1813 and 1834, reflected her need for money after she separated from her husband. The title might suggest a Gothic character, but this was set in contemporary England and, in many respects, was a conventional novel about social relationships, albeit with some limited Gothic features far from the supernatural, notably a secret marriage and related parentage. The extent to which the Devil could refer to much more than Satan was very clear from this novel. There was also the classic affirmation of Christian values, as with a Dean's remark at the christening of Edward Mackenzie: 'He is now become a Christian; Providence will not desert him – his destiny is in the hands of Heaven' (2), the sort of line cited by Hannah More. The two shudders of horror experienced by Edward at the funeral of his grandmother Margaret are conventional in their cause, relating as they do to contact with her dead body: looking at it before burial and touching 'the cold, cold hand' (11). This was a publication at the Minerva Press that was far from the edge. The shaming of sin was more to the point than its Satanism.

A benign supernaturalism was offered by Scott in *The Monastery: a Romance* (1820), his novel that followed *Ivanhoe*. Largely set at the fictional Monastery of Kennaquhair, which may well have been based on Melrose Abbey, this is an account of the Scottish Reformation that prominently includes the spectral White Lady of Avenel based on Friedrich de la Motte Fouqué's romance *Undine* (1811). In one of the more dramatic passages, the White Lady leads the hero to a fairy cavern where he takes the Bible from an unconsuming fire. There was no comparable figure in *The Abbot* (1820), the sequel and his next novel, which was set in the days of Mary Queen of Scots.

12. And So to Frankenstein

Mary Shelley was to provide a largely new edginess. In the 1804 Royal Academy exhibition, Fuseli had shown *The Rosicrucian Cavern* (1803), a painting which depicted the tomb of Christian Rosencreutz protected by an automaton. While this looked to the potential of machinery, automata were longstanding devices, and the Rosicrucians were an eighteenth-century movement.[4] Somewhat differently, Joshua Pickersgill's novel *The Three Brothers* (1803) had a role for the Devil, who provides Arnaud, a suffering hunchback, with a new, perfect body.[5] Mary Shelley read this soon before starting work on *Frankenstein* (1818). This novel might appear to look forward to the potential of scientific application and industrial society, but Mary Shelley also drew on a number of traditions and deployed a range of generic devices. This potential was increasingly asserted in the new age of steam, but was not restricted to it. Thus, on 2 July 1824, the first issue of the *North Devon Journal* announced:

> It is this desire for quick and incessant intercourse that has arisen in this kingdom within the last half a century, that has tended so much to increase our power as a nation.... The grand lever in all these astonishing inventions has been the press; for while with our steam engines we smile at the winds and disregard the operation of the ties, with the press we surpass the power of Archimedes; for we actually lift the universe – not the material world, certainly, but the world of thought – of mind – of conception! And by this power we shall be enabled, eventually, to overcome all the obstacles which prevent the great family of mankind from uniting cordially in the bonds of affection and brotherhood.

The context of *Frankenstein* was not only such developments, but also more specific literary interests against a troubled political background. Mary

---

4 Marie Roberts, 'Mary Shelley: Immortality, Gender and the Rosy Cross,' in Philip W. Martin and Robin Jarvis (eds), *Reviewing Romanticism* (New York, 1992), pp. 60–68.
5 Laura Kremmel, 'Suddenly Monstrous: Gothic Configurations of Disability and Justice in Joshua Pickersgill Jr's *The Three Brothers*,' *European Romantic Review*, 27 (2016), pp. 639–58.

Shelley (1797–1851), the daughter of radical writers, came to precocity and maturity as radicalism enjoyed a revival from the problems in which it had been cast by association with the French Revolution. The world of print proved particularly the source and means of opposition and radical arguments. Indeed, in 1812, William Brougham told the radical critic Leigh Hunt that the press was the real opposition to the Tory ministry of Robert Jenkinson, 2nd Earl of Liverpool. Although there was criticism in Gothic novels of the corrupt use of power, their writers were not really members of the 'radical underworld.'[6]

The overthrow of Napoleon, first in 1814, and then definitively in 1815, made the situation in Britain more volatile by ending the external threat and leading to demobilization and serious post-war economic problems. The press was increasingly polarized, while the government sought, by legislation and taxation, to limit dissent. The situation was to improve in the early 1820s with prosperity. George Huntingford, Bishop of Hereford reported a rallying of support at the time of George IV's coronation on 19 July 1821, adding a somewhat cynical take on popular motivation:

> I verily believe there existed throughout the nation a spirit of loyalty unparalleled for many years. In most places, measures were taken to make the lower orders substantially feel the importance of the day; they were feasted with what they seldom taste, and that most plentifully. Such language speaks home to them intelligibly, and the remembrance of the festival and of the occasion will be indelible.[7]

Moreover, aside from popular visits by George to Ireland (1821) and Scotland (1822), the Liverpool ministry's reconstruction in 1822 reaffirmed the resilience of the political system and its ability to absorb social,

---

[6] Ian McCalman, *Radical Underworld. Prophets, Revolutionaries and Pornographers in London 1795–1840* (Cambridge, 1988); Marcus Wood, *Radical Satire and Print Culture, 1790–1822* (Oxford, 1994); Kevin Gilmartin, *Print and Politics: The Press and Radical Opposition in Early Nineteenth-Century England* (Cambridge, 1996).

[7] Bishop of Hereford to Addington, 25 July 1821, Exeter, Devon CRO, 152 M/C 1821/OR 21.

12. And So to Frankenstein

economic and political pressures. The situation, however, had been very difficult in the late 1810s and was to become so anew from the late 1820s when a political crisis began that did not end until the passage in 1832 of the Great Reform Act.

The novels and plays of the period may appear overblown, but the life of the royal family suggests otherwise. There was a reality behind the sense of secrecy in élite circles, for secrets included the secret marriage in 1785 of George, Prince of Wales (later George IV) to Maria Fitzherbert, which was in defiance of the Royal Marriages Act of 1772. Furthermore, in 1827, Arthur Wellesley, 1st Duke of Wellington wrote to Sir William Knighton, the confidant of George IV soon after the death of George's brother, Frederick, Duke of York:

> Before I would take charge of the enclosed paper I was made certain that there was no male by which the unfortunate person to whom it related could bring under His Majesty's notice unless I could interest you in her favour; and I shall not think it proper that I should know of the circumstances therein stated without at least giving you the option of laying before the King, knowing as I do His Majesty's affection for his late brother, and how keenly he feels everything that can affect his reputation and honour.[8]

George's IV's personal life was lurid by any standards, with a series of affairs, illegitimate children, and a royal separation, while, if Carlton House and the Brighton Pavilion were scarcely castles, they were motivated by a desire for splendour. George's successor, William IV, had a rich and varied love life, including ten children by his liaison with the actress Dorothy Jordan. The eldest son, George FitzClarence, 1st Earl of Munster (1794–1842), was a drinker and gambler who became a Major General, had a strong sense of persecution, and committed suicide.

A more conventional, brooding take on Gothic fiction than *Frankenstein* was produced by Percy Bysshe Shelley. His verse drama *The Cenci*,

---

[8] Wellington to Knighton, 19 May 1827, draft, Southampton University Library, Wellington papers. Knighton's papers were destroyed by his widow.

written and published in 1819, was not, due to its theme of incest, performed in public in England until 1922. Evil Catholic clergy, parental rape, and a justified patricide, all play a role in this powerful tragedy. In the dedication, Percy Bysshe Shelley presented the work as 'a sad reality,' while the preface provided the standard provenance, beginning:

> A Manuscript was communicated to me during my travels in Italy, which was copied from the archives of the Cenci Palace at Rome, and contains a detailed account of the horrors which ended in the extinction of one of the noblest and richest families of that city during the Pontificate of Clement VIII, in the year 1599.

Darkness, and the underground, which are frequent themes of Gothic fiction, are brought in with reference to 'some of the most dark and secret caverns of the human heart.' There is also a critique of religion with an attack on 'Superstitious horror.' Differentiating it from Protestantism, Shelley explains Italian Catholicism as:

> interwoven with the whole fabric of life. It is adoration, faith, submission, penitence, blind admiration; not a rule for moral conduct. It has no necessary connection with any one virtue.

He adds a response to the Cenci Palace in Rome:

> a vast and gloomy pile of feudal architecture in the same state as during the dreadful scenes which are the subject of this tragedy.... One of the gates of the Palace formed of immense stones and leading through a passage, dark and lofty and opening into gloomy subterranean chambers, struck me particularly.

Earlier, in *Zastrozzi* (1810), Percy Bysshe Shelley had piled on classic features, including family feuds, incarceration, murder, suicide, the Inquisition, and revenge on a neglectful father in the shape of helping drive the father's other son to suicide. Driven by a diabolical intensity, the protagonist denounces religion and morality. The novel was rejected by *The Critical Review* as immoral as well as improbable.

12. And So to Frankenstein

Shelley continued with *St Irvyne; or, The Rosicrucian* (1811), in which the central figures are a lonely wanderer and a Rosicrucian alchemist. Bandits play a major role, as does an underground refuge, suicide, seduction attempts, and the misleading quest for immortality, a quest, in part prefiguring *Frankenstein*, that leads to the death of both men in a Providential storm. As in *Zastrozzi*, the epigraph is from Milton's *Paradise Lost*. Chapbook versions of *St Irvyne* followed in 1822 and the 1850s.

In *Posthumous Fragments of Margaret Nicholson* (1810) by Shelley and Thomas Hogg, there was, in 'The Spectral Horseman,' an engagement with forms of evil, not least:

… a shivering fiend that thirsting for sin,
Seeks murder and guilt when virtue sleeps,
Winged with the power of some ruthless king
….

The nightmare offered varied forms of horror, including:

… a fiend from the regions of Hell…
a ghost of the guilty dead,
… a yelling vampire reeking with gore;
…. A shapeless shadow that sleeps on the hill
…. The phantom courser…
…. the dragon, who, chained in the caverns…
shakes from his skeleton folds the nightmares,
Who, shrieking in agony, seek the couch
of some fevered wretch who courts sleep in vain.

In *The Daemon of the World* (1816), Shelley offered a grimmer account of evil on Earth including:

Hath then the iron-sceptred Skeleton,
Whose reign is in the tainted sepulchres,
To the hell dogs that couch beneath his throne
Cast that fair prey?

Compared to these, *Frankenstein* may seem quite tame or, rather, differently menacing.

Mary Shelley looked essentially in a different direction, not to apocalyptic images from the world of Christian millenarism, but rather to a troubling present of the problems posed by a quest to control the future. Although there were historical references, she did not turn primarily to past knowledge and threats, such as the satanic use of poison in Charlotte Dacre's *Zofloya* (30). Instead, in *Frankenstein*, electricity was one of the most dramatic instances of what appeared to be a new potential for humans. Frankenstein sees a transformation through science:

> these philosophers, whose hands seem only made to dabble in dirt, and their eyes to pore over the microscope or crucible, have indeed performed miracles. They penetrate into the recesses of nature, and show how she works in her hiding-places. They ascend into the heavens: they have discovered how the blood circulates, and the nature of the air we breathe. They have acquired new and almost unlimited powers; they can command the thunders of heaven, mimic the earthquake, and even mock the invisible world with its own shadows. (I,3)

This is a totally different challenge, one of man knowing God. Mary Shelley, however, traces out the new chaos that is created, notably for the Creature. The story becomes a strange murder story, with the Creature, at the close, presiding over the dead Frankenstein: 'in his murder my crimes are consummated; the miserable series of my being is wound to its close!' (III,7). 'Agony and remorse,' and understandably so for having 'murdered the lovely and helpless,' (III,7) are the Creature's living nightmare as it heads for the suicide that yet more places it outside the Christian span, and one of time as well as morality.

Thanks to the resonance of this particular work, our understanding of the Gothic quest for knowledge, public and secret, focuses on that described in *Frankenstein*, but that was largely a matter of the future. In practice, there was a very different science that appeared far more immediate and more aligned with that of the Gothic, namely that of geology. Geological discovery and speculation received much public attention, both due to its inherent interest

12. And So to Frankenstein

and because of its relationship with the historical framework of theology. Notably, William Buckland, who became Professor of Mineralogy at Oxford in 1813, published his proof of the biblical Flood, *Reliquuiae Diluvianae, or Observations on the Organic Remains Attesting the Action of a Universal Deluge* (1823), only for Charles Lyell, in his *Principles of Geology* (1830–3) to provide a fundamental challenge to biblical ideas such as the Flood. The Uniformitarianism he supported argued that current processes had acted over time, undermining biblical accounts of history. In turn, this thesis was to be challenged in the 1840s by a catastrophism in the shape of glaciation, and not the Flood.[9]

Geology leaves echoes in a number of Gothic works, including Byron's *Manfred* (1817), in which Arimanes, the diabolical figure, is described as follows in the 'Hymn of the Spirits':

> He moveth – earthquakes rend the world asunder./
> Beneath his footsteps the volcanoes rise. (II,iv)

In Dacre's *Zofloya* (1806), the denouement sees a transformative geological force:

> Suddenly a frightful noise like the rumbling of thunder was heard, - the cavern, and even the mountain itself, seemed to shake to the foundation! huge pieces from the walls, and from the roof, became as it were forcibly disjointed!

The mountains give way to a 'spacious plain' (33). This pattern had been seen in *The Monk*, in which Satan's arrival at the close of the novel is accompanied by 'a loud burst of thunder' and the prison shaking 'to its very foundations.' Soon after 'a violent earthquake rocked the ground.' In Radcliffe's *The Italian*, Vivaldi listens near midnight (characteristically) to:

> the hollow murmurs of Vesuvius, which threw up, at intervals its sudden flame on the horizon, and then left it to darkness.

---

9   Martin Rudwick, *Bursting the Limits of Time: The Reconstruction of Geohistory in the Age of Revolution* (Chicago, Ill., 2005) and *Worlds before Adam: The Reconstruction of Geohistory in the Age of Reform* (Chicago, Ill, 2008).

The solemnity of the scene accorded with the temper of his mind, and he listened in deep attention for the returning sounds, which broke upon the ear like distant thunder muttering imperfectly from the clouds. The pauses of silence, that succeeded each groan of the mountain, when expectation listened for the rising sound, affected the imagination of Vivaldi at this time with particular awe. (I,1)

In *The Italian*, moreover, Schedoni and his guide have differing responses to the history of a villa destroyed by an earthquake, and whether it was a judgment upon the immoral aristocratic owner or on the country as a whole (III,1). Set near Naples, Charles Maturin's *Fatal Revenge* (1807) has a clear reference to an explosion of Vesuvius in which 'the air and elements were in wondrous motion' (3). Later in the novel there was a link between geology and religion, in a nightmare revelation of Hell and punishment, with volcanoes as the means of justice:

> one night, when the evil ones were lording it in the upper air driven on by the flaky forks of the lightning, the sharp-bolted shot of the hail, and the hollo, and shout, and laughter of the revelling host of darkness, I shrunk into the recess of a mountain, and called upon its riven and rocky bowels to close upon me; but I was driven still onward; the sides of mountain groaned under the fire-shod and hooky feet of my pursuers. I pressed on through the dark passages, through secrets of nature never seen by sun, clogged by the dews, parched with the airs, seared with the meteor fires of this dungeon of the fabric of the world; till through an aperture that would admit all the armies, I flew into a vast plain, in the centre of the mountain.... in elder time, stood a vast city, with all its inhabitants; they were idolatrous and wicked, and invaded the powers, and studied the arts of the dark and nether world.
>
> Therefore the supreme power had in his wrath caused a vast body of volcanic fire to rise out of the centre of the city, which had consumed it, with all its inhabitants, in one night, while the stones, and mineral masses, and solid fire spreading around,

12. And So to Frankenstein

and arching over it, formed a mountain around it, and hid its name, and place, and memory from man for ever and ever. It was now the favoured haunt of unclean spirits. (16)

This was geology in a fashion reconciled with scripture, an approach that was more resilient than might be appreciated. Edward Nares, the Professor of Modern History at Oxford from 1813 to 1841, was among those who wrote at book-length in favour of such a synthesis.

Geology was also of note due to its ideas of an inconstant, unstable world, whose every frame is unsettled, and also that of an only limited control by God. Volcanoes and earthquakes, the sublime as acute disruption,[10] brought this instability to the fore, *Fatal Revenge* referring to 'masses of bold, tumultuous darkness' from Vesuvius (4); and did the same for a lack of clarity over any predictability about the present and the future. This lack of predictability looked also to the past which was the frame for so many stories, not least due to the role of past inheritance issues in a landed system based on dynasticism. Usurpation focused this unpredictability.

By presenting such an unpredictability in the past, it was clear that it was also pertinent for the present, and therefore a threat to any sense of clarity that might be enjoyed by readers. Geological uncertainty was thrust to the fore when the setting was in a volcanic region, and, unlike Britain and France, both Sicily and southern Italy provided great potential for this. The challenge was encouraged by ideas of primeval conflict in the shape of competing dinosaurs which, indeed, led Tennyson in 1850 to refer to Nature as 'red in tooth and claw.'

Geology continued to play a part in novels later in the century. In *Dracula*, Van Helsing explains the Count's unique power as one of the Un-Dead:

> With this one, all the forces of nature that are occult and deep and strong must have worked together in some wondrous way. The very place, where he have [sic] been alive, Undead for all these centuries, is full of [the] strangeness of the geologic and chemical world. There are deep caverns and fissures that reach

---

10 David McCallam, *Volcanoes in Eighteenth-Century Europe: An Essay in Environmental Humanities* (Liverpool, 2019).

none know whither. There have been volcanoes, some of whose openings still send out waters of strange properties, and gases that kill or make to vivify. Doubtless, there is something magnetic or electric in some of these combinations of occult forces which work for physical life in [a] strange way. (24)

The attempt to reconcile religion and geology was more significant, because the former faced problems. That had always been the case, but was more so in this period. The early nineteenth century saw the dismantling of much of the legal privilege of Establishment (official status as the state church) for the Church of England, Wales and Ireland, and the Presbyterian church in Scotland (the Church of Scotland), with the strength of the Catholic Question, which in part focused on this issue,[11] ensuring that Gothic anti-Catholicism had a political resonance.

Thereafter, these churches experienced challenges from a number of directions: from social and economic change, from other faiths, from government, from intellectual challenges, and from growing disbelief. Religious factors were crucial, and not some product of other elements. The 1843 Disruption shattered the unity of the Established Church of Scotland, with the Kirk losing about a third of its ministers. Social and economic change led to major population moves, particularly the expansion in number, wealth and importance, of the industrial cities, such as Bradford, Leeds and Manchester, which greatly stretched existing church provision. In many cases, there were insufficient church buildings, or the mission of the churches did not strike a response with people who were adapting to a rapidly altering society.

Nevertheless, industrialisation and urbanisation were also linked to religious revival in some areas. Indeed, there was a powerful movement for reform, with committed clerics seeking to make Christian teaching more accessible. 'Slum priests' took the Church's message to the urban poor, and bishops insisted on clergy working through cholera outbreaks. More generally, Anglican church interiors were rebuilt in order to replace box pews, which belonged to families, with rows of identical, open pews, most of which were rent-free and open to all.

---

11   G.I.T. Machin, *The Catholic Question in English Politics 1820 to 1830* (Oxford, 1964).

12. And So to Frankenstein

Britain remained very much a Christian country, a key context for Gothic novels, although after Catholic Emancipation in 1829, it largely ceased to be a confessional state as far as the law was concerned. Jewish immigration from Eastern Europe became important in the late nineteenth century, leading to an upsurge in anti-Semitism, but the Jews largely settled in major urban centres, especially London. The vast bulk of the population remained Christian, and most subscribed at the very least to the formal requirements of Christian living.

This provided a background to the use of fiction in order to throw light not only on moral and ethical questions, but also on the very nature of being and of how the material and the immaterial interacted. At one level, the Gothic novel was about death in life, the death of evil, the reality of ghostliness, transcendence across time, and a Christianity which much of the Church hierarchy did not address directly.

The Gothic novel also was about satisfying a readership. The Gothic canon commonly ignores the 1820s and 1830s, either stopping with the 1810s, notably *Frankenstein*, or overstepping the 1820s, 1830s and 1840s, in order to move on to the Sensation Novels. This is a mistake as Gothic fiction remained important to readers, not least the many who visited circulating libraries.

Frankenstein has been seen as encouraging a New Gothicism, one related to an intensification of feeling and an imaginative expansion. The horror of Maturin's *Melmoth the Wanderer* (1820) sees a soul abandoned in return for 150 extra years of life, only for the protagonist, having failed to find another to take over the bargain, to have no redemption and, instead, to be taken by demons amidst sounds of 'indescribable horror' (39). The episodic story includes harsh imprisonment in a monastery, a monk who is a parricide, the brutal prison of the Inquisition, and a Jewish scholar who lives in a secret chamber with the skeletons of his family. This novel had an enormous subsequent reputation, notably in the nineteenth century, with Balzac writing a sequel and Delacroix producing, in 1831, a painting of a scene from the novel that in turn was used by Oxford University Press as the cover for its World's Classics 1981 paperback edition of Radcliffe's *The Italian*. Maturin's preface indicated the inspiration of one of his own sermons:

> At this moment is there one of us present, however we may have departed from the lord, disobeyed his will, and disregarded his

word – is there one of us who would, at this moment, accept all that man could bestow, or earth afford, to resign the hope of his salvation? – No, there is not one – not such a fool on earth, were the enemy of mankind to traverse it with the offer!

He continued by nothing debate over what should be included, with part of the novel:

> …censured by a friend to whom I read it, as containing too much attempt at the revivification of the horrors of Radcliffe Romance, of the persecutions of convents, and the terrors of the Inquisition. I defended myself, by trying to point out to my friend, that I had made the misery of conventual life depend less on the startling adventures one meets with in romances, than on that irritating series of petty torments which constitutes the misery of life in general, and which, amid the tideless stagnation of monastic existence, solitude gives its inmates leisure to invent, and power combined with malignity, the full disposition to practice.

'The Wanderer's Dream,' which is the prelude to the last chapter, sees the protagonist on a precipice looking at a fiery ocean which sends up 'sulphurous rain':

> The whole glowing ocean below was alive – every billow bore an agonizing soul, that rose like a wreck or a putrid corse [corpse] on the waves of earth's oceans – uttered a shriek as it burst against that adamantine precipice – sunk – and rose again to repeat the tremendous experiment! Every billow of fire was thus instinct with immortal and agonizing existence, - each was freighted with a soul, that rose on the burning wave in torturing hope, burst on the rock in despair, added its eternal shriek to the roar of that fiery ocean, and sunk to rise again – in vain, and – for ever!

Continuing with the passage given in the preface to this book, this was the Gothic as Christian and the Christian as Gothic.

12. And So to Frankenstein

A different form of cosmic sensation as physical shock was provided by Francis Danby's *The Opening of the Sixth Seal* (1828), a painting shot through with threat about the opening of that Seal, an episode from the Book of Revelation that precedes the Apocalypse, one beginning with a great earthquake and the stars falling upon the Earth, and following with the heavens departing and the mountains and islands moving.

In practice, alongside *Frankenstein* and its influence, there was a continuance of the pre-existing patterns, with, in particular, the new editions and reprints of earlier works, as with *The Castle of Otranto* in 1824, and the short stories of the 1820s taking on earlier tropes. There was a decline, however, in the appearance of longer Gothic novels. As manliness was increasingly understood in terms of self-discipline and a civilising treatment of women,[12] so there was less tolerance of different conduct, which led to a lack of acceptance of many of the stereotypes of Gothic fiction. Yet, often closely related to new work, adaptations and shorter versions were an important part of Gothic publication, as was plagiarism. There was a range in approach from the moral to the disreputable.[13]

Novelists such as William Child Green, Francis Lathom, and Sarah Scudgell Wilkinson were all very active in producing new works. Green was from the small group of Gothic novelists born in the first decade of the century, in his case 1802, and thus not experiencing the direct impact of Radcliffe or Lewis. His Gothic novels include *The Maniac of the Desert* (1821), *Secrets of Cabalism, or Ravenstone and Alice of Huntingdon* (1821), *The Sicilian Boy* (1824), *The Prophecy of Duncannor, or, The Pool of Blood* (1826), *The Abbot of Montserrat; or, The Pool of Blood* (1826), and *Ailbey the Tempter: A Tale Wild and Wonderful* (1831). Set in medieval Spain, moral strictures were foregrounded in *The Abbot of Montserrat*, with the emphasis on redemption through penitence.[14] This was an Evangelical Gothic.

12　Martin Wiener, *Men of Blood: Violence, Manliness and Criminal Justice in Victorian England* (2006).
13　Franz Potter, *The Monster Made By Man: A Compendium of Gothic Adaptations* (Plymouth, New Hampshire, 2004), *The History of Gothic Publishing, 1800–1835. Exhuming the Trade* (Basingstoke, 2005), and *Gothic Chapbooks, Bluebooks, and Shilling Shockers, 1797–1830* (Cardiff, 2019).
14　Franz Potter, *The History of Gothic Publishing, 1800–1835* (Basingstoke, 2005), pp. 97–8.

An overlap can be seen between shorter Gothic works and the rising weight of publication in all formats devoted to crime, notably Sunday newspapers, particularly *Lloyd's Weekly News* (launched in 1842), the first British paper with a circulation of over 100,000, and with over 400,000 by 1862.[15] Murder, in particular, played a major role, both reflecting and making the developing reading audience,[16] which fed through into the market for short Gothic tales, a market that remained active.

15 Judith Knelman, 'Subtly Sensational: A Study of Early Victorian Crime Reporting,' *Journal of Newspaper and Periodical History*, 8 (1992), pp. 28–33.
16 Jon Klancher, *The Making of English Reading Audiences, 1790–1832* (Madison, Wisconsin, 1987).

13. ENTER MESSRS COLLINS AND DICKENS

> 'The broken ground of the heath looked wild enough in the mysterious light, to be hundreds of miles away from the great city that lay beneath it .... every drop in my body was brought to a stop by the touch of a hand laid lightly and suddenly on my shoulder from behind me.'
> Wilkie Collins, *The Woman in White* (1860) The First Epoch

Widely treated as the first Sensation Novel, as well as the foundation of the British detective story, the highly successful *The Woman in White* (1860) took Gothic plots from the settings of Italian and British abbeys and castles (and often ruined ones at that) in the past, and placed them in present-day Britain. In practice, the latter had been a setting in British Gothic novels from the outset and, prior to *The Woman in White*, it was also already seen in Dickens's novels, notably *Bleak House* (1854) and *Little Dorrit* (1857), before Dickens himself turned to horror in *The Mystery of Edwin Drood* (1870).

Collins meanwhile had referred in *Basil: a story of Modern Life* (1852) to 'the secret theatre of home.' This was melodrama at home, and from novelists who also produced plays, stories acted around the reader, and, as such, different from classic Gothic fiction. Indeed, the Sensation Novel tended to rely on the metaphorical skeleton in the cupboard, and not the actual one in the castle chapel, and this contrast ensured a difference in characters and tone, as well as plot and narrative features. Thus, in Collins' *No Name* (1862), there is the usual Gothic theme of dispossession, and again the beneficiary is an uncle, although, in this case, the negligent failure of a father to change his will to the benefit of his illegitimate daughters is the major cause. In response, the illegitimate Magdalen Vanstone uses conspiracy and deceit to regain her position. Illegitimacy was an aspect of the uncertainty not only of dynasticism, but also of landownership as a whole, and, more generally, families. There were indeed many illegitimate children born within families as well as outside the marital context. Illegitimacy was far more pronounced in Sensation than Gothic novels.

There is some Gothic language in *No Name*, as in discerning 'through the ominous darkness of the future, the lurking phantoms of Terror and Crime, and the black gulfs behind them of Ruin and Death' (IV,1), but the supernatural is not really foregrounded; although, in his preface, Collins writes: 'Here is one more book that depicts the struggle of a human creature, under those opposing influences of Good and Evil, which we have all felt, which we have all known.' In turn, Collins' epistolary novel *The Black Robe* (1881) presents Father Benwell, a Jesuit Catholic priest, in a villainous role, motivated by an attempt to gain Vange Abbey, the family home of the protagonist, Romayne, for the Catholic Church, and seeking to undermine Romayne's marriage to that end by revealing that his wife Stella had, unwittingly, had an earlier bigamous marriage.[1] This was again an issue of family legitimacy, but as part of a broader question of confessional legitimacy.

As with so many Gothic novels, identity with Collins, and not only in these two novels, is issue and means, narrative and outcome, a matter underlined in the number of novels in which parenthood, particularly fatherhood, was a mystery. This theme joined Gothic novels, such as Radcliffe's *The Italian*, not only to many standard nineteenth-century ones, for example Dickens's *Nicholas Nickleby* (1839), in which the villainous Ralph Nickleby is revealed as the father of the unfortunate Smike, but also to a wide tranche of non-Gothic eighteenth-century novels, such as Henry Fielding's *Tom Jones* (1749). In *The Moonstone* (1868), Collins offers a rather different plot, but one in which mystery and suspense are more clearly prioritized, as well as an atmosphere derived in large part from a single setting.

Society meanwhile was changing greatly. From 1851, the majority of the British population lived in towns, and London was the phenomenon of the age. As such, there was an atmosphere different to that of the eighteenth-century novel, one of mass industry and expanding cities. This helped produce fog as the modern indistinct, not the mist of a spectral landscape centred on medieval ruins, but a fog that sprang from unprecedented industrialization and the burning of coal. In 'The Truth, The Whole Truth,

---

1   Maureen Moran, *Catholic Sensationalism and Victorian Literature* (Liverpool, 2007).

and Nothing But the Truth' (1873), Rhoda Broughton referred to London as 'this great smoky beehive.' Fog provided the cause, means and evidence of a visual lack of clarity that captured the slippage of sin, a fall that existed even if the categories of judgment might strain. Ghosts, vampires, and others were part of this slippage, with evil, in its various forms, exploiting the resulting possibilities. Knowledge in this context could literally be haunting.

Madness was much in play in the Victorian Sensation Novel, as was the very different unfixing offered by the use of subjectivity, especially through multiple narrators. Sleepwalking brought the two together in *The Moonstone*, and could lead to consideration of madness which was an issue in Mary Braddon's debut novel *Three Times Dead* (1860), in her very successful *Lady Audley's Secret* (1862), in which disappearance and insanity play roles, and in her *Aurora Floyd* (1863). These novels are set in part in stately homes, and present false identity and bigamy, both of which confuse legitimacy, as well as other crimes. Personal experience played a role. In 1861, Braddon began living with the publisher John Maxwell, whose wife Mary was confined in a mental asylum. A pact with the Devil was central to Braddon's *The World, the Flesh and the Devil* (1891).[2]

Ellen Wood's *East Lynne* (1861) was another prime instance of the Sensation Novel, again with murder, false identities, and adultery all playing a role. Such novels were satirized in W.S. Gilbert and Thomas Reed's comic musical play *A Sensation Novel* (1871), one of implausibility and a lack of authorial control. With Arthur Sullivan, Gilbert was to take this approach forward in *Ruddigore; or, The Witch's Curse* (1887). Wicked ancestors and a past family curse laid by a witch on the persecuting Sir Rupert Murgatroyd played central roles in this operetta, which included the established Gothic device of pictures coming to life in the picture gallery in Ruddigore Castle, in this case *en masse*, as well as the brilliant song 'When the Night Wind Howls' sung by the dead Sir Roderic Murgatroyd in which the first four verses offer a grisly perspective:

When the night wind howls
In the chimney cowls,

2 Anne-Marie Beller, *Mary Elizabeth Braddon: A Companion to the Mystery Fiction* (Jefferson, N.C., 2012).

And the bat in the moonlight flies,
And the inky clouds,
Like funeral shrouds,
Sail over the midnight skies –

When the footpads quail
At the night-bird's wail,
And black dogs bay at the moon,
Then is the spectre's holiday –
then is the ghost's high noon!

As the sob of the breeze
Sweeps over the trees
And the mists lie low on the fen,
From grey tomb-stones
Are gathered the bones
That once were women and men,

And away they go,
With a mop and a mow,
To the revel that ends too soon,
For cock crow limits our holiday –
The dead of the night's high noon!

 The operetta is a protracted and successful spoof on horror, one that looks to such twentieth-century versions as the 1973 film *Theatre of Blood* starring Vincent Price, a masterpiece of cascading overacting, not least as the protagonist is an actor.
 Far from rigidly separated categories, the Gothic novel, penny dreadfuls, vampire novels, melodrama, and Sensation Novels all overlapped and interacted, all being part of a broader professional authorship that sought to engage with a potential mass audience in a competitive marketplace.[3]
The range of Gothic fiction included Emily Brontë's *Wuthering Heights*

---

3 William Rowland, *Literature and the Marketplace: Romantic Writers and Their Audiences in Great Britain and the United States* (Lincoln, Nebraska, 1996).

(1847), notably the potent figure of Heathcliff and his 'half-civilised ferocity' (10), his obsession with the dead Catherine, the storm-scoured Yorkshire moorland, and the roles of mystery and nightmare. The following year, Charlotte Brontë's *Jane Eyre* (1848) presented a mystery at Thornfield Hall, one of secret rooms concealing Bertha Mason, Edward Rochester's first wife. Again, insanity and control were both key themes. Bertha, the daughter of a West Indian merchant-planter's 'creole' wife, meaning of racially-mixed origins, is decried by Rochester as a horrific figure linked to a threatening environment:

> ... giant propensities ... the true daughter of an infamous mother .... A wife at once intemperate and unchaste ... her excesses ... prematurely developed the germs of insanity.... One night I had been awakened by her yells ... it was a fiery West-Indian night.... The air was like sulphur-streams – I could find no refreshment anywhere. Mosquitoes came buzzing in and hummed sullenly round the room; the sea, which I could hear from thence, rumbled dull like an earthquake – black clouds were casting up over it; the moon was setting in the waves, broad and red, like a hot cannon-ball – she threw her last bloody glance over a world quivering with the ferment of tempest.

The Caribbean is presented as sickly beautiful, with the lunacy in the novel rooted there, notably as a result of slavery in the form of miscegenation. A deeply disturbing marginal world of dark secrets is transposed to England. There is also a touch of the Gothic, with the threatening figure of Mr Brocklehurst towering over Jane with tales of the sudden deaths of naughty children.

Dark secrets are also present in the work of Edgar Allan Poe (1809–49), an American whose writings drew on British as well as German influences and had influence in Britain. Insanity and control were again central elements. A ruined home, a medieval romance, and an underground vault, play a role in Poe's *The Fall of the House of Usher* (1839). He influenced the evolution of detective fiction and also of horror literature, being a formative influence on H. P. Lovecraft (1890–1937), a specialist in 'weird fiction' who played a major role in developing occult themes. These and other works underlined the extent to which, alongside any decline in Gothic literature, there was innovation, not least as the form found new audiences, influenced other literary modes, supernaturalised or internalised evil, and developed regional characteristics, as in predestination with the Scottish Gothic, from Hogg through to Robert Louis Stevenson.

Very differently, sorcery took a part in one of the most successful novels of the age, Edward Bulwer-Lytton's *The Last Days of Pompeii* (1834). This story was inspired by a lurid and very popular 1830–33 painting of that title by the Russian Karl Bryullov (1799–1852), a major figure in Russian Romanticism who spent time in Italy. Lytton's cast includes the Witch of Vesuvius; Arbaces, an Egyptian sorcerer and high priest of Isis, who is provided with poison by the Witch; Ione who Arbaces repeatedly seeks to seduce; Apaecides, Ione's brother, who is murdered by Arbaces; and Calenus, a blackmailing priest of the corrupt cult of Isis. Arbaces is straight out of Gothic fiction, not least in imprisoning the good female characters, notably Ione, who is his ward, only to be wounded by an earthquake and later killed by lightning. Egypt brought in a setting of the occult that reflected ancient mystery but also the new knowledge of the period. There were two operatic versions of the novel in the 1850s.

Horror and the supernatural were part of the repertoire of Lytton, notably with *The Haunted and the Haunters; or, The House and the Brain* (1859) and *A Strange Story* (1862), and, very differently, as an element in *The Coming Race* (1871), a major early work of science fiction. Indeed, *The Coming Race* showed how the supernatural could readily be developed into the sense of new challenges from the edges of human consciousness. An admirer of the novels of Mary Shelley, Bulwer Lytton, one of the leading novelists of the century, was disturbed by *Doppelgängers*, and they served in his life and work to suggest the presence of an evil threat.[4]

The nature of overlapping categories was also very much seen in Dickens's *The Mystery of Edwin Drood* (1870), a novel itself made far more mysterious by being unfinished, and with the likely solution a matter of controversy. The novel is a mystery, one in which a murder story is central, but there are also elements of horror – notably, from the outset, during an opium-infused dream, the setting of which Dickens researched by visiting

---

4   A.C. Christensen (ed.), *The Subverting Vision of Bulwer Lytton: Bicentenary Reflections* (Newark, Del., 2004).

13. Enter Messrs Collins and Dickens

an opium den in London's dockland. The chapter closes in the old cathedral of Cloisterham (modelled on Rochester, Kent):

> and then the intoned words, "WHEN THE WICKED MAN – " rise among groins of arches and beams of roof, awakening muttered thunder. (1)

Hoarse rooks are present, there is a clerk who is 'like a fabulous Familiar' called into existence 'by a magic spell' (11), and there are the potent dangers of sexual attraction:

> "… to-night when he watched my lips so closely as I was singing, besides feeling terrified I felt ashamed and passionately hurt. It was as if he kissed me, and I couldn't bear it, but cried out…. I am too frightened to be left by myself."
>
> The lustrous gipsy-face drooped over the clinging arms and bosom, and the wild black hair fell down protectingly over the childish form. There was a slumbering gleam of fire in the intense dark eyes…. Let whomsoever it most concerned look well to it! (7)

Fog swirls, and the dark is feared:

> Ask the first hundred citizens of Cloisterham, met at random the streets at noon, if they believed in Ghosts, they would tell you no; but put them to choose at night between these eerie Precincts and the thoroughfare of ships, and you would find that ninety-nine declared for the longer round…. (12)

There is a visit to the crypt, and a disappearance, both established features in Gothic novels.

The roles of the dark and of a cathedral as settings provide an urban background to *Edwin Drood*, in contrast to the ruined, often monastic, rural settings of most Gothic novels. From Dickens, there is a downplaying of ghosts which are present only in the imagination, while the personal tensions of the cathedral city provide a way to ground the story, as do the chapter titles. The rook is introduced as 'that sedate and clerical bird' and 'some occult importance' is mocked (2).

The unfinished nature of *Edwin Drood* means that it is unclear how far there would have been a judgment call, but, explicitly or implicitly, Christianity certainly provided one in many other horror stories. Thus, in Lettice Galbraith's 'In the Séance Room,' published in a popular 1893 anthology, *New Ghost Stories*, the evil protagonist, the seductive, hypnotic, physically attractive Dr Valentine Burke, can apparently evade justice, but his words 'were registered by a higher power than that of the criminal court, damning evidence to be produced one day against the man who had prostituted his spiritual gift to mean and selfish ends.' Believing, instead, only 'in matter and myself,' the conventional props of a materialist, Burke's evil is revealed by a séance, which leads him to 'the exact admixture of physical courage and moral cowardice' that takes him to suicide.

As a background to the novels of the period, partial church attendance revealed by the Religious Census of 1851 suggested to commentators that there was a crisis of faith. The Census of Religious Worship was the first (and last) attempt by government to record all places in England and Wales where public worship was held, the frequency of their services, the extent of their accommodation, and the number of people in them. 34,467 places of worship were identified and the census revealed nearly 11 million attendances at church on census Sunday, 30 March (60.8 per cent of the population) of which 48.6 per cent were in Anglican churches and 51.4 per cent in others, a return that led to Anglican anger. The Anglicans did best in the rural South and in small towns, while Catholics and Nonconformists were most successful in the cities. Working-class attendance was lower than clerics would have liked, with John Davies, Rector of St Clement's Worcester, reporting that his working-class parishioners 'seldom ever attend Sunday Morning Service. The Saturday Market and the late payment of wages on the evening of that day contribute probably in no small degree to produce this remark.' Drink thus kept devotion at bay.

In his poem 'Dover Beach' (1867), Matthew Arnold, the influential Professor of Poetry at Oxford, regretted that:

The Sea of Faith
Was once, too, at the full, and round earth's shore

13. Enter Messrs Collins and Dickens

Lay like the folds of a bright girdle furl'd.
But now I can only hear
Its melancholy, long, withdrawing roar,
Retreating to the breath
Of the night-wind, down the vast edges drear
And naked shingles of the world.

Indeed, in *The Way We Live Now* (1875), Anthony Trollope has Melmotte as his protagonist, using a name that recalls Charles Maturin's Melmoth, and the corrupt financier evades justice by committing suicide by means of prussic acid in his brandy-and-soda (83). There is none of the anguish or drama of the soul seen with Maturin's Melmoth, and the same was true of Dickens' corrupt financier Merdle in *Little Dorrit* (1857), who again turns to suicide. This is not given the horrific connotations seen in classic Gothic novels.

The 1851 census in practice indicated the role of local circumstances and the greatly contrasting character of religious activity. Indeed, there was re-Christianisation as well as secularisation. Religious validation continued to be important for the key turning points in life, such as birth (baptism), marriage and death; and making a good and Christian death was an important aspect of the latter. Private judgment in religious matters was increasingly stressed by Protestants. Under pressure from the ritualists of the Oxford Movement and from Evangelicals, the Church of England was strengthened by the different Broad Church approach, which was favoured by Queen Victoria (r. 1837–1901). Moreover, the major Christian churches, especially the Church of England, the Catholic Church, and the Methodists, still had much life in them, not least in asserting legitimacy by contesting their rivals' accounts of the past. This was a process in which both fiction and history played a role, not least accounts of the medieval Church and the Reformation.[5] New churches were energetically constructed in an effort to reach out to new congregations, especially in the expanding cities. Furthermore, in Scotland there was a huge building programme by United Presbyterian and Free Kirks alongside Church of Scotland places of worship. Britain also saw

---

5   Miriam Burstein, *Victorian Reformations: Historical Fiction and Religious Controversy, 1820–1900* (Notre Dame, Ind., 2014).

the rise of new religious forms, including both Pentecostalism and the Salvation Army.

Meanwhile, the Gothic style became more prominent in architecture, especially in church-building, where the case was pushed hard by Augustus Pugin (1812–52), an architect who saw Gothic as the quintessentially Christian style. His arguments and designs hit home at the right moment as, after a long period in which relatively few new churches had been built, there was a period of massive church-building, both Protestant and Catholic. There was also much secular building in the Gothic style, especially from the 1850s. Works included Charles Barry's Houses of Parliament, finished in 1860, George Gilbert Scott's Midland Grand Hotel at St Pancras (1865–71) and the Albert Memorial (1872), and George Edmund Street's Royal Courts of Justice (1874–82).

In addition, the strong drive for missionary work in the outside world was matched by a powerful sense of the need for such efforts in Britain, notably in the slums. Aside from the commitment to Christian mission, seen with the popularity of 'slum priests,' such as Charles Lowder, the founder in 1855 of the Society of the Holy Cross, there was a marked attempt to improve the institutional framework of the churches, an attempt that also captured the interest in reform. For example, alongside many new churches, there was extensive improvement to existing church buildings. Far more effort was devoted to training clerics than hitherto and the number of Anglican clergy increased from 14,613 in 1841 to 24,232 in 1891, which meant that most parishes had resident incumbents. Attention was also devoted to organisation. New Anglican dioceses and parishes were created. In Cornwall, where a diocese was created at Truro in 1877, more than fifty new churches were built between 1870 and 1900. Chelmsford was selected in 1913 for the new cathedral for Essex. Derby became a diocese in 1914 and Guildford in 1927. There was also much expansion by the Catholic Church and by the Nonconformists.

Religious scenes, not least those painted by the Pre-Raphaelites, were frequently reproduced in the engravings that decorated many walls, from the loftiest to the most humble dwellings. As with Gothic architecture, and the interest in the poetry of Geoffrey Chaucer, they could suggest a Romantic medievalism that was at odds not only with Liberal utilitarianism[6]

---

6   Simon Skinner, *Tractarians and the 'Condition of England': The Social and Political Thought of the Oxford Movement* (Oxford, 2005).

but also with the sensationalist and troubling accounts of Gothic novels.

The various religious groupings were keen to develop church music. Leading composers, such as Sir Hubert Parry, who wrote the chorus *Jerusalem* (1916), to words by William Blake, and Sir Charles Villiers Stanford, both played a major role in the British choral tradition, while the output of Sir Arthur Sullivan included *Onward Christian Soldiers* (1871) and the oratorio *The Light of the World* (1873), and Sir Edward Elgar wrote *The Dream of Gerontius* (1900). Yet, in a different version of the challenge earlier posed by geology, the evolutionary ideas associated with Charles Darwin confounded Christian conceptions of time and purpose.

There was pressure for change in other respects. In the British Isles, the movement toward both Whiggery and Tory reform from the late 1820s ensured a different historical context for fiction. A progressivist account of history made the Middle Ages seem redundant and anachronistic to many commentators, and this had implications for the Gothic. Thus, in Edward Quin's *Historical Atlas* (1830), a work reprinted or re-edited in 1836, 1840, 1846, 1856 and 1859, progress was associated with the rise of the middle class, the urban entrepreneurs essentially omitted from the Gothic novel. For the 1100–1294 map, Quin wrote:

> Notwithstanding the gross superstition which prevailed, the undefined state of regal power and popular rights, and the many atrocious acts which were perpetrated, Europe was fast emerging from the state of barbarism in which it had been sunk for several centuries. In England, France, Germany and Italy, the Commons or third estate, began to be recognized and respected; industry and commerce were acquiring their due weight and estimation, and through the study of jurisprudence, the rights of persons and of property were better understood.

The period 1294–1498 was described in clearly teleological terms: 'The darkness of the middle ages was dispelled and the way cleared for the progress of the Protestant religion by the light of science, literature, and commerce.'[7] Similarly, in his *Atlas of Universal Historical Geography* (1854),

7   Edward Quin, *Historical Atlas*, pp. 41, 47.

Edward Gover wrote of the close of the fourteenth century: 'The darkness of the medieval period was now dispelling, and the way cleared for the progress of religion, science, literature, and commerce,' while 'liberal and enlightened forms of policy' were praised.[8]

A changing country meant a transformed context for the Gothic. In the British Isles, the extensive 'fringes' of uncertainty were modernized by the Victorian state, thus making Gothic survivals more unusual, if not bizarre. In *Northanger Abbey*, Catherine Morland comes to appreciate that 'human nature, at least in the midland counties of England,' was not 'to be looked for' in 'Mrs Radcliffe's works.'[9] The geography of this somewhat ludicrous remark, itself a joke at Catherine's expense, could have been totally expanded in the Victorian period, in part as a result of the rapid mid-century expansion of the railway and of rail-linked transportation. The bridges that spanned estuaries and rivers, and the tunnels that punched through hills, transformed the physical environment. Old fortresses, such as Berwick and Fort William, became railway stations. Engineering became more central to British knowledge and achievement, and affected the élite in fiction in a way that would not have been deployed earlier in the century. Thus, in *Dracula* (1897), Lord Godalming, a positive figure, uses a steam launch in order to approach Dracula's castle via the Sereth and Bistritza Rivers. In a presentation of the British élite as encompassing the new technological order, and capable of rejecting the decadent Continental count, Godalming is able to fire up: 'He is an experienced hand at the work, as he has had for years a launch of his own on the Thames, and another on the Norfolk Broads' (26). Godalming is also an amateur fitter, able to repair the launch when it has an accident forcing its way up the Bistritza.

The British perception of the continent also changed. The image of Italy altered with the *Risorgimento*, which saw in 1860–70 a liberal unification of the country applauded in Britain, with Giuseppe Garibaldi being a celebrity when he visited England in 1864 and treated as a hero for radicalism. The classic physical sites of terror and horror in Gothic novels, castles and monasteries, were brought under the control of a liberal state that had no need for an Inquisition and scant requirement for the old aristocratic families, especially those of Sicily and southern Italy. The change in

8   Edward Gover, *Atlas of Universal Historical Geography*, p. 17.
9   *Northanger Abbey*, II, 10.

13. Enter Messrs Collins and Dickens

Italy as a setting for Gothic fiction was seen with Arthur Conan Doyle. In his non-Holmes short story 'The New Catacomb' (1922), he presented the Roman catacombs as separate from 'the modern Rome, the long double chain of the electric lamps, the brilliantly lighted cafés, the rushing carriages, and the dense throng upon the footpaths,' in what becomes a brilliant, logically-explained, horror story. In one respect, evil is driven to the borders of Europe, as with Dracula's Transylvania (modern north-west Romania), the version at the end of the nineteenth century of the Swiss Alpine setting in its early years; but, even in Transylvania, British culture, the epitome of modernity, was available.

The foreign was often now, at least in part, modern, as in the United States. In the preface to his *Edgar Huntley; or, Memoirs of a Sleep-Walker* (1799), the American novelist Charles Brockden Brown (1771–1810) rejected the idea of what he termed 'puerile superstition and exploded manners; Gothic castles and chimeras,' only to offer, instead, a cave, which becomes a natural place of imprisonment. In *Dracula*, Bram Stoker offered a modern account of America with Quincey Morris of Texas, a hero who is thus addressed by Renfield:

> you should be proud of your great state. Its reception into the Union was a precedent which may have far-reaching effects hereafter, when the Pole and the Tropics may hold allegiance to the Stars and Stripes. The power of Treaty may yet prove a vast engine of enlargement, when the Monroe doctrine takes its true place as a political fable. (18)

Thus, the entire New World may come under American sway. The struggle with Dracula is one for an Anglo-American world. Morris, 'always the one to arrange the plan of action' (23) and described by Van Helsing as 'all man' (24), acclaims his belief in Winchester rifles, which are added to the armory. This is in line with the geopolitical-cultural-ethnic axis seen by many High Imperialists of the Arthur Conan Doyle generation. Morris swears to do his duty, being the first to do so (25), and is bravely killed in the struggle.

However, alongside an America that was a triumphant modern rejection of a Gothic European past, a vison that was to lead to the particularly ridiculous horror film *Billy the Kid Versus Dracula* (1966), there was also an American Gothic of brooding threat and nightmare. Old houses frequently featured in the American Gothic, not least in what became, in the twentieth century, a distinctive Southern Gothic, one that drew on the defeat of the Confederacy in the Civil War, and offered an often macabre account of decline, with the plantation replacing the castle. There was a separate Gothic strand in and about New Orleans, one that came to focus on voodoo and, eventually, vampirism

In the nineteenth century, the change in the exotic was seen in a Britain that was involved as an imperial power in Africa, India and the Pacific; rather than in Catholic Europe. As a consequence, the exotic locale of a magical past and a supernatural present changed. Set in 1850, the very close of *The Moonstone* referred to 'the wild regions of Kattiawar,' a province 'but little known to Europeans.' The narrator, Murthwaite, visits the sacred city of Somnauth, a place of 'magnificent desolation,' destroyed in the eleventh century, a backdrop for an Ozymandias, but, now, in this case, a pilgrimage setting to honor the God of the Moon, in the forehead of which the yellow diamond gleamed.

At the same time, there was a degree of humor on offer, not only in Gilbert and Sullivan's *Ruddigore*, but also in novels, such as Charlotte Riddell's *Fairy Water: A Christmas Story* (1873), which began with the conventional approach:

> We found ourselves in a cellar, or dungeon ... behind us was the concealed door by which we had entered; facing it was another door, which stood open; this latter gave ingress to three other small chambers. Out of one of these opened an archway, leading to what seemed a subterraneous passage; out of another a steep flight of stone steps descended to unknown depths. (10)

In turn, Mr Tuft observes that: 'dirt, dust, damp, mildew, are the usual tenants of concealed apartments nowadays.' In the event, a ring is found 'taken off a skeleton finger discovered in that ghastly heap of dust' (10), but the tone throughout the novel is light and easy; and there is no fear. So also with her *The Uninhabited House* (1875), in which a haunted house leads to legal action against an owner for failing to reveal this element to the tenants. There is a character 'all-powerful for evil' and 'a great horror of darkness upon me' (14), but the panic is all within bounds. Making horror domestic also made it easier to control.

So also to a degree with the widespread attempt to apply intellectual insights into phenomena as varied as ghosts and aspects of religious teaching. The resulting discussion did not necessarily lead, however, to an end to what critics thought irrational. Instead, there was a marked development in publications about such fields as spiritualism. 'True' ghost stories also excited interest, as in Charlotte Crowe's *The Night Side of Nature* (1848). Interest in 'doubles' and the consequences of a duality of identity, were seen in James Hogg's *The Private Memoirs and Confessions of a Justified Sinner* (1824), Collins, as in *The Woman in White* and *Armadale* (1864), and two major literary works of (very different) menace, Robert Louis Stevenson's *The Strange Case of Dr Jekyll and Mr Hyde* (1886), a work later illustrated by Mervyn Peake, and Oscar Wilde's *The Picture of Dorian Gray* (1890).[10] Wilde even fashioned himself along Gothic lines, life imitating art. Established in 1882, the Society for Psychical Research sought to investigate the paranormal, including haunted houses.

Meanwhile, as the nature of horror in Victorian society was probed in both senses, there was a reading of the past of Gothic fiction. Much seemed redundant and ridiculous and was therefore discarded from attention and libraries. At the same time, a ranking and chronology of the literature was established. In particular, Sheridan Le Fanu's piece on 'Forgotten Novels' in *The Living Age* (1862) praised *The Castle of Otranto* as 'a happy attempt to combine an interesting story with a glimpse of life in the feudal times, and invest both with interest of a fearfully supernatural character,' and claimed that its reputation remained high. He also found vitality still in Charlotte Smith's *The Old Manor House*, but argued that Smith's other novels had not done well. Ann Radcliffe's 'works are still sought.' Le Fanu complained about 'the impotent conclusion of the *Mysteries of Udolpho*, but captured the impact of a youthful read:

---

10 John Herdman, *The Double in Nineteenth-Century Fiction* (Basingstoke, 1990); Rachel Sims, 'Insanity and the *Doppelgänger* in Wilkie Collins' *The Woman in White* and Mary Elizabeth Braddon's *Lady Audley's Secret*,' in Irina Lyubchenko and Fiona Ann Papps (eds), *Schizo, The Liberatory Potential of Madness* (Brill, 2016), pp. 135–44.

we got into the dark subterranean passage, and beheld by the light of the torch, which would on no inducement burn clear for ten seconds, the grim Barnardino, half-dragging, half-leading, the white-muslined heroine along. Oh, what a contrast between the russet-booted, flapped-hatted, buff-gauntled, bearded brigand, and the shrinking, terrified beauty! And what a scene of sweet terror, where she is reading the fearful tale in the large stately b ed in a corner of the vast room, the flickering lamp flinging the immense shadows to the farther regions of the dim apartment, and the terrors of the story enhanced by these noises, so weak, yet so distinct in the palpable silence! Ah! what is that sudden click? What projects that awful shade?

There is far more criticism of Francis Lathom, whose *Midnight Bell* was summarized at length in a way that made it appear ridiculous, with the conclusion:

If we multiply Mr Lathom's forty volumes by the thousand and forty novel writers who flourished, vegetated rather, along with him, and imagine, that the novel-reading public had to devour all that mess, dreadful their destiny would have been. But the Misses Porter had begun to contribute some healthier additions to the meal, in 1793, and Miss Edgeworth some more healthy still in 1798, and others followed their example; and this was gradually pushed aside the unhealthy mass of mental diet, till Sir Walter Scott in 1814, joined the givers of the feast, and spread satisfaction and happiness over the countenances of all who paid for, or were invited to the entertainment.[11]

This, however, was misleading, as many of the themes of the earlier literature were still found in popular works, not least children's literature. Apparently haunted sites, villains, and providential escapes all played a part. The penny blood serial works of the 1840s-70s were succeeded by the penny dreadfuls of the 1860s-1900s, a genre aimed at the market of young

11 *The Living Age*, 73 (1862), pp. 233–42.

13. Enter Messrs Collins and Dickens

men.[12] The sequential publication of stories in magazine issues was important in a formal tightening up that changed the nature of plots, with repeated cliffhangers introduced in a disciplined way, instead of a more baggy and extended terror. To a degree, there was a parallel with Alfred Harmsworth's ambition for the *Daily Mail* which he founded in 1896, and which the Prime Minister, Robert Cecil, 3rd Marquess of Salisbury, condemned as a newspaper produced 'by office boys for office boys.' It was also more successful and lasting than many other newspapers.[13] In so many respects, the condescension of both past and present hides, or at least misrepresents, broader cultural contours.

12 Anthony Mandal, 'Gothic Fiction, From Shilling Shockers to Penny Bloods,' in Dale Townshend and Angela Wright (eds), *The Cambridge History of The Gothic II* (Cambridge, 2020), 139–61.
13 Andrew Roberts, *The Chief: The Life of Lord Northcliffe, Britain's Greatest Press Baron* (London, 2022).

14. ECHOES IN WHITBY

The locations for Gothic horrors ranged greatly as the nineteenth century drew to a close, with Gothic themes revived and developed in such works as Robert Louis Stevenson's *The Strange Case of Dr Jekyll and Mr Hyde* (1886), Oscar Wilde's *The Picture of Dorian Gray* (1891), and Henry James's *The Turn of the Screw* (1898), all of which offered different types of the surreal from that in *The Castle of Otranto*. The most lasting of the surreal horrors of this period in its impact was Bram Stoker's *Dracula* (1897), one in which evil is on the attack. In contrast, Arthur Conan Doyle's *The Hound of the Baskervilles* (1902) represented the more conventional type of horror story, with a rational solution to what was a Gothic tale. Evil is human, not supernatural, in that story, and there was no equivalent to his interest in spiritualism.

As discussed by Stoker in *Dracula* (18), the belief in vampires was longstanding. It became more prominent in the 1730s, in turn being attacked in the *Encyclopédie*, the repository of liberal learning and fashionable views, in an article that appeared in 1765. Moreover, in 1772, Voltaire condemned the 1746 book on vampires by the cleric and scholar Augustin Calmet and queried how it was possible to write a book on, or believe in, vampires. From this perspective, *Dracula* and, more particularly, the response to it, appear as a late Victorian pathology with roots specific to that period. On this, as on so much else, however, Voltaire's righteous scorn was a misleading guide to popular attitudes. Belief in vampirism continued during the eighteenth and nineteenth century, with panics in parts of Europe in the 1730s, 1750s, and 1770s. A variant of concern about vampirism could also be found in the center of European consciousness, Paris, in 1749–50. It was widely believed that children were seized and killed in order to provide blood for baths to help Louis XV of France combat leprosy.

Blood was a theme and image guarded by stigmas, both due to its role in the Eucharist and the prohibition, in laws divine and law, of murder.

14. Echoes in Whitby

There were also a series of inhibitions about blood relating to health and good taste. This restrictive code was frequently breached in Gothic fiction, and there were many references in it to blood, which gave the novels some of their drama.

The taste of blood, however, largely remained a taboo, or at the least, a different breach in order and decency. Vampirism, indeed, was a particular challenge for writers – one, moreover, that drew its structural significance on that previously played by Satan. Vampirism came to play a literary and artistic role in Gothic fiction, in part as a dangerous tempter, one linked with sexual and medical threats.[1] Indeed, this became a significant strand in Romantic storytelling and iconography, and an aspect of the age of nightmare. There is a disturbing character in the depiction of Geraldine in Coleridge's unfinished poem *Christabel*, which was published 1816, although written in 1797–1800. The possibly demonic Geraldine does not pray, cannot cross the threshold of a house, and weakens the heroine Laura, albeit in an unspecified fashion. Byron's 'Fragment' and John Polidori's more considered *The Vampyre; A Tale* (1819), were followed by a series of works including James Rymer's *Varney the Vampire, or, The Feast of Blood* (1847) and Sheridan Le Fanu's *Carmilla* (1872).[2]

Byron's 'A Fragment' represents an engagement with the imaginative East, being set near Ephesus. Polidori's *The Vampyre*, a longer work, began in London, proceeding via Rome to Athens, and introduced vampires and the foolish mocking of their threat by an Englishman, Aubrey. He is attacked by a vampire 'whose strength seemed superhuman.' Aubrey's mysterious mentor, Lord Ruthiven, dies, but returns from the dead to resume his vampirism in London, taking Aubrey's sister to marriage and destruction. This is a very different satanic figure to the namesake of Dacre's *Zofloya*.

In *Varney the Vampire*, which originally appeared in weekly numbers, the vampire, Sir Francis Varney, was again a member of the élite. His end was particularly memorable and re-introduces yet again a classic site in the Gothic imagination, for his suicide involved casting himself into Mount

1   James Twitchell, *The Living Dead: A Study of the Vampire in Romantic Literature* (Durham, North Carolina, 1981).
2   Christopher Frayling, *Vampyres: Lord Bryon to Count Dracula* (London, 1991).

Vesuvius. The story was not terribly well-written, but helped develop the portrayal of vampires, with Varney having fangs, hypnotic abilities, and great strength, as well as leaving puncture wounds and approaching his female victims by nighttime entry through windows.

Dracula juxtaposed the interest in vampires with a range of factors from more traditional Gothic novels, including those of the mystery and the more general sense of a past with which it is interacting. In part, there was the theme of blood, one seen frequently in Gothic novels, but more recently gripping the imagination with horror in the Jack the Ripper killings of 1888 in London, the mystery of which strengthened and sustained the gruesome interest.

Dracula was also reminiscent of the engagement with a mysterious Continent seen in the earlier Gothic novels, in that it began in a distant and exotic part of Europe, one that involved considerable journeying. Appropriately, as Dracula's Transylvania took the place of the formerly-Catholic Mediterranean, Jonathan Harker's rail journey presented this engagement with the past: 'Sometimes we saw little towns or castles on the top of steep hills such as we see in old missals' (1). He moved on to glimpsing 'mighty rifts in the mountains' (1).

Yet Dracula's castle also had much of the modern, not least an extensive library on English matters which reflected the Count's interest in the country where he was planning to settle and feast, in a version of the *translatio imperii* theme seen with Batoni's portrait of Colonel Gordon in Rome (see chapter one). Indeed, Dracula reads a Bradshaw's Railway Guide in his library. That is a counterpoint to the proud sense of blood-and-soil nationalism that characterizes Dracula's response to Transylvania, and, more generally, the role of a Gothic medievalism as the basis for contemporary proto-nationalism, or at least identity. Dracula boasts:

> In old days there were stirring times, when the Austrian and the Hungarian came up in hordes, and the patriots went out to meet them – men and women, the aged and the children too – and wailed their coming on the rocks above the passes, that they might sweep destruction on them with their artificial avalanches. (2)

14. Echoes in Whitby

Dracula seeks an old estate in England, and Harker accordingly finds Carfax in Purfleet near London, the modern centre of empire: 'It is surrounded by a high wall, of ancient structure, built of heavy stones, and has not been repaired for a large number of years. The closed gates were of heavy old oak and iron, all eaten with rust.' This is an aspect of a story introduced with the idea of the battle of time: 'unless my senses deceive me, the old centuries had, and have, powers of their own which mere "modernity" cannot kill' (3).

In *Dracula*, as in other Gothic novels, the power of a living past turns dream-like images and episodes into narrative. In *Dracula*, this power is an introduction to successive dreams and nightmares, culminating in Dracula's warning to Harker about 'bad dreams for those who sleep unwisely' (3). Soon after, three young women approach him by moonlight:

> The fair girl ... bent over me, fairly gloating. There was a deliberate voluptuousness which was both thrilling and repulsive, and as she arched her neck she actually licked her lips like an animal, till I could see in the moonlight the moisture shining on the scarlet lips and on the red tongue as it lapped the white sharp teeth.... I closed my eyes in a languorous ecstasy and waited – waited with beating heart. (3)

The reversion to animal is in part a case of evolution going backwards, a disturbing theme also present in the specific case of the Count. This throughout is a challenging aspect of the novel, although one that is not always notable at the first reading. The ambivalent sexuality of the episode is enhanced when Dracula intervenes, saying of Harker 'when I am done with him you shall kiss him at your will' (3). Harker faints. These three vampires recur in the story, but never with the same power.

Religious imagery is frequent in *Dracula*, Harker for example describing Dracula, his deceitful host, as having 'a smile that Judas in hell might be proud of' (4). Transylvania is referred to as 'where the devil and his children still walk with earthly feet. At least God's mercy is better than that of these monsters, and the precipice is steep and high. At its foot a man may sleep – as a man' (4).

Unlike Frankenstein's monster or, indeed, the partly sympathetic features of Francis Varney, Dracula is clearly satanic, and, indeed, Harker refers to his creating 'a new and ever-widening circle of semi-demons to batten on the helpless' (4). Symptomatically, Dracula arrives in Britain in the midst of a storm. His arrival is at Whitby, a place already, as Stoker noted, used by Walter Scott in his poem *Marmion* (1808). *Marmion* has elements of the Gothic, in that there is a villain who seeks to seduce the heroine, a duel, an exile, a dishonest nun who is walled up alive for breaking her vows, a real battle (Flodden, 1513), and a happy ending. Whitby Abbey is presented by Stoker as 'a most noble ruin, of immense size, and full of beautiful and romantic bits; there is a legend that a white lady is seen in one of the windows' (6). A big graveyard run by the parish church is also described. An old fisherman refers disparagingly to reports of curses, ghosts, apparitions, harbingers of death, and hobgoblins, but also claims that tombstones provide false accounts and mocks the standard idea of the Day of Judgment. The churchyard provides the setting for the assault on Lucy by Dracula with his 'white face and red, gleaming eyes' (8). Lucy subsequently has many bad dreams as well as anemia, and this leads Van Helsing to write of 'spiritual pathology' (10), with a comparison to nature: 'It is something like the way Dame Nature gathers round a foreign body an envelope of some insensitive tissue which can protect from evil that which it would otherwise harm by contact' (10). This is a form of environmentalism, which Seward continues with the remark: 'If this be an ordered selfishness, then we should pause before we condemn anyone for the vice of egoism, for there may be deeper roots for its causes than we have knowledge of' (10).

There are up-to-date items in a novel set in the Age of Steam, such that characters can readily move from one part of Europe to another, and there are such instances of the here-and-now as cyclists, the Underground [London tube], a phonograph diary, typewriting, small electric lamps, aerated bread and a steam launch. The dark is becoming less prominent in urban spaces,[3] while Van Helsing speaks of having 'the resources of science' (18). Yet, aside from the phonograph diary being compared to 'a soul crying out to almighty God' (17), the root of the magical struggle between Good and Evil is ages old. Van Helsing, who deploys the Host, for the use of which

---

3   A. Roger Ekirch, *At Day's Close: Night in Times Past* (New York, 2005).

14. Echoes in Whitby

he has an indulgence (16), is in no doubt that there is a struggle against ancient, non-Christian evil:

> ... he raised his arms again, as though appealing to the whole universe. "God! God! God!" he said. "What have we done, what has this poor thing done, that we are so sore beset? Is there fate amongst us still, sent down from the pagan world of old, that such things must be, and in such way?.... Devils or no devils, or all the devils at once, it matters not; we fight him all the same." (11)

Subsequently, Van Helsing refers to Mina Harker as: 'one of God's women, fashioned by His own hand to show us men and other women that there is a heaven where we can enter, and that its light can be here on earth' (14), the two, linked prepositions. Van Helsing presents continuation rather than transformation: 'we see around us every day the growth of new beliefs, which think themselves new; and which are yet but the old, which pretend to be young' (14). Explaining that 'the teachings and the records of the past give proof enough for sane peoples,' Van Helsing describes Dracula as having a cunning that was:

> the growth of ages ... he have still the aids of necromancy ... and all the dead that he can come nigh to are for him at command ... he can at times vanish and come unknown ... to fail here ... we become as him; we henceforward become foul thins of the night like him – without heart or conscience, preying on the bodies and souls of those we love best.... We go on for all time abhorred by all ... an arrow in the side of Him who died for god. (18)

Van Helsing is later to say that the 'old physicians took account of things which their followers do not accept' such as 'witch and demon cures' (20).

The challenge posed by evil ensured a need for brutal responses. Explaining that he must kill the vampire Lucy in her sleep, Van Helsing adds: 'I shall cut off her head and fill her mouth with garlic, and I shall drive a stake through her body' (15). His language is apocalyptic: 'this night our feet must tread in thorny paths; or later, and for ever, the feet you love must walk in paths of flame!' (15). And Van Helsing adds, in a swipe at scientific confidence, a swipe that borrows from *Hamlet*: 'There are mysteries which men can only guess at, which age by age they may solve only in part' (15). That thesis was a mirror of the plots in Doyle's later 'scientific' adventure novels.

The indicators are the normal ones of Gothic fiction. Thus, the mission to Lucy's tomb recorded in John Seward's diary begins:

> It was just a quarter before twelve o'clock when we got into the churchyard over the low wall. The night was dark, with occasional gleams of moonlight between the rents of the heavy clouds that scudded across the sky.

In turn, having found the coffin empty:

> it seemed fresh and pure in the night air after the terror of that vault. How sweet it was to see the clouds race by, and the passing gleams of the moonlight between the scudding clouds crossing and passing – like the gladness and sorrow of a man's life; how sweet it was to breathe the fresh air, that had no taint of death and decay; how humanizing to see the red lighting of the sky beyond the hill, and to hear far away the muffled roar that marks the life of a great city. (16)

This was very much the city as civilization, of London as the centre of the latter, and of the threat from outside. This approach was to look from Dracula to twentieth-century civilizational challenges such as Fu Manchu who, against a background of rising concern in the Anglosphere about a 'Yellow Peril,' appeared in *The Mystery of Dr Fu-Manchu* (1913) by Arthur Henry 'Sarsfield' Ward. Ward, who wrote under the pseudonym Sax Rohmer, was influenced by Edgar Allen Poe, while his first published work, 'The Mysterious Mummy,' a short story, captured interest in a different exotic location. The Fu Manchu adventures, in which the genesis and genius of evil are those of the 'Yellow Peril,' have the heroes, Denis Nayland Smith and Dr Petrie, modelled on those who combat Dracula.

14. Echoes in Whitby

Lucy is explained in *Dracula* as a bridge between life and death, good and evil:

> ... the foul Thing which had taken Lucy's shape without her soul.... It is her body, and yet not it ... the curse of immorality; they cannot die. (16)

This approach is then linked to female sexuality as threat: 'the bloodstained, voluptuous month ... the whole carnal and unspiritual appearance, seeming like a devilish mockery of Lucy's sweet purity' (16). Her destruction is presented as a liberation:

> when this now Un-Dead be made to rest as true dead, then the soul of the poor lady whom we love shall again be free. Instead of working wickedness by night and growing more debased in the assimilation of it by day, she shall take her place with the other Angels ... restore Lucy to us as a holy, and not an unholy, memory.... Strike in God's name... the mercy-bearing stake. (16)

Arthur is described as looking 'like a figure of Thor,' the Norse god of thunder, as he drives the stake into Lucy. Lucy is returned to a 'holy calm,' and Arthur able to kiss her, before Van Helsing and Seward cut off her head and fill the mouth with garlic (16). This is more 'Gothic' or stark than the horrors of the 1790s, and more physically immediate than most of the latter. Van Helsing accounts for his knowledge as: 'out of the love and experience of the ancients and of all those who have studied the powers of the Un-Dead' (16). The tone of horror is varied by moving from Dracula – 'this Thing is not human – not even beast' (17), to the psychiatric patient Renfield who swallows flies and spiders:

> I used to fancy that life was a positive and perpetual entity, and that by consuming a multitude of live things, no matter how low in the scale of creation, one might indefinitely prolong life. At times I held the belief so strongly that I actually tried to take human life ... for the purpose of strengthening my vital powers

by the assimilation with my own body of his life through the medium of his blood-relying of course, upon the scriptural phrase, "For the blood is the life." (18)

There is then a reference to the commercialism of Victorian society in the shape of 'Clarke's World-Famed Blood Mixture' which claimed to cleanse the blood, and used the scriptural adage in its advertising, vulgarizing 'the truism to the very point of contempt' in the words of Stoker. Ironically, it was the Church itself that was failing to preserve the weight of Scripture; and thus the laity had to act against Dracula. Looked at differently, the Church included such laity, who were modern crusaders against Evil. As Mina Harker noted, with reference to Seward: 'the world seems full of good men – even if there *are* monsters in it' (17).

Commercialism is not always castigated in the novel. A hungry and tired Jonathan Harker gets 'a cup of tea at the Aerated Bread Company' (A.B.C.) (20), thus anticipating such luminaries as Bill Owen, a teahouse detective in Baroness Orczy's *The Old Man in the Corner* (1908), and Tommy Beresford in Agatha Christie's *The Secret Adversary* (1922). The self-service A.B.C. tea shops operated from 1864, and proved particularly useful for unaccompanied women. Mass-produced aerated bread, which forced carbon dioxide into the dough under pressure, avoided the labour of manual kneading, while fermentation was also less expensive.

Animals are part of the world of struggle. Dracula offers Renfield 'rats ... millions of them' on which to prey for food, and shows 'a dark mass spread over the grass, coming on like the shape of a flame of fire ... and I could see that there were thousands of rats with their eyes blazing red' (12). Later, as both description and an aspect of his threatening reverse-evolution, one that is a parallel to the spectral intervention in other novels, Dracula is compared to a panther (23).

In the fight against him, good animals are of use as well as good men. In Essex, the intrepid band find themselves threatened by swarming rats: 'the lamplight, shining on their moving dark bodies and glittering, baleful eyes, made the place look like a bank of earth set with fireflies.... The rats were multiplying in thousands' (19). In a passage redolent of the British class-system, Lord Godalming blows a whistle and three terriers arrive. Implausibly, they drive off the thousands of rats, and bring the group relief in

14. Echoes in Whitby

their spirits. There are frequent references to hunting as in 'Stop the earths' (exits) and running down 'our old fox' (22), and with the hunting cry 'Tally Ho'. (23)

The pace of the book and the intensity of the horror are revived by a sighting of Dracula attacking Wilhelmina Harker, which is described with a greater physicality than that of most of the Gothic genre:

> With his left hand he held both Mrs Harker's hands, keeping them away with her arms at full tension; his right hand gripped her by the back of the neck, forcing her face down on his bosom. Her white nightdress was smeared with blood, and a thin stream trickled down the man's bare breast which was shown by his torn-open dress.... His eyes flamed red with devilish passion; the great nostrils of the white acquiline nose opened wide and quivered at the edge; and the white sharp teeth, behind the full lips of the blood-dripping mouth, champed together like those of a wild beast.

The Sacred Wafer and the crucifixes, repeatedly a source of power, lead Dracula to flee, leaving finally as a bat, and Mina remains, 'her eyes ... mad with terror' and a stream of blood trickling from her throat. Indeed, Dracula earlier felt able to boast to Mina of his powers: 'me who commanded nations, and intrigued for them, and fought for them, hundreds of years before they were born' (21). In a perversion of the Christian message, he continues that she is now: 'flesh of my flesh; blood of my blood; kin of my kin; my bountiful wine-press for a while; and shall be later my companion and my helper.'

The economy of good versus evil is clearly expounded by Van Helsing: 'God does not purchase souls ... and the Devil, though he may purchase, does not keep faith. But God is merciful and just' (23). Linked to this, there is a clear differentiation between God and man. Van Helsing explains to Mina that she may bear the mark she received as a result of driving out diabolical influences:

> till God himself sees fit, as He most surely shall on the Judgment Day to redress all wrongs of the earth and of His children that

He has placed thereon.... Till then we bear our Cross, as His Son did in obedience to his will. It may be that we are chosen instruments of His good pleasure, and that we ascend to His bidding as that other through stripes and shame; through tears and blood; through doubts and fears, and all that makes the difference between God and man. (22)

The struggle is not bounded by human time on Earth. Dracula, moreover, deploys time: 'My revenge is just begun! I spread it over centuries, and time is on my side' (23). Indeed, there is the danger that he might sleep for a century and thus avoid the retribution of the band of human crusaders (26). This provides Van Helsing with an opportunity to provide a gloss on evolution, presenting that in terms of the struggle between humans and Dracula, with God playing a key role:

I have hope that our man-brains that have been of man so long and that have not lost the grace of God, will come higher than his child-brain that lie in his tomb for centuries, that grow not yet to our stature, and that do not work selfish and therefore small.... There is this peculiarity in criminals. It is so constant, in all countries and at all times, that even police, who know not much from philosophy, come to know it empirically, that *it is*. That is to be empiric. The criminal always work at one crime – that is the true criminal who seems predestinate to crime, and who will of none other. This criminal has not full man-brain. He is clever and cunning and resourceful; but he be not of manstature as to brain. He be of child-brain in mind. Now this criminal of ours is predestinate to crime also; he too have child-brain, and it is of the child to do what he have done.... The Count is a criminal and of criminal type. Nordau and Lombroso would so classify him, and *qua* criminal he is of imperfectly formed mind.... His past is a clue ... it may be that, as ever is in God's Providence, the very thing that the evil doer most reckoned on for his selfish good, turns out to be his chiefest harm. (25)

14. Echoes in Whitby

With only one of his sheltering earth-boxes left, Dracula flees London for Transylvania and Castle Dracula, and the rest of the action takes place in the Balkans, the novel thus returning to its setting at the start.

As in so many Gothic novels, there is, in *the Hound of the Baskervilles*, a dream-like quality. This is in part a matter of the light and fog on Dartmoor, but also of a terrain that initially seems 'like some fantastic landscape in a dream.' There is 'the long, gloomy curve of the moor, broken by the jagged and sinister hills.' Holmes, however, introduces the note of witty scepticism that is so rare in many Gothic novels: 'A devil with merely local powers like a parish vestry would be too inconceivable a thing.' An evil on Dartmoor is much more to the fore in the anonymous and genuinely haunting short story 'The Whisper in the World,' published in *All the Year Round* in 1880.

Very differently, the Berkshire Gothic setting in 'Shoscombe Old Place,' a short story from 1927, triggers a question that Holmes finds very interesting:

> … what is master doing down at the old church crypt at night … the haunted crypt … an old ruined chapel in the park. It's so old that nobody could fix its date. And under it there's a crypt which has a bad name among us. It's a dark, damp, lonely place by day, but there are few in that county that would have the nerve to go near it at night.

Holmes and Watson surreptitiously come into the park at night, and, in true Gothic form, in an episode handled at some length, enter the chapel:

> … It was pitch-dark and without a moon … a dark mass loomed up in front of us which proved to be the ancient chapel. We entered the broken gap which was once the porch, and our guide, stumbling among heaps of loose masonry, picked his way to the corner of the building, where a steep stair led down into the crypt. Striking a match, he illuminated the melancholy place – dismal and evil-smelling, with ancient crumbling walls of rough-hewn stone, and piles of coffins, some of lead and some

of stone, extending upon one side right up to the arched and groined roof which lost itself in the shadows above our head ... the gate of death.

Holmes and Watson examine the graves, the oldest of which is apparently Saxon, before coming to a coffin which, on the pattern of so many of the novels, Holmes jemmies open: 'There was a rending, tearing sound as it gave way, but it had hardly hinged back and partly revealed the contents before ...' That is not the end of the drama: 'In the glare of the lantern I saw a body swathed in a sheet from head to foot, with dreadful, witch-like features.... The dim, glazed eyes staring from a discoloured and crumbling face,' a classic Gothic moment. However, in this case, the placing of the body turns out to be a benign deception. Doyle could play with the Gothic of established historical sites, but this was at a time when castles in Britain were losing their past Gothic aura of decay. Instead, there was a widespread attempt to preserve them. Having purchased Taunton Castle in 1874, the Somerset Archaeological Society restored it, as did William, Lord Armstrong with Bamburgh Castle in 1894. George, Marquess Curzon bought and helped restore Bodiam and Tattershall castles, giving them to the National Trust in 1925.

In 'The Sussex Vampire' (1924), Holmes, the voice of reason, takes aim at the belief in vampires and, therefore, at *Dracula*:

> What have we to do with walking corpses who can only be held in their grave by stakes driven through their hearts? It's pure lunacy.

Watson counterpoints sensibly:

> But surely the vampire was not necessarily a dead man? A living person might have the habit. I have read, for example, of the old sucking the blood of the young in order to retain their youth.

Holmes responds:

> You are right ... But are we to give serious attention to such things? This Agency stands flat-footed upon the ground, and

14. Echoes in Whitby

there it must remain. The world is big enough for us. No ghosts need apply.

Holmes as the antithesis to Watson in this instance captures in practice a central theme in Gothic novels. Alongside unexplained horrors come, more commonly, those in which there is an explanation, one located, however, much due to human evil, in the material and rational. The latter, indeed, is part not only of the story's resolution but also of its eventual tone. This approach was unwelcome to the many who sought a more vivid palette. The contrast aided tension. As Edith Nesbitt pointed out in her short-story, 'Man-size in Marble' (1887), 'Nowadays a "rational explanation" is required before belief is possible.' In being fascinated, instead, possibly with the horror from a different world, of the imagination and of a reality without rules, it is necessary to remember that we are dealing with fiction.

Separately, with both Doyle and Stoker, there is an 'edge of empire' feel. In his Holmes stories, but even more in some of the other Doyle ones, notably those set in Sudan, there is the heroism of an imperial people.[4] In *Dracula*, there is a related situation, one of British, American and Dutch individuals operating in a Balkans where the local powers cannot control Dracula and maintain the rule of law; and, in this case, God is under serious challenge. This leads in *Dracula* to the denouement, one predicted by Seward: 'We ride to death of someone. God alone knows who, or where, or what, or when, or how it may be' (27). Amidst driving snow, the good concentrate on the wagon carrying Dracula and its 'gypsy' escort. Technology plays its role with the use of the Winchester repeating rifles. The gypsies are not able to outthink their opponents as in *A Fistful of Dollars* (1964), where the man with nothing more than a pistol, played by Clint Eastwood, defeats the man with the Winchester by outthinking and tricking him. In *Dracula*, in what is a somewhat perfunctory closing clash, the gypsies give in (27).

Dracula offered a clear illustration of a world that one of the major educators of the elite, H. Montague Butler, then a very successful Headmaster

---

[4] Jeremy Black, *The Game is Afoot: The Enduring World of Sherlock Holmes* (Lanham, Maryland, 2022).

of Harrow, warned of in his hymn 'Lift up your hearts!' (1881). The dichotomy offered was scarcely an optimistic view of the life of many:

> Above the level of the former year,
> The mire of sin, the weight of guilty fears,
> The mist of doubt, the blight of love's decay
> ....
> Above the swamps of subterfuge and shame,
> The deeds, the thoughts, that honour may not name,
> ....
> Low lies the best till lifted up to heaven.

Stoker gave evil deeds and thoughts names and, in Dracula, a voice. In doing so, Stoker provided both adventure story and Christian message, which was the case as a whole, directly or indirectly, of the Gothic revival.

15. CONCLUSIONS

> 'Instantly a loud noise was heard, resembling a clap of thunder, and the steel shivered into a thousand pieces.'

The impact of a small golden cross laid on a constellated mirror used for satanic purposes by Matilda in *The Monk* (III,12) is a classic instance of the struggle between Good versus Evil that was central to the Manicheanism of the Gothic novel. So also with Harker placing a crucifix over the head of his bed to provide protection in Dracula's castle, and the repeated use of the Host in that novel.

That stance may not conform to many modern understandings, and clearly much else was involved in both writing and reception, not least, in the case of *Dracula*, adventure and pornography. Yet, the moral universe of the Gothic was also significant. *The Monk* was not a spoof: the sinful Ambrosio cannot take refuge in atheism and deny the soul's immortality, and cannot help feeling the existence of a God and sense Hell's imminence. Fearful of being burnt alive at the *auto da fe* to which he is sentenced by the Inquisition, this fear leads Ambrosio to turn to Satan, and there is a theological discussion about the possibility of Ambrosio ever winning pardon. Seeking to exploit Ambrosio's despair, Satan is initially unsuccessful, but then 'the God-abandoned' makes over his soul and is carried away. Satan then reveals that Elvira, who Ambrosio had killed, was his mother, and Antonia therefore his sister, and that he had exploited Ambrosio's vanity, and deliberately put Matilda in this path. At the close of the very different, non-Satanic *The Italian*, Radcliffe, nevertheless, has the villain Schedoni commit suicide, and therefore damns his soul, putting him beyond the possibility of redemption.

The tone varied between the novels of the period, let alone between Gothic novels. Thus, William Combe's *The Devil Upon Two Sticks in England* (1790), which was based on *Le Daible Boiteux* (1707) by A. R. Le

Sage, was facetious, while, among Gothic novels, in contrast to *The Monk* comes:

> In reviewing this story, we perceive a singular and striking instance of moral retribution. We learn, also, that those who do only THAT WHICH IS RIGHT, endure nothing in misfortune but a trial of their virtue, and from trials well endured derive the surest claim to the protection of heaven. (16)

The closing words of Radcliffe's *A Sicilian Romance* captured the highly contained terrors of that novel. Like that of Austen, Radcliffe's work was within the established moral compass, whereas the revolutionary era saw challenges to it. Separately, but related to this, the Romantic aesthetic of freeing artists and their creations from the constraints of the ordinary encouraged and was encouraged by the imaginative reshaping of 'Gothicists.'[1]

Dreams, which tended to be focused as nightmares, expanded the possibilities for such reshaping. Thus, in *The Italian*, Vivaldi dreams of a monk:

> ... something of that strange and indescribable air, which we attach to the idea of a supernatural being, prevailed over the features; and the intense and fiery eyes resembled those of an evil spirit, rather than of a human character. He drew a poniard from beneath a fold of his garment, and, as he displayed it, pointed with a stern frown to the spots which discoloured the blade; Vivaldi perceived they were of blood! He turned away his eyes in horror. (III,5)

The dream turns out to predict a meeting with a real monk who shows him spots of blood on such a dagger (III,5). Vivaldi wonders about the dream and meeting, providing Radcliffe with an opportunity to row back from the marvellous:

> These reflections led Vivaldi to various conjectures relative to the visit he had himself received from the monk, the dream that

---

1 George Dekker, *The Fictions of Romantic Tourism. Radcliffe, Scott, and Mary Shelley* (Stanford, Calif., 2005), p. 3.

had preceded it, the extraordinary means by which he had obtained admittance to the prison, the declaration of the centinels, that not any persons had passed the door, and many other unaccountable particulars.... he almost fancied, as he had formerly done, that he beheld something not of this earth. "I have heard of the spirit of the murdered," said he, to himself – "restless for justice, becoming visible in our world –" But Vivaldi checked the imperfect thought, and, though his imagination inclined him to the marvellous, and to admit ideas which, filling and expanding all the faculties of the soul, produce feelings that partake of the sublime, he now resisted the propensity, and dismissed, as absurd, a supposition, which had begun to thrill his every nerve with horror. (III,7)

This was an insightful account of the imagination and the thrilling energy of horror, but also a positioning of audience response. Subsequently, Vivaldi's imagination is discussed by Schedoni, who describes him as:

especially liable to superstition.... The opinions you avowed were rational ... but the ardour of your imagination was apparent, and what ardent imagination ever was contented to trust to plain reasoning, or to the evidence of the senses? It may not willingly confine itself to the dull truths of this earth, but, eager to expand its faculties, to fill its capacity, and to experience its own peculiar delights, soars after new wonders into a world of its own!

Vivaldi acknowledges the truth of this remark (III,11).

A sense of boundaries surpassed, one that prefigures (although not in the Gothic use of moral, and still more religious, terms and ideas) the modern ability to synthesise experience, was captured by Maturin in *Fatal Revenge* when, under the influence of the 'supernatural eloquence' of the evil Father Schemoli, the protagonist feels himself floating:

over the confines of the invisible world, over the formless, and the void. I felt it with a wild and terrible joy – a joy that made me as strange to myself, as every thing around me was; a joy that from the very giddiness of its elevation, precluded me from measuring the height to which it had raised me – the remote point at which I stood from the common feelings and habits of human nature.... I have heard of beings, who, with unnatural strength of feeling, would hang on a bare and single point of rock to see the ocean in a storm; would rush out to cross the forky lightnings in their dance, or howl to the storm as it bent the forest, or shook the mountains to their base.

Schemoli, however, seeks to lead the protagonist to murder.

Horror was scarcely separate for a culture that saw Hell as a real place. The *Westminster Journal* was not alone in 1773–4 in publishing articles on the need, in light of thunder and lightning, to contemplate the Day of Judgment and the Torments of Hell.[2] Such beliefs continued in the nineteenth century, however much social patterns were disrupted by large-scale urbanization. London and other cities might build an underground, but the underworld was a world that was deep in the collective psyche and the individual imagination, the two interacting to sustain each other. This was a world of decay, evil, and spirits, one to which bodies were consigned once their souls had departed, but death was not a close. Instead, as Gothic novelists repeatedly argued, there was a presence of the dead in life, these unquiet souls, indeed often murder victims, but also of the undead and other diabolical agents. The Gothic novelist could use this idea with great effect in order to shock in style, but also to probe a range of issues, notably social anxieties.

Criticism of Gothic novels was at one time widespread, a criticism, moreover, that was also seen with disparaging remarks about medievalism. The novels were condemned for a number of factors including repetition, sensationalism, poor characterization, and weak plotting.[3] This hostile approach has been less prominent in recent decades, not least as a consequence of greater engagement with the vitality, as well as variety, of the Gothic

2 *Westminster Journal*, 19 June 1773, 9, 16 April 1774.
3 Elizabeth Napier, *The Failure of Gothic: Problems of Disjunction in an Eighteenth-Century Literary Form* (Oxford, 1987).

15. Conclusions

world, and with its ethos and commercial logic. As far as characterization and plotting are concerned, there is room for greater interest in the role of narrative structure, parallel to Umberto Eco's essay *The Narrative Structure in Ian Fleming* (1965; English version 1966), in which a comparison was made between the James Bond novels and Wagner's operas, both seen as operating successfully because their use of clear structures, including of characterization, triggered responses with the employment of a consistent narrative structure and of recognizable settings, characters, events and themes all being significant.

Causation in the literature, however, is not synonymous with the existence of structure, and the first has offered too much too readily in the discussion of Gothic novels, as with the commonplace that horror literature rests on anxieties stemming from radical change such as that in Britain from the late eighteenth century. In practice, the nature of change in a Britain that remained monarchical, religious, and conservative, was conditional. Indeed, Britain, unlike France and (differently) Germany did not see the dissolution of its *ancien régime* in the years of political and ecclesiastical change beginning in 1828,[4] which, in Britain, were in fact years of a decline in the quantity and quality of Gothic literature. Moreover, there were many reasons why such causative links should be drawn with care, not least avoiding a crude historicism. This need is particularly notable as the range of Gothic works in general attention has expanded, in both literary fiction and other formats.

The placing and analysis of Gothic fiction has been etched from different perspectives, which is an aspect of the more general problem of 'locating' the period 1750–1850, and, linked to this, understanding and discussing issues of modernity and the revolution.[5] Gothic studies as an academic field indeed lends itself to a variety of approaches. Aside from the stress on particular novels, there are readings that are partly or particularly gender, religious, socio-economic,[6] political, aesthetic, and psychological

---

4   Jonathan Clark, *English Society 1660–1832. Religion, ideology and politics during the ancient regime* (Cambridge, 2000), pp. 527–46.
5   Jeremy Black, 'Locating 1750–1850,' *Consortium of Revolutionary Europe; Selected Papers* (2004), pp. 31–45.
6   Montague Summers, *The Gothic Quest. A History of the Gothic Novel* (1938);

in their emphasis, with the Gothic novel seen as a response to a range of developments, from the Industrial and French revolutions to Enlightenment historiography,[7] and also the reading of the Gothic by later commentators, similarly, a product of a range including psychoanalytic and Marxist criticism and the relationship with Romanticism, not least the idea of the Gothic as an aspect of a popular Romanticism, as well as with the development of melodrama.[8] The reading of time as linear or, in contrast, with eruptions from the past is also significant,[9] not least bringing Dracula into the frame.

Time in the Gothic novel is a matter not simply of narrative structure, plot-artifice and explanatory method, but also an interaction with the religious struggle of good versus evil. The sense of the reality and proximity of Hell was reinforced by evangelical religion. This was different to, but on a continuum with, the contrast between Enlightenment rationalism and, on the other hand, Providentialism and the Romantic attention to the sublime.

There is also a contrast geographically, from the balance between the parts of the British Isles, not least the emphasis on, and reading of, the different Irish, Scottish and Welsh perspectives,[10] to the extent to which there is a willingness to look at Continental sources, parallels and comparisons, as well as the American tradition. Indeed, the emphasis on English Protestantism as a seedbed for the Gothic, as in Alison Milbank's important book,[11] should be complemented by a consideration of these points.

As Milbank shows, the diversity of this Protestantism could encompass a number of strands in the Gothic, but, expressed differently, these strands

---

Robert Mayo, 'How Long Was Gothic Fiction in Vogue?,' *Modern Language Notes*, 58 (1943), pp. 58–64.

7 Jonathan Dent, *Sinister Histories. Gothic Novels and Representations of the Past, from Horace Walpole to Mary Wollstonecraft* (Manchester, 2016).

8 Peter Brooks, *The Melodramatic Imagination* (New Haven, Conn., 1976).

9 Dale Townshend and Angela Wright (eds), *Ann Radcliffe, Romanticism and the Gothic* (Cambridge, 2014).

10 Emerson Loomis, 'The Problem of the Gothic Novel in Wales,' *National Library of Wales Journal*, 13 (1963).

11 Alison Milbank, *God and the Gothic: Religion, Romance, and Reality in the English Literary Tradition* (Oxford, 2018).

15. Conclusions

could easily take precedence over an explicitly Protestant approach. Thus, in Radcliffe's *The Italian*, which saw the culmination of her critique of Mediterranean Catholicism, there was, aside from that very clearly Protestant position, a commitment to Enlightenment values, one, indeed, that is given to the Catholic protagonist. Observing the Roman Inquisition by which he was imprisoned:

> Vivaldi lost every selfish consideration in astonishment and indignation of the sufferings, which the frenzied wickedness of man prepares for man, who, even at the moment of infliction, insults his victim with assertions of the justice and necessity of such procedure. "Is this possible!" said Vivaldi internally, "Can this be in human nature! – Can such horrible perversion of right be permitted! Can man, who calls himself endowed with reason, and immeasurably superior to every other created being, argue himself into the commission of such horrible folly, such inveterate cruelty, as exceeds all the acts of the most irrational and ferocious brutes. Brutes do not deliberately slaughter their species; it remains for man only, man, proud of his prerogative of reason, and boasting of his sense of justice, to unite the most terrible extremes of folly and wickedness! (II,6)

While directed at the Inquisition, this argument was also pertinent for a European civilization tearing itself apart in an intractable conflict, that of the French Revolutionary Wars, which had started in 1792. Radcliffe more generally seeks to use her characters to make universal points about human nature, as with Schedoni in *The Italian*, a Catholic priest, who is driven by pride, 'the master-spring of his mind' (II,8).

A rather different comprehension was offered by Sarah Scudgell Wilkinson in one of her bluebooks, with a particularly marvellous catch-all title, *The Eve of St Mark; or, the Mysterious Spectre: Describing the Murder of Lady Bertha de Clifford by a Jealous and Disappointed Suitor; and Suicide of her Father: Her Singular Re-appearance after the Lapse of a Whole Century – Surprising Events in Consequence of their Marvellous Incident – Descent of the Steward of the De Clifford Family into the Vaults of Mowbray Church; Remarkable Discovery there, and the Marriage of Earl de Clifford with the*

Steward's Daughter, Margaret. A Romance (1820). This title very much conveyed market recognition, but obviously could not match *The Italian* which was released at 15 shillings for three volumes.

It is easy to mock the Gothic, but in the preface to *Fatal Revenge* (1807), Charles Maturin responded to those who 'most piteously bewailed … the present style of novels,' and, instead, argued the case for novels seeking to unlock 'every store of fancy and of feeling' and, in particular, '*the fear arising from objects of invisible terror.*' He added a pertinent Shakespearean reference to *The Tempest*: 'The wand and robe of Prospero have often been snatched by Caliban; but, in a master's hand, gracious Heaven! what wonders might it work!'

Horror fantasy continued to take a Gothic approach in the twentieth century, not least with Denis Wheatley's *The Devil Rides Out* (1934), a work that also appeared as a serial in the *Daily Mail* and later, in 1968, as a film. The plot focuses on a Devil-worshipping cult able to call up the Angel of Death and seeking the Talisman of Set, a diabolical icon. The heroes resemble the group who fight Dracula, although the villain, Mocata, lacks the Count's physical presence, while his servant is referred to in a racist fashion, as a 'bad black,' probably a Malagasy (1). The wise hero, the Duc de Richelieu, hammers out:

> Despite our electricity, our aeroplanes, our modern scepticism, the power of Darkness is still a living force, worshipped by depraved human beings for their unholy ends in the great cities of Europe and America to this very day. (3)

J.R.R. Tolkien's different *The Lord of the Rings* (1954–5) proved even more successful. In this, the ring that is fought for transcends space and cannot be expressed or explained in it. The potential of this ring is expressed in the verse opening the work:

> … One Ring to rule them all, One Ring to find them,
> One Ring to bring them all and in the darkness bind them
> In the Land of Mordor where the Shadows lie

15. Conclusions

Mordor, the dominion of the evil Sauron, is an imaginative realm as much as a place; and it, Mount Doom, and the Dark Tower are far more potent than Dracula's realm and castle. At the climax of the book, Sauron acts with Satanic energy:

> His Eye piercing all shadows looked across the plain.... At his summons, wheeling with a rending cry, in a last desperate race there flew, faster than the winds, the Nazgûl, the Ringwraiths, and with a storm of wings they hurtled southwards to Mount Doom.

And so on with the reiterated success of fantasy fright in more recent culture, as with Philip Pullman's trilogy *His Dark Materials* (1995–2000). The Gothic novel was the modern historical entry to this literature, one that repurposed conventional Christian accounts in order to provide a new age of nightmare. We are still in its shadows.

SELECTED FURTHER READING

Alexander, Michael, *Medievalism: The Middle Ages in Modern England* (2007).

Baldick, Chris (ed.), *The Oxford Book of Gothic Tales* (1992).

Bearden-White, Roy, *Into The Darkness: An Anthology of Gothic Fiction* (2019).

Bearden-White, Roy (ed.), *Blood Lines: An Anthology of Vampire Fiction* (2019).

Blakey, Dorothy, *The Minerva Press, 1790-1820* (1939).

Bloom, Clive (ed.), *The Palgrave Handbook of Steam Age Gothic* (2021).

Bundock, Chris and Elizabeth Effinger (eds), *William Blake's Gothic Imagination: Bodies of Horror* (2018).

Burke, Edmund, *A Philosophical Enquiry into the Origin of our Idea of the Sublime and Beautiful* (1756).

Clery, E.J. *The Rise of Supernatural Fiction, 1762-1800* (1995).

Cox, Jeffrey (ed.), *Seven Gothic Dramas, 1789-1815* (1992).

Cutchins, Dennis and Dennis Perry (eds), *Adapting Frankenstein: The Monster's Eternal Lives in Popular Culture* (2018).

Davenport-Hines, Richard, *Gothic: Four Hundred Years of Excess, Horror, Evil and Ruin* (1998).

Davison, Carol Margaret and Marie Mulvey-Roberts (eds), *Global Frankenstein* (2018).

Dekker, George, *The Fictions of Romantic Tourism: Radcliffe, Scott, and Mary Shelley* (2005).

DeLamotte, Eugenia, *Perils of the Night: A Feminist Study of Nineteenth-Century Gothic* (1990).

Selected Further Reading

Dent, Jonathan, *Sinister Histories: Gothic Novels and Representations of the Past, from Horace Walpole to Mary Wollstonecraft* (2016).

Drakakis, J. and Dale Townshend (eds), *Gothic Shakespeares* (2008).

Elliott, Kamilla, *Portraiture and British Gothic Fiction: The Rise of Picture Identification, 1764-1835* (2012).

Ellis, Markman, *The History of Gothic Fiction* (2001).

Frank, Frederick, *The First Gothics* (1987).

Frayling, Christopher, *Vampyres: Lord Byron to Count Dracula* (1991).

Frayling, Christopher, *Nightmare: The Birth of Horror* (1996).

Geary, Robert, *The Supernatural in Gothic Fiction: Horror, Belief and Literary Change* (1995).

Georgieva, Margarita, *The Gothic Child: A Study of the Gothic Novel in the British Isles, 1764-1824* (2011).

Greenaway, Jonathan, *Theology, Horror and Fiction: A Reading of the Gothic Nineteenth Century* (2021).

Groom, Nick, *The Gothic. A Very Short Introduction* (2012).

Harris, Katherine (ed.), *The Forgotten Gothic: Short Stories from British Literary Annuals, 1823-1831* (2012).

Hay, Daisy, *The Making of Mary Shelley's Frankenstein* (2018).

Hoeveler, Diane, *Gothic Riffs: Secularizing the Uncanny in the European Imaginary, 1780-1820* (2010).

Hogle, Jerrold (ed.), *The Cambridge Companion to Gothic Fiction* (2002).

Hogle, Jerrold (ed.), *The Cambridge Companion to the Modern Gothic* (2014).

Horner, Avril and Sue Zlosnik, *Gothic and the Comic Turn* (2005).

Kiely, Robert, *The Romantic Novel in England* (1972).

Lévy, Maurice, *Le Roman Gothique Anglais 1796-1820* (1968).

Milbank, Alison *God and the Gothic: Religion, Romance, and Reality in the English Literary Tradition* (2018).

Milbank, Alison, *Daughters of the House: modes of the Gothic in Victorian Fiction* (1992).

Miles, Robert, *Gothic Writings 1750-1820: A Genealogy* (1993).

Morin, Christian, *The Gothic Novel in Ireland, c.1760-1829* (2018).

Mowl, Timothy, *Horace Walpole: The Great Outsider* (1996).

Napier, Elizabeth, *The Failure of Gothic: Problems of Disjunction in an Eighteenth-Century Literary Form* (1987).

Norton, Rictor, *Mistress of Udolpho: The Life of Ann Radcliffe* (1999).

Paulson, Ronald, *Representations of Revolution 1789-1820* (1983).

Peck, Louis, *A Life of Matthew G. Lewis* (1961).

Potter, Franz, *The History of Gothic Publishing, 1800-1835* (2005).

Punter, David, *The Literature of Terror: A History of Gothic Fictions* (1980, 2nd ed., 1996).

Purves, Maria, *The Gothic and Catholicism: Religion, Cultural Exchange and the Popular Novel, 1785-1829* (2009).

Raven, James, *The Business of Books: Booksellers and the English Book Trade, 1450-1850* (2007).

Raven, James, *The English Novel, 1770-1829* (2 vols, 2000).

Roberts, Marie, *Gothic Immortals: The Fiction of the Brotherhood of the Rosy Cross* (1990).

Sage, Victor, *Horror Fiction in the Protestant Tradition* (Basingstoke, 1988).

Sedgwick, Eve, *The Coherence of Gothic Conventions* (2nd ed., 1986).

Shapira, Yael, *Inventing the Gothic Corpse: The Thrill of Human Remains in the Eighteenth-Century Novel* (2018).

Townshend, Dale and Glennis Byron, *The Gothic World* (2013).

Townshend, Dale and Angela Wright (eds), *Ann Radcliffe, Romanticism and the Gothic* (2014).

Townshend, Dale and Angela Wright, *The Cambridge History of the Gothic Volumes 1-2* (2020).

Volz, Jessica, *Visuality in the Novels of Austen, Radcliffe, Edgeworth and Burney* (2017).

Ware, Malcolm, *Sublimity in the Novels of Ann Radcliffe* (1963).

Watt, James, *Contesting the Gothic: Fiction, Genre and Cultural Conflict, 1764-1832* (1999).

Weber, Ingelborg, *Der englische Schauerroman. Eine Einführung* (1983).

Wright, Angela, *Gothic Fiction: A Reader's Guide to Essential Criticism* (2007).

Wright, Angela, *Britain, France and the Gothic, 1764-1820: The Import of Terror* (2013).

Index

A
Abaellino (Lewis), 113, 141–42
The Abbess (Ireland), 64, 130, 133
The Abbey of Clugny (Meeke), 126–27
The Abbey of St Asaph (Kelly), 122–23
The Abbot (Fouqué), 174
The Abbot of Montserrat (Green), 187
abduction and imprisonment
    in Beckford's *Azemia*, 128
    in Bonhôte's *Bungay Castle*, 125
    in Bulwer-Lytton's *The Last Days of Pompeii*, 194
    in *Count Roderic's Castle*, 122
    in Crandolph's *The Mysterious Hand*, 168
    in Curties' *Ethelwina*, 132
    and false imprisonment, 86
    in Fuller's *The Convent*, 49
    in Godwin's *Things as They Are*, 121
    and the Inquisition, 142–43
    in Ker's *Adeline St Julian*, 133
    in Ker's *Edric, the Forester*, 173
    in Maturin's *Melmoth the Wanderer*, 185
    and medievalism, 157
    in *The Monks and the Robbers*, 130
    in nunneries, 145
    in Parson's *The Castle of Wolfenbach*, 149
    in Radcliffe's *The Castles of Athlin and Dunbayne*, 100
    in Radcliffe's *The Italian*, 104–5
    in Roche's *The Children of the Abbey*, 125, 127
    in Wilkinson's *The Fugitive Countess*, 171
abusive power, 47–48
Account of Ireland (Wakefield), 4
adaptations and shorter versions, 187
Addington, Henry, 36
Adeline St Julian (Ker), 133
adultery, 191
The Adventures of Miss Sophia Berkley, 11
Aikin, Anna, 42–43
Aikin, John, 43
Akenside, Mark, 6
alarm and uncertainty, 12, 17, 40, 71, 80, 91, 109, 125, 127, 129, 183, 189, 200
The Albigenses (Maturin), 161
Alfred, 49
Allan the Freebooter, 169
All the Year Round (magazine), 217
Almagro and Clause, 123, 128
The Alps (Keate), 36
Amelia (Fielding), 34
American Gothic, 201–2. *See also* Poe, Edgar Allan
American War of Independence, 57
Analytical Review, 139
Ancient Architecture Restored and Improved (Langley), 24
An Angel's Form and a Devil's Heart (Davenport), 170, 174
Anglican churches, 184, 196–98
The Animated Skeleton, 130–32

anti-Catholicism, 30, 36, 42, 86, 128, 141, 149, 164, 184
anti-clericalism, 83, 142, 145
antiquarianism, 30
anti-Semitism, 185
apocalyptic ideas, 3–4
apocalyptic paintings, 116
archetypes in Gothic fiction, 47
Armadale (Collins), 203
Arminian Magazine, 50
Arnold, Matthew, 196–97
artistic references, 68, 72–73
Arundel Castle, 32
Ashe, George, 13–14
Astrologer's Magazine, 84
astrological and occult beliefs and practices, 2–3, 136. *See also* Providence
atheism, 89
Atlas of Universal Historical Geography (Gover), 199–200
Aurora Floyd (Braddon), 191
Austen, Jane, 36, 90, 97, 108, 147–53, 200
authenticity, 51, 64
automaton, 175
Azemia (Beckford), 128

B
Baillie, Joanna, 79
ballads, 51, 136, 171
Ballin, Rosetta, 64–65
Balsamo, Giuseppe, 40
bandits, 33, 56, 87, 130–32, 157, 164, 170, 174, 179
Barbastal, 125
The Bard (Gray), 25–26
The Bard (Martin), 26
Baroness Orczy, 214
Barozzi (Smith), 170, 174
Barry, James, 66
Bartauld, Anna. *See* Aikin, Anna

Basil (Collins), 189
Batoni, Pompeo, 22, 208
Beaulieu Abbey, 36
Beckford, William, 10, 32, 73, 128, 136
Berkeley, St George, 13–14
Berkshire by-election of 1776, 47–48
Berrow's Worcester Journal, 3
Bertram (Maturin), 77–78, 161
best practice, 50–51
Billy the Kid Versus Dracula (film), 201–2
Bird, John, 123–25
Birmingham Commercial Herald, 94
Bishop of Durham, 91
The Black Castle (Barrett), 78
The Black Robe (Collins), 190
Blair, Robert, 23, 131
Blake, William, 33, 92, 168
Blenheim Palace, 52
blood as theme and image, 206–8
bluebooks, 80, 128, 154, 171, 227–28
body-snatching, 127
Bolebec, Hugh de, 164
Bonhôte, Elizabeth, 126
Book of Martyrs (Foxe), 35
border superstitions, 172–73
Boydell, John, 66–67
Braddon, Mary, 191
Breval, John, 14
Brewer, George, 157
Britain
 Age of Nightmare in, 1
 attack on Christianity in France, 113
 body-snatching in, 127
 castles in, 218
 and causation in the Gothic novel, 225
 change in society, 190
 change in the exotic, 202
 as a Christian country, 185

and exploration, 51
and the French Revolution, 88–96, 163–64, 176
German literature in, 136
Gothic themes in British culture, 37–38
Gothic tourism, 35
heroines under risk in, 104
historical novels located in, 173
history and literature, bridging of, 102
ideological partisanship in Britain, 82–84
and medievalism, 30, 52–55
perception of the continent, 199–201
Poe's influence in, 193
and Providence, 7
rise of new religious forms, 197–98
and ruins, 23
setting in British Gothic novels, 189
translation of empire, 22
and wildness, 32
women in, 150
British Enlightenment, 3
Broad Church approach, 197
Brontë, Charlotte, 167, 193
Brontë, Emily, 192–93
Brothers, Richard, 89
Brougham, William, 176
Brougham Castle (Harvey), 170, 172–73
Broughton, Rhoda, 190–91
Brown, Charles Brockden, 201
Brown, Mather, 32
Browne, Richard, 1–2
The Brownie of Bodsbeck (Hogg), 172
Brydone, Patrick, 101
Bryullov, Karl, 194
Buckland, William, 181

Bulwer-Lytton, Edward, 58–59, 194
Bungay Castle (Bonhôte), 126
Bürger, Gottfried, 136
The Burial of the Princes in The Tower, 27–28
Burke, Edmund, 5, 57, 84, 88, 112–15, 156, 160
Burney, Fanny, 11

C
Cadogan, Charles, 100–101
Calmet, Augustin, 206
Caribbean conquests, 7, 193
caricatures, 72–73, 76
Carlisle, Anthony, 127
Carmilla (Le Fanu), 41–42, 207
Carte, Thomas, 25–26
Castle Howard, 52
The Castle of Hardayne (Bird), 123–25
The Castle of Inchvally (Cullen), 121
The Castle of Ollada (Lathom), 126
The Castle of Otranto (Walpole), 7, 9–22, 32, 39–59, 62, 64, 67, 75, 77, 89, 125, 141, 187, 203, 206
The Castle of Wolfenbach (Parsons), 148–49
castles, 9, 34–35, 54, 111, 122, 123, 126, 134, 189, 218
The Castles of Athlin and Dunbayne (Radcliffe), 99–100
The Castle Spectre (Lewis), 77, 140–41
catastrophism, 181
cathedral, 79, 195–96
Catherine, Duchess of Leeds, 105–6
Catholic Church, 1–2, 23, 30, 37, 41–42, 83–84, 110, 113, 117–18, 128, 133, 142, 166, 178, 196–98. *See also* anti-Catholicism
Catholic Emancipation, 94–95, 185
Catholicism, Mediterranean, 227
Catholic Question, 184
Cato Street Conspiracy of 1820, 90

The Cavern of Death, 121
caverns, 16, 49, 121, 125, 134, 149, 151, 168, 174, 178–79, 181, 183–84
Cecil, William, 101
Cecilia (Burney), 11
Cenci, Beatrice, 72
The Cenci (Shelley), 72, 177–78
Census of Religious Worship, 196
The Champion of Virtue (Reeve), 9, 43–46, 48
chapbooks, 50, 80, 125, 140, 154, 158, 170–71, 179
characterization, 79, 111, 224–25
Charles, 11th Duke of Norfolk, 32
Charles, Earl of Dalkeith, 81
Chatterton, Thomas, 25
Cheap Repository for Moral and Religious Tracts (More), 147
The Children of the Abbey (Roche), 97, 127
Cholmondeley, George, 14
Christabel (Coleridge), 207
Christianity, 77, 113, 116, 144, 185–86, 196
Christie, Agatha, 214
Church, 117–18, 165–66, 184–85, 196–98, 214
church music, 198–99
Church of England, 184, 197
The Church of St Siffrid (Hervey), 127
clandestine marriage, 133
Classical remains in Sicily, 100–101
A Classical Tour through Italy and Sicily (Hoare), 14
Classicism, 23–24, 27
Coleridge, Samuel Taylor, 139, 153, 207
Collins, Wilkie, 189–90, 203
Colman, George, 28
Combe, William, 221–22
The Coming Race (Lytton), 194

commercialism of Victorian society, 214
competitiveness, 27
Concise History of England (Wesley), 55, 65
"Condition of England" novels, 167
Confessions of the Nun of St Omer (Dacre), 157–58
Conjurors' Magazine, 84
conservatism, 6–7, 19, 82–84, 88–89, 94–95, 112, 160
conspiracy, 84, 90
consumerism of public interest, 43
continuity, 6, 41, 58, 88–89, 116
control of the Church, 117–18
The Convent (Fuller), 49
The Convict, or Navy Lieutenant (Parsons), 149–50
Cooke, Thomas, 79–80
correspondence, 57–58
Count Kaunitz, 83
The Count of Narbonne (Jephson), 50, 77
Count Roderic's Castle, 122
country settings, 33–34
Count Ugolino and his Children in the Dungeon (Reynolds), 60–61
Covent Garden, 77
cover-ups, 31
Coxe, William, 37
Cozens, John Robert, 100
Crandolph, Augustus Jacob, 164–69
Crawley, John, 14
criminality and social disruption, 5
The Critic (Sheridan), 11
Critical Review, 20–22, 51, 110, 123, 133, 137, 139, 178
criticism of Gothic novels, 224–25
Crookenden, Isaac, 170
Cross, J. C., 79
Crowe, Charlotte, 203
Crucifixion, 4

Cruickshank, Isaac, 72–73
crypt, 123, 195, 217
Cullen, Stephen, 121
Cumming, John, 4
Curties, Thomas, 132–33

D
Dacre, Charlotte, 41, 113, 118, 157–60, 180–81, 207
The Daemon of the World (Shelley), 179–80
Daily Mail, 205, 228
Danby, Francis, 187
dark comedy, 130
darkness, 15–16, 31, 102–3, 131, 178, 195
Darwin, Charles, 199
Davenport, Selina, 170, 174
Davies, John, 196
Death on the Pale Horse (West), 73
De Montfort (Baillie), 79
Despard Conspiracy, 90
The Devil Rides Out (Wheatley), 228
The Devil Upon Two Sticks in England (Combe), 221–22
dialogue in the Gothic novels, 58
Dickens, Charles, 66, 85, 167, 189–90, 194–97
disappearance, 130–31, 162, 191, 195
dispossession, 189
Disruption of 1843, 184
divine intervention, 2–3, 41
divine providence, 151–52
Domenichino, 68–69
Don Juan (Byron), 95–96
door that cannot be opened, 102
Doppelgängers, 194
Dorchester and Sherborne Journal, 93
"Dover Beach" (Arnold), 196–97
Doyle, Arthur Conan, 50, 201, 206, 212, 217–19
Dracula (Stoker), 4, 11, 18, 42, 110, 167, 183–84, 200–201, 206, 208–20, 221
Drake, Nathan, 62
The Dream (Baillie), 79
dreams and nightmares, 4–5, 8, 17, 48, 109–10, 124–25, 133–34, 137–38, 158–59, 167, 179, 207, 209, 222–23
Drury Lane Theatre, 64, 66, 77, 79, 89
Dryden, John, 101
dynasticism, 15, 31–32, 65, 74–75, 89, 107, 183. *See also* illegitimacy

E
earthquakes, 41, 43, 180–83, 187, 193–94
East Lynne (Wood), 191
ecclesiastical style of the Gothic, 23–24
Eco, Umberto, 225
economic issues, 1, 91–92, 176–77, 184
Edgar (Sicklemore), 130–32
Edgar Huntley (Brown), 201
Edric, the Forester (Ker), 173
Edward II, 31
Edward III, 25, 27–28, 132
Edward III Crossing the Somme (West), 27
Edward V, 55
Eidophusikon, 77
E. Johnson's British Gazette and Sunday Monitor, 152
electrical phenomena, 39
electricity, 39, 44, 180
Emmeline (Smith), 56
emotional realism, 46
emotions, 71, 106–8
Enabling Act of 1788, 80
Encyclopédie, 206
England, 19–20, 35, 42, 53, 64, 74,

90, 126, 156, 164, 172, 174, 178,
    193, 196
The English Garden (Mason), 23
English Protestantism, 226–27
English Renaissance fiction, 113
English travelogues, 34
Enlightenment, 85–86, 119, 146,
    166, 226–27
enormous threatening limb, 17
Established Church of Scotland, 184
Ethelwina (Curtie), 130, 132–33
Ethwald (Baillie), 79
Evangelical Gothic, 187
Evangelical Magazine, 50
Evangelicals/evangelicalism, 49–50,
    71, 93, 197, 226
Evelina (Burney), 11
The Eve of St Marco (Soane), 174
The Eve of St Mark (Wilkinson), 153,
    227–28
evil
    and Age of Nightmare, 1
    and apocalyptic ideas, 3
    in Brewer's *The Witch of
        Ravensworth*, 157
    and British perception of the continent, 201
    challenge posed by, 210–11
    in Crandolph's *The Mysterious
        Hand*, 166
    in Dacre's *Zofloya*, 159–60
    dialogue in the Gothic novels, 58
    in *Dracula*, 206
    versus evil, 213
    and fog, 191
    in Galbraith's "In the Séance
        Room," 196
    good *versus*, 46, 70, 137, 151,
        215, 221, 226
    in *The Hound of the Baskervilles*,
        206, 217
    in Lewis's *The Monk*, 143–46
    in Maturin's *Fatal Revenge*, 163
    and plausibility in fiction, 45
    in Radcliffe's *The Italian*, 119
    and religious admonition, 41
    in Shelley's "The Spectral Horseman," 179
exoticism, 10, 54–55, 144, 202, 212
experience and reality, relationship between, 147
exploration, 51

F
Fairy Water (Riddell), 202
fall of Constantinople, 87
fall of Rome, 81–82
The Fall of the House of Usher (Poe),
    193
false identities, 191
false imprisonment. *See* abduction and
    imprisonment
false sentiment, 114–15
Falstaff Examining his Recruits (Hogarth), 65
familial relationships, 106
famine years, 91–92
Fatal Revenge (Maturin), 5, 56, 69–71,
    88, 136, 161–63, 182–83, 223–
    24, 228
fears of night, 167–68. *See also* darkness
Fielding, Henry, 26, 34, 65, 105, 166,
    190
Filial Piety (Rowlandson), 76
Fingal (Macpherson), 51
A Fistful of Dollars (film), 219
Fitzherbert, Maria, 177
Five Pieces of Runic Poetry (Percy), 51
Foedera (Rymer), 30
fog, 190–91, 195
Fonthill Abbey, 73
foreign countries, 32, 55, 104
foreign travels, 35, 101

Index

forests, 16–17, 34, 78–79, 149
Fouqué, Friedrich de la Motte, 174
Fox, Joseph, 127–28
Foxe, John, 35
"Fragment" (Byron), 207
Fragments of Ancient Poetry collected in the Highlands (Macpherson), 51
France, 28–29, 52, 77, 81–96, 106, 113, 133, 165. *See also* French Revolution
Frankenstein (Shelley), 38, 79–80, 121, 172–88
Frederick, Prince of Wales, 75
free will, 138. *See also* human agency
French Revolution, 1, 3, 7, 61, 63, 73, 81–96, 163–64, 176, 227
The Fugitive Countess (Wilkinson), 171
Fullarton, William, 101
Fuller, Anne, 49
fun in the Gothic, 153
Fuseli, Henry, 60–61, 66–67, 175

G
Gaelic poems and ballads, 51
Galbraith, Lettice, 196
gap in time in science fiction, 107
Gaston de Blondeville (Radcliffe), 67
General History of the Christian Church (Walmesley), 3
geology, 101, 180–84, 199
George, Lord Lyttelton, 26–27
George, Prince of Wales, 49, 75–76, 177
George FitzClarence, 1st Earl of Munster, 177
George II, 75
George III, 19, 25, 27, 31, 33, 37, 48, 75, 89–90, 93, 94
George I of Britain, 74–75
George IV, 37, 57–58, 176–77. *See also* George, Prince of Wales
Germany, 53, 135–36, 225

G.G. and J. Robinson, 129
ghosts
    applying intellectual insights to, 203
    and Baillie's *De Montfort*, 79
    in *Count Roderic's Castle*, 125
    in Crandolph's *The Mysterious Hand*, 168
    in Curties' *Ethelwina*, 132
    in German literature, 136
    and Gothic abbeys, 36–37
    in Kahlert's *The Necromancer*, 121
    in Ker's *Edric, the Forester*, 173
    in Ker's *The Heiress di Montalde*, 133
    in Maturin's *Fatal Revenge*, 162
    and medieval abbeys, 125
    in Meeke's *The Abbey of Clugny*, 127
    in Palmer's *The Haunted Cavern*, 125
    in Radcliffe's *Gaston de Blondeville*, 67
    in Radcliffe's *The Italian*, 105
    in Radcliffe's *The Mysteries of Udolpho*, 102–3, 114
    in Sicklemore's *Edgar*, 131
    and slippage of sin, 191
    in "Terrorist Novel Writing," 134
    in Wilkinson's *Priory of St Clair*, 171
    See also hauntings
Gibbon, Edward, 22, 32, 81, 87, 116
Gifford, William, 147
Gilbert, W. S., 191, 202
Gilpin, William, 34, 56
Gleanings through Wales, Holland and Westphalia (Pratt), 115
Glorious Revolution of 1688-1689, 30, 156
Gloucester Journal, 90
Godwin, William, 121–22

Gondez the Monk (Ireland), 64, 133–34
good lordship, 47
Gordon, William, 22, 208
Gore, Charles, 100
Gormenghast (Peake), 111
Gothic abbeys, 34–35, 36–37, 85–86, 122–23
Gothic architecture, 24, 85, 110, 198
Gothic Romance, 11–13, 20–22, 42, 44–45, 50, 77, 97–98, 112, 173–74, 207, 222. *See also* historical romances; *The Mysteries of Udolpho* (Radcliffe); sentimental fiction; sublime
Gover, Edward, 199–200
Grasing, William, 4
Grasville Abbey (Moore), 123, 128–29
The Grave (Blair), 131
graveyard poets, 23
Gray, Thomas, 25–26
Great Reform Act, 177
Green, William Child, 187
Grenville, Richard, 88
The Grey Friar (Lipscomb), 164–65
guidebooks and journals, 101
Gunpowder Plot of 1605, 84

H
Hackert, Jacob Philipp, 100
Hadfield, James, 89
Hall, James, 101
Harmsworth, Alfred, 205
Harvey, Jane, 157, 170, 172–73
The Haunted Cavern (Palmer), 125–26
The Haunted Priory (Cullen), 121
hauntings, 48, 79, 102–3, 121, 127, 131, 134, 149, 171, 173, 191, 202–4. *See also* ghosts
Hayman, Francis, 65
Hearne, Thomas, 30, 100
heaven in *The Old English Baronet*, 31

The Heiress di Montalde (Ker), 126, 133
Hell, 182, 224, 226
Henderson, John, 66
Henry, 2nd Viscount Palmerston, 76
Henry, Viscount Bolingbroke, 25
Henry II, 26
Henry III, 11, 110, 164
Henry the Second, or the Fall of Rosamond (Hull), 26
Henry V, 25, 29, 46
heroism, 29, 49, 65, 97–100, 104–5, 108, 112, 219
Hervey, Elizabeth, 127
Highland Scotland, 100, 126, 172
Hill, Brian, 101
His Dark Materials (Pullman), 229
Historical Atlas (Quin), 199
historical novels, 64–65, 126, 128, 164, 173
historical romances, 170
historical settings, 13
An Historical Tour of Monmouthshire (Coxe), 37
history and literature, bridging of, 64, 102
The History of Amanda. Written by a Young Lady, 11
History of England (Carte), 25–26
The History of Sir William Harrington (Hull), 27
History of the Life of Henry the Second (Lyttelton), 26
An History of the Mitred Parliamentary Abbie (Willis), 36
History of the Present State of Electricity (Priestley), 39
The History of the Reign of the Emperor Charles the Fifth (Robertson), 113
Hoare, Richard Colt, 14, 37
Hogarth, William, 15, 65
Hogg, James, 172, 203

Index

Hogg, Thomas, 179
homosexuality, 162
Horatio, Lord Nelson, 93–94, 163
horror and terror
   in *The Animated Skeleton*, 130
   and blood theme, 208
   in Bulwer-Lytton, 194
   and Christianity, 196
   classic physical sites of, 200–201
   and Crandolph's *The Mysterious Hand*, 165–68
   in *Dracula*, 213–15
   and drama, 77
   and Hell as a real place, 224
   in *The Horrors of Oakendale Abbey*, 127
   and humour, 153
   in Lewis's *The Monk*, 138
   in Maturin's *Melmoth the Wanderer*, 185
   nature of in Victorian society, 203
   in Radcliffe, 223
   in Radcliffe's *The Mysteries of Udolpho*, 110–11, 114
   and revenge tragedy, 37
   Ruddigore; or, The Witch's Curse as spoof on, 192
   in Shelley's "The Spectral Horseman," 179
   in Walpole's *The Castle of Otranto*, 17
   in Walpole's *The Old English Baronet*, 30–32
horror fantasy, 228–29
The Horrors of Oakendale Abbey, 127
The Hound of the Baskervilles (Doyle), 50, 206, 217–19
Hull, Thomas, 26–27
human agency, 138
Hume, David, 32
humour, 11, 65, 153, 202
Hunt, Leigh, 176

Huntingford, George, 36, 176
Hurd, Richard, 25
hypocrisy, 114, 145

I

The Idea of a Patriot King (Bolingbroke), 25
illegitimacy, 189–90
imagination, 5, 9, 23, 37, 39, 60–61, 64, 76, 96, 105, 116, 147–48, 150, 173, 223
imprisonment. *See* abduction and imprisonment
incest, 15, 42, 72, 110, 165, 170, 178
industrialisation, 171, 184, 190
infidelity, 91
inheritance, 23, 57, 65, 89, 96, 110, 128–29, 133, 157, 170, 183
Inquisition, 81, 111, 117–19, 142–44, 164, 174, 185–86, 200, 221, 227
"In the Séance Room" (Galbraith), 196
Ireland, William Henry, 64, 133–34
Ireland/Irish Gothic, 19–20, 30, 33–34, 41–42, 89, 90, 94, 163, 172, 176, 184, 226
Isle of Devils (Lewis), 141
The Italian (Radcliffe), 111, 115–20
   architectural preferences, 69
   in Austen's *Northanger Abbey*, 148
   critique of Mediterranean Catholicism, 227
   and dreams, 4–5, 222–23
   and fatherhood, 190
   and geology, 181–82
   heroism and humour, 65
   and the Italian Wars, 113
   loss of meaning in, 151
   market recognition of, 228
   and morality, 15, 221
   painterly qualities in, 71–72
   and the past, 53
   quotations from Shakespeare, 62

references to illustrations, 98–99
response to *The Monk*, 137
and Rome, 81–82
shorelines in, 56–57, 104
sinister passages in, 17
socially benign views of the good, 46–47
and Southern Italy, 14
sublime in, 6
villains in, 97–98
Italian Catholicism, 178
Italy, 6, 13–14, 22, 52, 56, 81, 85, 98, 100–101, 113, 116, 119, 183, 200–201
Ivanhoe (Scott), 173–74

J
Jackson's Oxford Journal, 28
Jacobitism, 19–20, 49, 52
James, 1st Duke of Monmouth, 74
James, Henry, 206
Jane Eyre (Brontë), 193
Jenkinson, Robert. *See* Robert, 2nd Earl of Liverpool
Jephson, Robert, 77
The Jesuit (Patrick), 128
Jewish immigration from Eastern Europe, 185
Joan of Arc (Southey), 28–29
John, 1st Duke of Marlborough, 52
John, Lord Brudenell, 14
John, Lord Glenorchy, 52
Johnson, Samuel, 61, 63–64
Jones, Thomas, 26, 65
Joseph Andrews (Fielding), 34
A Journey made in the Summer of 1794 (Radcliffe), 115
Julia of Louvain (Cross), 78–79

K
Kahlert, Karl Friedrich, 121
Keate, George, 36

Kelly, Isabella, 122–23
The Kentish Barons (North), 78
Ker, Anne, 126, 133, 173
King Lear in the Tempest Tearing off his Robes (Romney), 65
Knight, Richard Payne, 100
The Knight of the Rose (Peacock), 53–54

L
Lady Audley's Secret (Braddon), 191
Lady Macbeth Sleepwalking (Fuseli), 66
The Lady's Magazine, 129–30
Lampedusa, Giuseppi, 37–38
landed nobility, 96, 183
landscape, 32, 34–35, 56, 71, 97, 100, 111, 115. *See also* ruins
Lane, William, 149, 154
Langley, Batty, 24
The Last Days of Pompeii (Bulwer-Lytton), 58–59, 194
Lathom, Francis, 90, 126, 148, 187, 204
The Lay of the Last Minstrel (Scott), 37
Le Daible Boiteux (Le Sage), 221–22
Lee, Sophia, 128
Leeds Intelligencer, 82
Leeds Mercury, 49
Le Fanu, Sheridan, 41–42, 203, 207
legitimacy, 23, 89, 112, 190, 197
Leland, Thomas, 11–12
Lemoine, Ann, 125, 171
Lemoine, Henry, 84
Lenore (Bürger), 136
The Leopard (Lampedusa), 37–38
Le Sage, A. R., 221–22
Letters on Chivalry and Romance (Hurd), 25
Lewis, Matthew, 10, 42, 62, 77, 123, 135–46, 187. *See also* individual works by
liberty, 6

Licensing Act of 1737, 80
The Life and Adventures of Launcelot Greaves (Smollett), 7, 11, 55, 128
Lipscomb, George, 164–65
Literary Hours (Drake), 62
Little Dorrit (Dickens), 189, 197
The Living Age (magazine), 203–4
Lloyd's Weekly News, 188
London, England, 33–34, 47, 76–77, 79–80, 185, 190–91, 195, 207–8, 212, 224
"London" (Blake), 92
London Chronicle, 82–83
Longsword, Earl of Salisbury (Leland), 11–12
Lord Byron, 51, 95–96, 140, 158, 181, 207
The Lord of the Rings (Tolkien), 228–29
Lord Pelham, 96
Louis XVI, 75, 83
Loutherbourg, Philip James de, 77
Lovecraft, H. P., 193–94
Lowder, Charles, 198
loyalist Gothic, 24
Ludlow Castle, 54
lunacy, 193
Lussington Abbey (Rouviere), 155–57
Lyell, Charles, 181

M
Macbeth (Martin), 116
Macbeth (Shakespeare), 62, 66–67, 73, 76, 79, 138, 157
Macbeth, Banquo and the Witches (Fuseli), 61
Macbeth and the Witches (Reynolds), 66
Macpherson, James, 51
Madeline, or The Castle of Montgomery (Kelly), 123
madness, 74–75, 79, 191

Magna Carta, 6, 32, 156, 164
male Gothic, 140, 173. See also *The Monk* (Lewis)
Manfred (Byron), 181
"Man-size in Marble" (Nesbitt), 219
Marchmont (Smith), 57
Marmion (Scott), 210
Martin, John, 26, 116
Martyn of Fenrose (Summersett), 154–55
Mason, William, 23
Matthias, Thomas James, 139
Maturin, Charles, 5, 8, 17, 56, 69–71, 77–78, 80, 88, 136, 161–63, 182–83, 185–86, 197, 223–24, 228
Maxwell, John, 191
Meades, Anna, 27
medical care, 40
medievalism, 11–13, 24–30, 50, 52, 76–77, 96, 157, 164–65, 173, 198, 208, 224
Meeke, Mary, 126–27, 130
Melmoth, the Wanderer (Maturin), 8, 17, 161, 185–86, 197
melodramatic aspects of Gothic novels, 5, 7, 64, 192, 226
mélodrame, 77
Melrose Abbey, 37, 174
Memoirs of Sir Roger De Clarendon (Reeve), 27
Methodist movement, 49–50
Middle Ages, 6, 25, 27, 30, 42, 58, 141, 164, 199
middle class, 199
The Midnight Bell (Lathom), 90, 126, 148–49, 204
Milbank, Alison, 226–27
millenarianism, 1, 3, 41, 83, 89, 95
Minerva Press, 36, 122, 123, 125, 126–27, 128, 130, 149, 174
miscegenation, 193
Miscellaneous Pieces in Prose (Aikin), 42–43

Mischianza, 24
missionary work, 198. *See also* slum priests
modernity, 30, 201, 225
modern realism, 12
monasteries, 34–35, 79, 86, 106–7, 110, 117, 134, 161, 185, 200
The Monastery (Scott), 37, 174
The Monitor (newspaper), 7
The Monk (Lewis), 135–46
    accounts of Revolutionary atrocities, 87
    anti-Catholicism in, 86
    and dreams, 4
    ecclesiastical style of the Gothic, 23–24
    geology in, 181
    mercy in, 151
    and morality, 221–22
    and the past, 53
    and Radcliffe's *The Italian*, 115–16
    sexuality in, 18–19
    troubled villains in, 10
    and urbanisation, 33
    women in, 118
The Monk of Udolpho (Curties), 133, 140
The Monks and the Robbers, 130
Montagu, Elizabeth, 47, 53
Monthly Mirror, 139–40
The Monthly Review, 20, 49, 134
The Moonstone (Collins), 190–91, 202
Moore, George, 123, 128–29, 143
morality, 10, 26, 31–32, 39–40, 159, 170, 178, 180, 187, 221–22
More, Hannah, 147, 174
More Ghosts!!! (Patrick), 128
Mosse, Henrietta (née Rouviere), 6, 33–34, 55, 62–63, 155–56
Mrs Siddons as the Tragic Muse (Reynolds), 66

murder
    in Baillie's *De Montfort*, 79
    in Baillie's *The Dream*, 79
    and blood, 206
    in Brewer's *The Witch of Ravensworth*, 157
    in *Count Roderic's Castle*, 122
    in Crandolph's *The Mysterious Hand*, 165
    in Cullen's *The Haunted Priory*, 125
    in Curties' *Ethelwina*, 132
    in Dickens's *The Mystery of Edwin Drood*, 194
    and dynastic inheritance, 65
    in Ireland's *Rimualdo*, 134
    in Maturin's *Fatal Revenge*, 162
    in *The Monks and the Robbers*, 130
    in Moore's *Grasville Abbey*, 129
    and newspapers, 188
    in Parsons, 149–50
    in Radcliffe, 224
    in Radcliffe's *A Sicilian Romance*, 152
    in Radcliffe's *Gaston de Blondeville*, 67
    in Radcliffe's *The Mysteries of Udolpho*, 110
    in Reeve's *The Champion of Virtue*, 46
    in Shelley's *Frankenstein*, 180
    in Shelley's *Zastrozzi*, 178
    in Sleath's *The Orphan of the Rhine*, 122
    in Summersett's *Martyn of Fenrose*, 155
    in Wood's *East Lynne*, 191
The Murder of the Princes in the Tower (Northcote), 27
Murray, John, 147
Murray House (Parsons), 149–50
The Mysteries of Udolpho (Radcliffe), 9–10, 29, 68–69, 90, 97–98, 100,

Index

102, 110–15, 137, 148, 172, 203–4
The Mysterious Freebooter, 126
The Mysterious Hand (Crandolph), 164–69
The Mysterious Mother (Walpole), 42, 116
The Mysterious Warning (Parson), 148–50
mystery, 9, 12, 65, 102, 190
The Mystery of Dr Fu-Manchu (Ward), 212
The Mystery of Edwin Drood (Dickens), 66, 189, 194–96

N
Napoleon, 1, 51, 93, 163, 176
Nares, Edward, 96, 160–61, 183
narrative structure, 225–26
The Narrative Structure in Ian Fleming (Eco), 225
nationalism, 30
national prayer days, 3
The Necromancer (Kahlert), 121
Needham, John, 40
Neo-Classicism, 24
Nesbitt, Edith, 219
Netley Abbey, 36
Netley Abbey (Warner), 36–37
Newbattle Abbey, 37
"The New Catacomb" (Doyle), 201
New Ghost Stories, 196
New Gothicism, 185
New Jerusalem, 89
newspapers, 28, 50, 171, 188, 205
"The New Year's Present of the Men" flysheet, 90–91
Nicholas Nickleby (Dickens), 190
The Night-Hag visiting the Lapland Witches (Fuseli), 61
Nightmare (Fuseli), 60
Nightmare Abbey (Peacock), 153

nightmares. *See* dreams and nightmares
The Night Side of Nature (Crowe), 203
Night Thoughts (Young), 23
No Name (Collins), 189–90
North, Francis, 78
Northanger Abbey (Austen), 147–48, 150–51, 153, 200
Northcote, James, 27–28
North Devon Journal, 175
nunnery, 49, 78–79, 133, 145
nuns, 87–88, 97, 117–18, 141, 145, 210

O
Observations and Remarks in a Journey through Sicily and Calabria in the Year (Hill), 101
Observations on Modern Gardening (Whately), 23
Observations on Reversionary Payments (Price), 40
occult. *See* astrological and occult beliefs and practices
Okehampton Castle, 54
The Old English Baron (Reeve), 9, 29, 33, 43, 55, 89, 108, 155
The Old English Baronet (Walpole), 30–32
The Old Irish Baronet (Rouviere/Mosse), 6, 33–34, 55, 62–63, 85–86, 142–43, 155
The Old Man in the Corner (Orczy), 214
The Old Manor House (Smith), 57, 154, 203
"The Old Woman of Berkeley" (Southey), 136
"On the Supernatural in Poetry" (Radcliffe), 54, 67
The Opening of the Sixth Seal (Danby), 187

organisation, 198
The Orphan of the Rhine (Sleath), 122, 148
Ossian cult, 50–51
Owenson, Sydney, 37
Oxford Gazette, 28
Oxford Movement, 197
Ozymandias (Shelley), 38

P
pagan beliefs, 41–42
painterly qualities in Radcliffe, 34, 67–68, 71–72
paintings, 22, 24, 26–27, 32, 61–73, 116, 144, 165, 185, 187, 194. *See also* scene-painting
Palmer, John, Jr., 125–26
Pamela (Richardson), 34
paranormal, 66, 203
parenthood, 190
Paris, France, 33, 79, 81–82, 206
Parsons, Eliza, 148–49
past, 38, 44–45, 52–55, 64–65, 103, 183, 203, 208, 226
Pastorini Prophecies, 90
Patrick, F. C., 128
Patriot King theme, 25
Peacock, Lucy, 53–54
Peacock, Thomas Love, 153
Peake, Mervyn, 111, 203
Peake, Richard, 79–80
Pennant, Thomas, 35–36, 63
penny blood serial works, 204
penny dreadfuls, 192, 204–5
Perceval, 94–95
Percy, Thomas, 51
Philosophical Enquiry into the Origin of Our Ideas of the Sublime and the Beautiful (Burke), 5
Pickersgill, Joshua, 175
The Picture of Dorian Gray (Wilde), 203, 206

Pilkington, Laetitia, 125
Pittite system, 94–95
plagiarism, 187
plausibility in fiction, 44–45
playwrights, 61–62
The Pleasures of Melancholy (Warton), 23
plotting of Gothic novels, 83–84, 90, 111, 173, 224–25
Poe, Edgar Allan, 193, 212
Polidori, John, 207
politics, 57, 86, 88–89, 94–95, 135–36, 175–77. *See also* Jacobitism
Popham, Home, 163
Porter, Jane, 164
portraits, 50
post-Enlightenment, 146
Posthumous Fragments of Margaret Nicholson (Shelley and Hogg), 179
power, 121–22, 176
Pratt, Samuel, 115
predestination, 138, 146, 194
pre-Revolutionary France, 90
pre-Romanticism, 51, 108
Presumption (Peake), 79–80
Price, Richard, 3, 40
Pride and Prejudice (Austen), 150
Priestley, Joseph, 3, 39, 83
primitivism, 51
Principles of Geology (Lyell), 181
Priory of St Clair (Wilkinson), 170–71
prison conditions, 86. *See also* abduction and imprisonment
The Private Memoirs and Confessions of a Justified Sinner (Hogg), 203
prophecies, 4, 14, 50–51, 95
Protestantism, 3, 41–42, 83, 178, 197, 226–27
Providence, 7–8, 15, 40, 48, 49–50, 125, 160
providentialism, 2–3, 226
publication and theatre, 78

Index

Pugin, Augustus, 198
Pullman, Philip, 229
The Pursuits of Literature (Matthias), 139

Q
Quarterly Review, 147
Queen Charlotte, 89
Quin, Edward, 199

R
Radcliffe, Ann, 97–120
    and Austen, 147–48, 150–51
    Catholicism in, 42
    conservatism in, 7
    device of explaining the apparent supernatural, 126
    female Gothic represented by, 140
    and human nature, 227
    impact of, 187
    influence of, 122
    and Lewis, 137
    loyalist Gothic, 24
    painterly qualities, 34, 67–68, 71–72
    and reading of the past of Gothic fiction, 203–4
    and reason, 85–86
    and Shakespeare, 62
    and shorelines, 56–57
    sublime in, 6, 32–33
    on Windsor Castle, 54
    See also individual works by
Radcliffe, William, 82, 99
radicalism, 61, 86, 95, 141, 176
"Raising Evil Spirits" (Cruickshank), 72–73
Rayland Hall (Smith), 154
Raymond (Sicklemore), 136
Raymond and Agnes, 140
readership, 171, 185
Reading Mercury, 3, 28
realism, 9, 12, 28, 44–46
reason, 4, 47, 61, 86, 108, 152
The Recess (Lee), 128
re-Christianisation, 197
redemption, 50, 110, 144–46, 185, 187, 221
Reed, Thomas, 191
Reeve, Clara, 9, 27, 29, 33, 43–48, 54–56, 89, 108, 155
Reflections on the Revolution in France (Burke), 112–13, 160
reform, 94–95, 169, 184, 198–99
Reformation, 37, 97, 166, 197
Regency Crisis of 1788–9, 74–76
Reid, William Hamilton, 84
Reinhard, Johann, 136
Religious Census of 1851, 196
religious context of *The Mysterious Hand,* 165–66
religious imagery in *Dracula,* 209
religious positioning of Gothic writing, 4
religious scenes in art, 198
religious setting of *A Sicilian Romance,* 48–49
religious validation, 111, 197
Reliques of Ancient English Poetry (Percy), 51
Reliquuiae Diluvianae (Buckland), 181
Remarks on Several Parts of Europe (Crawley), 14
Remarks on the Writings and Conduct of J.J. Rousseau (Fuseli), 60
Reni, Guido, 72
republicanism, 89
retribution, 31–32, 41, 50, 103, 216, 222
Reveley, Willey, 9, 14
revenge tragedy, 37
Revolutionists, 76
Reynolds, Joshua, 60–61, 65–66
Richard, 3rd Duke of York, 26–27

Richard III, 15, 75
Richard III (Shakespeare), 76
Richard III Visited by Ghosts (Fuseli), 61
Richard Plantagenet, a Legendary Tale (Hull), 26–27
Richardson, Samuel, 34
Riddell, Charlotte, 202–3
Rimualdo (Ireland), 64, 133–34
rioting townspeople, 87
The Rise and Dissolution of the Infidel Societies in this Metropolis (Reid), 84
Risorgimento, 200
Robert, 2nd Earl of Liverpool, 95, 176
Robert Cecil, 3rd Marquess of Salisbury, 205
Robertson, William, 113
Roche, Regina Maria, 97, 127, 148
Rolls, John, 2
Rolls of Parliament, 30
Roman catacombs, 201
The Romance of the Forest (Radcliffe), 34–35, 56, 62, 97, 100, 105–10
Roman Empire, 22
Roman Forum, 116
Roman Inquisition, 227
Romney, George, 65–66
The Rosicrucian Cavern (Fuseli), 175
Rosicrucians, 175
Rouviere, Henrietta, 6, 33–34, 55, 62–63, 155–56
Rowlandson, Thomas, 76
Rowley, Thomas, 25
Royal Academy, 60–61, 175
royal family, 177
Royal Marriages Act of 1772, 177
Ruddigore (Gilbert and Sullivan), 191–92, 202
ruins, 22, 23, 34–38, 52–54
The Ruins of Netley Abbey (Keate), 36
Rymer, James, 207–8
Rymer, Thomas, 30

S
Santa della Pietà, 117
Santa-Maria (Fox), 127–28
Santon Barisa, 137
Satan, 77, 139, 141, 143–46, 160–61, 174, 181, 207, 221
satire, 12, 128, 140
scene-painting, 77
science, 39–42, 180–81
science fiction, 39–40, 107
Scotland/Scottish Gothic, 19–20, 30, 42, 52, 99–100, 172, 176–77, 184, 194, 197, 226
Scott, Walter, 37, 80, 126, 140, 147, 154, 172–74, 204, 210
The Scottish Chiefs (Porter), 164
Scottish Reformation, 174
secrecy, 133, 149, 162, 177, 193
The Secret Adversary (Christie), 214
secret doors, 167–68
secret passages, 78–79
secret societies, 84
secular architecture, 198
secularisation, 197
A Sensation Novel (Gilbert and Reed), 191
Sensation Novels, 11, 58–59, 185, 189–92
Sense and Sensibility (Austen), 147, 151
sentimental fiction, 5, 10–11, 29, 57, 109, 127
September Massacres of 1792, 81
sexuality, 10, 18–19, 36, 43, 92, 102, 104, 107, 109, 131, 137–38, 141, 195, 209, 213. *See also* morality
Shakespeare, William, 43, 61–67. See also individual works by
Shelley, Mary, 61, 79, 121, 175–76, 180, 194
Shelley, Percy Bysshe, 38, 72, 112, 153, 158, 177–79

Index

Sheridan, Richard Brinsley, 11
shorelines, 56–57, 104
A Sicilian Romance (Radcliffe), 32–34, 48, 56, 68–69, 85–87, 100, 101–5, 148, 151–52, 222
Sicily, 13–14, 20, 32–33, 100–101, 130, 183, 200
Sicklemore, Richard, 130–32, 136
Siddons, Sarah, 66
Sir William Walworth ... Killing Wat Tyler (Northcote), 27
slave trade, 3, 57, 86, 193
Sleath, Eleanor, 122, 148
sleepwalking, 133, 191
slum priests, 184, 198
Smith, Catherine, 174
Smith, Charlotte, 56, 57, 154, 203
Smollett, Tobias, 7, 11, 55, 65, 128
Soane, George, 80, 174
social and economic change, 184. *See also* urbanisation
social élite, 55, 96, 108, 177, 200
socially benign views of the good, 46–47
Society for Psychical Research, 203
The Son of Ethelwolf: An Historical Tale (Fuller), 49
sorcery, 194
Southcott, Joanna, 50
Southern Gothic, 202
Southey, Robert, 28–29, 136
Spain, 32, 133, 145, 164, 187
Spanish Catholicism, 142
species, 39–40
"The Spectral Horseman" (Shelley), 180
The Spectre of Lanmere Abbey (Wilkinson), 170
The Spirit of the Public Journals for 1797, 134
spontaneous generation, 40
The Statue Room (Ballin), 64–65

status, 5, 149
Stevenson, Robert Louis, 203, 206
St Irvyne (Shelley), 179
St James's Chronicle, 92–93
Stoker, Bram, 4, 201, 208–18, 219–20. See also *Dracula* (Stoker)
St Patrick's Purgatory, 1–2
The Strange Case of Dr Jekyll and Mr Hyde (Stevenson), 203, 206
strange sounds, 106, 111, 126
subjectivity, 191
sublime, 5–6, 10, 29, 33, 42–43, 47, 67–69, 71, 76–77, 98, 100, 101–2, 112, 168, 183, 226
subterranean, 16, 79, 114, 123, 125, 134, 145, 157, 178, 202–4
The Subterranean Cavern (Pilkington), 125
The Subterraneous Passage (Wilkinson), 170
suicide, 23, 42, 65, 110, 133, 152, 155, 177–78, 180, 196–97, 207–8, 221
Sullivan, Arthur, 191, 199, 202
supernatural
  in Austen, 150
  in Bulwer-Lytton, 194
  in Bürger's *Lenore*, 136
  in Collins' *No Name*, 190
  and drama, 76–77
  explaining the apparent, 126
  and Gothic tourism, 36
  in Harvey's *Brougham Castle*, 173
  and heaven, 31
  in *The Horrors of Oakendale Abbey*, 127
  in Ker's *Adeline St Julian*, 133
  in Lewis's *The Castle Spectre*, 141
  in Lewis's *The Monk*, 138
  and the male Gothic, 140
  in Maturin's *Melmoth the Wanderer*, 18–19

in Radcliffe's *The Italian*, 115–16
in Radcliffe's *The Mysteries of Udolpho*, 112, 114
in Scott's *The Monastery*, 174
in Walpole's *The Castle of Otranto*, 9, 12
See also ghosts
superstition, 35–36, 85–86, 105, 121, 129, 142, 172–73, 178, 201, 223
The Surrender of Calais (Colman), 28
"The Sussex Vampire" (Doyle), 218
Swinburne, Henry, 101
Switzerland, 32, 79

T
A Tale of Two Cities (Dickens), 85
Tales of Wonder (Lewis), 136
tapestries, 162
technology, 44, 219
Tegg, Thomas, 171
Temora (Macpherson), 51
Tempest (Shakespeare), 65, 228
tension in the Gothic novel, 18, 48, 173, 219
"Terrorist Novel Writing," 134
Terror of 1793–4, 82
Teuthold, Peter, 121
Theatre of Blood (film), 192
theatre(s), 66, 76–80, 101, 136, 140–42
theatricality of the Gothic, 66, 71, 140–41
Theodosius de Zulvin (Moore), 129, 143
Things as They Are (Godwin), 121–22
Thomas Earl of Surrey defending himself before Henry VII after Bosworth (Brown), 32
The Three Brothers (Pickersgill), 175
Three Times Dead (Braddon), 191
time in the Gothic novel, 107, 163, 216, 226

Times, 84–85
time travel, 103
Titania's Awakening and Bottom (Fuseli), 61
Tolkien, J. R. R., 228–29
Tom Jones (Fielding), 34, 89, 190
torture, 133–34, 142–43
Tour of Scotland (Pennant), 35
Tour through Sicily and Malta (Fullarton), 101
Townsend, Joseph, 32
translatio imperii theme, 208
translation of empire, 22
Transylvania, 201, 208–9, 217
Travels in the Two Sicilies (Swinburne), 101
trial and execution, 29
Trollope, Anthony, 197
"The Truth, The Whole Truth, and Nothing But the Truth" (Broughton), 190–91
Turner, J. M. W., 165
The Turn of the Screw (James), 206

U
Ulysses Deriding Polyphemus (Turner), 165
uncles, 162, 189
Undine (Fouqué), 174
Uniformitarianism, 181
The Uninhabited House (Riddell), 202–3
United States, 84, 201
unpredictability, 100, 183
urban entrepreneurs, 199
urbanisation, 33, 184, 224
usurpation, 19–20, 28, 46, 74–76, 93, 99, 122, 129, 130–31, 132, 162, 183

V
vampires/vampirism, 43, 136, 139,

162–63, 191, 202, 206–12, 218–19. See also *Dracula* (Stoker)
The Vampyre (Polidori), 207
Varney the Vampire (Rymer), 207–8
Vathek (Beckford), 10
veil, 43, 69, 148
The Veiled Protectress (Meeke), 127
verisimilitude, 44, 102
victimhood, 29, 49, 92, 104, 135, 171. See also heroism
Victoria, Queen, 197
villains/villainy, 10, 15, 49, 64–65, 73, 97–100, 112, 117, 122, 127, 131, 149–51, 165, 204, 210. See also bandits
The Vindictive Monk (Crookenden), 170
Visits from the World of Spirits (Lemoine), 84
volcanoes, 100–101, 181–84
Voltaire, 206
A Voyage to Sicily and Malta (Dryden), 101

W
Wakefield, Edward, 4
Wales/Welsh Gothic, 25–26, 30, 42, 184, 196, 226
Wallace, William, 164
Walmesley, Charles, 3
Walpole, Horace, 7, 9–22, 24, 30, 39, 42–46, 50, 52, 56, 62, 75, 78, 99–100, 116, 137
Walpole, Robert, 9, 19
Ward, Ann. See Radcliffe, Ann
Ward, Arthur Henry "Sarsfield," 212
Warner, Richard, 36–37
war news, 90
Wars of the Roses of 1455–87, 74
wartime Gothic novels, 93–94
Warton, Thomas, 23

Waverley (Scott), 172–73
The Way We Live Now (Trollope), 197
Weekly Register, 91, 152
Wesley, John, 2–4, 39, 50, 55, 65, 168
West, Benjamin, 24, 27, 73, 168
Western Times, 118
Westminster Journal, 83, 224
Whately, Thomas, 23
Wheatley, Denis, 228
White Lady of Avenel, 174
white magic, 103–4, 111
Who's the Murderer? (Sleath), 122
Wilde, Oscar, 203, 206
The Wild Irish Girl (Owenson), 37
wildness, 32–33
Wilkinson, Sarah Scudgell, 153, 170–71, 187, 227–28
William, 6th Lord Craven, 48
William, Duke of Cumberland, 75
William, Duke of Portland, 94
William, Lord Grenville, 95
William Cecil, Lord Burghley, 96
William IV, 177
Willis, Browne, 36
Willoughby, 4th Earl of Abingdon, 48
Wilson, Richard, 54
Winchcombe Henry Hartley, 48
Windsor Castle, 24, 54
The Witch of Ravensworth (Brewer), 157
Wollstonecraft, Mary, 135
The Woman in White (Collins), 189, 203
woman seized and incarcerated in an asylum theme, 7
women, 11, 73, 107, 118, 127, 135, 140, 148–50, 187, 213. See also abduction and imprisonment; heroism
Wood, Ellen, 191
Wordsworth, William, 33
The World, the Flesh and the Devil (Braddon), 191

The Worst of Stains (Summersett), 155
Wrongs of Woman (Wollstonecraft), 135
Wuthering Heights (Brontë), 192–93

Y
Young, Edward, 6, 23
Young, William, 14

Young England movement, 30
Young Frankenstein (film), 153

Z
Zastrozzi (Shelley), 178–79
Zofloya (Dacre), 113, 118, 157–60, 180–81, 207